# LIVING THE PAST

# LIVING THE PAST

❧

RECONSTRUCTION

RECREATION

RE-ENACTMENT

AND

EDUCATION

AT

MUSEUMS AND HISTORICAL SITES

by

Beth Goodacre and Gavin Baldwin

MIDDLESEX UNIVERSITY PRESS

Thanks to all our unknown colleagues in The Sealed Knot Society.

First published in 2002 by Middlesex University Press

Middlesex University Press is an imprint of
MU Ventures Limited,
Bounds Green Road, London N11 2NQ

A CIP catalogue record for this book is available from
The British Library

ISBN  1 898253 43 9

Cover and book design by Helen Taylor
Manufacture coordinated in UK from the Editors CRC by
Book-in-Hand Limited, London N6 5AH.

---·—

National Museum of American History, Washington, United States.
Overheard remark. GB's observation notes on visit.

**Dad, I hate this history stuff!**

A student during her first year of teaching practice with a Year 1
group of children, had a boy in her class come up to her and ask if
she had seen a particular television programme the night before.
She told him that she hadn't.

**He frowned and after, a short pause, asked why. I explained that I
hadn't got a television (I lived in halls of residence). He seemed
confused. He thought for a while and then asked: 'Are you from the
past, Miss?'**

(Teacher Jennie Phillips, 'Soundbites',
*Times Educational Supplement*, 6 August 1999, p.16)

Visit to Old Sydney Town 'the biggest heritage park in N.S.W.
Australia.'
Costumed character, gaoler. Speaking to crowd of visitors - adults
and children - crowded into a cell in the recreated gaol. He had
been describing conditions and punishments for convicts. Invites
questions.
GB's observation notes. Transcript.

**Gaoler:   ... right anybody got, I'll say that again....anybody like to
ask anything, about absolutely anything they have seen
today, have not seen, would like to see or would like to
know anyway**

---·—

# CONTENTS

Introduction                                                                        1

PART ONE – LIVING HISTORY, EDUCATION AND MUSEUMS

*Chapter one*    Making history come alive                                          7

*Chapter two*    History education in schools, museums
                 and at historic sites                                             28

*Chapter three* Peopling Historical Space:
                 the contexts of the living history approach                       46

PART TWO – THE EXPERIENCE OF LIVING HISTORY

*Chapter four*   Introduction:
                 Design of the study and sources
                 of information                                                     63

*Chapter five*   The setting of living history                                     68

*Chapter six*    The visitors                                                       91

*Chapter seven*  The interpreters                                                  111

PART THREE  REFLECTIONS ON LIVING HISTORY

*Chapter eight*  A closer look at the language of interaction                      139

*Chapter nine*   A closer look at living history and identity                      167

*Chapter ten*    Conclusion                                                         200

*Appendix I*                                                                        204

*Appendix II*                                                                       210

*Bibliography*                                                                      215

*Index*                                                                             221

✣

# ACKNOWLEDGMENTS

We have received a great deal of help in undertaking this research and writing the book. We especially wish to thank Peggy Howells and Mark Howells at Colonial Williamsburg; Eric White, Neil Cunningham and Peter O'Connell at Old Sturbridge Village; John Kemp and Michael Hall at Plimoth Plantation; Rob Richter at Mystic Seaport and Jane Malcolm Davis and colleagues at Hampton Court Palace for giving us so much of their time and for agreeing to be interviewed.

We are also grateful to Ruth Serner for allowing us to draw on her experiences of first person interpretation, and to Stacy Roth and Debbie Gibson for their personal correspondence. Colin and Sally Mitchell have provided invaluable help with their careful proof reading and helpful suggestions and Marion Locke and the staff of Middlesex University Press have skillfully managed the design of the book and its production.

Without the support and encouragement of our colleagues in the School of Lifelong Learning and Education at Middlesex University this project would have been impossible. We particularly thank Richard Andrews, Trevor Corner, Richard Tufnell and John Whomsley.

❧

# INTRODUCTION

## WHAT THE BOOK IS ABOUT

This book is essentially about the past. As such, it is about something that is no longer with us but continues to assert a huge influence on our daily lives through the traces it has left behind. These traces may be found physically in our environment, symbolically in our customs and institutions and psychologically in our own conscious and subconscious memories. As these traces are only partial representations of the past they have to be constructed into a form which can usefully explain the influence of the past on us. This form is called history.

This book is also, therefore, about history. In our society history takes many forms. It can be written in a book, presented on television in the form of a documentary, accessed through the Internet or stored in multi-media dimensions on a CD-ROM. Whatever its format, someone, individual or in a group, has interpreted the past which is constructed and then communicated.

This book is also, therefore, about construction and interpretation. The particular form of history which we have chosen to analyse is what is commonly known as 'living history'. In this format people put on period costumes. Some of them adopt the persona of someone who lived in former times whilst others demonstrate bygone crafts and technology. Some speak in a way which they imagine people to have spoken and admit knowledge only of concepts current in their reconstructed time. Others use modern language and feel free to explain historical differences to their audiences. Whatever the technique used their aim is to communicate something of their understanding of the past to other interpreters and the visiting public.

This book is also, therefore, about communication. One of the claims made for 'living history' is that it enables a human relationship to develop between the modern visitor and someone 'from another time'. This form of communication, like all interpersonal interaction is exceedingly complex as it is multi-sensory. The main mode is, however, through spoken language.

This book is also, therefore, about language. There has been no consideration of the structures of language used in 'living history'. Some consideration has been given to effective communication for exponents of 'living history' but this has tended to be based on commonsense interpersonal skills rather than any form of linguistic analysis. In this book, Beth Goodacre (referred from now on as BG) refers to recent research from

Australia in Systemic Functional Linguistics (SFL) to discover more about the way in which language is used to communicate this particular form of history.

This book is also about identity. The images of the past and the individual and collective memories which influence us daily help to form the ways in which we see ourselves and others. If these images are constructed into history which is interpreted and communicated, then that history can tell us something about who we are and in turn, who other people are. As there are numerous interpretations of the past then there are numerous opportunities for defining ourselves and others. History, therefore, offers us a vital opportunity for identity exploration. This exploration can be seen as the development of a critical relationship with the past which, in the terms of this book, is explored through living history and expressed through language. If this process is to be understood, however, knowledge and understanding about the past and how the past is constructed into history must be discussed. This form of discussion might be called education.

This book is also, therefore, about education. This is seen as taking place in a number of institutions with varying degrees of formality at different stages in one's life. Formal History education might most commonly take place in school but can also be found in museums and at historical sites.

This book is also, therefore, about places. 'Living history' is to be found in a setting that is often, although not always, purposefully constructed to support the interpretation. The setting contributes enormously to the version of history that is conveyed. In this book we draw examples from England, the east coast of the United States, and Australia. Notice that the authors have been identified as 'we' and are constructing this book.

This book is also, therefore, about writing a book. It is, like all other forms of history, a construction from traces of the past interpreted from our own perspectives. In this case, BG comes from a background of social psychology and literacy education and Gavin Baldwin (from now on referred to as GB) from a background of history and History education. We have both been primary school teachers and teacher educators.

This book is also therefore about ourselves.

**INTENDED READERSHIP**

In general, we see the potential readership as all those interested in the interpretation and communication of history, whether they are 'history professionals' or visitors to museums and historical sites. Specifically our intention is that this book will be of interest to:

- exponents of 'living history';
- museum professionals incorporating 'living history' into the interpretation of their collections;
- teachers trying to help children and young people develop a meaningful relationship with the past through exciting and stimulating teaching.

In addition, we are hoping that the book will be read by the growing number of visitors to museums and sites, who are fascinated by the past and the way in which it is presented. We would like to raise some questions in their minds about what is presented and how it is done.

The ideas in this book are not intended to be the final word on 'living history' as a means of exploring and communicating the past but as a part of a dialogue. The reader may violently disagree with our definitions of history and communication, may contradict our interpretation of 'living history' interactions, and dispute tentative conclusions. Our intention is that this can be done with more insight and understanding than before reading the book.

## THE BOOK'S STRUCTURE AND ORGANISATION

The book is organised into three parts:

Part 1  looks at background issues of definition, History and museum education, and the presentation of the past;

Part 2  analyses living history by considering the setting, visitor and interpreter;

Part 3  reflects upon living history in terms of the language used and its contribution to identity exploration.

### Part 1

In Chapter One we consider ideas of recreation, reconstruction and re-enactment and look at various ways in which living history can be defined and used.

In Chapter Two we move on to discuss History education as it can be found in schools, museums, and historical sites.

Chapter Three continues this analysis by looking at ways in which the past is presented in museums and at historical sites, setting up a continuum of communication. This places 'living history' as the most developed form of two-way interaction for communicating about the past.

### Part 2

Here we reach the central analysis. Examples of 'living history' drawn from our own visits, publications, and the Internet are analysed to explore the complexity of the phenomena of living history.

Chapter Four outlines the methodology and discusses our source material.

Chapter Five examines the range and types of setting in which 'living history' takes place.

Chapters Six and Seven analyse the interaction firstly by considering the visitor and then the interpreter.

### Part 3

Chapters Eight and Nine give us the opportunity to develop our own specific interests in relation to 'living history'.

In Chapter Eight BG analyses the language forms used to communicate between interpreter and visitor and in Chapter Nine GB demonstrates some of the ways in which 'living history' might contribute to identity exploration.

In Chapter Ten we outline our conclusions.

## ON FINISHING THE BOOK

We acknowledge that this has been a personal journey of discovery for both of us and hope that it will be illuminating for you as reader. We have met many dedicated and fascinating individuals on our odyssey and would like to thank them all for their generosity of time and spirit.

Beth Goodacre and Gavin Baldwin
July 2001

# PART ONE

———

# LIVING HISTORY, EDUCATION AND MUSEUMS

## Chapter one

❧

## MAKING HISTORY COME ALIVE

We have used the subheading: *reconstruction, recreation, re-enactment and education at museums and historical sites* with our title to help clarify the scope of the book. This is also because we are aware in these days of electronic data bases and information search engines as well as library data systems, that titles of books can be searched not only by the words of their title but also by what comes after a colon. The three words with their re- prefix are important. It is worth keeping in mind that the prefix doesn't have just one meaning but three, that of:

- doing or being back to a former state;
- doing something again;
- doing it again but in a better way.

We will be discussing this later in greater detail, but constructing or creating or enacting the past is also to re-present the past in a form as near as possible to what is known - or even to perceive it as being ' better' than it was. What we are intrigued by is the presentation of the past by or through such representation, particularly by means of discourse - written and spoken. In constructionist terms, this is the means by which, in this case, the 'past' can be accessible for discussion and even for practical use.

The three 're' terms used in the representation of the past describe how a period or event in the past can be re-enacted, recreated and reconstructed by those living in the present. The usage of the three terms by different groups, such as, for instance, museum and education staff, publicists for historical houses, or those involved in reliving battles or past historical events, indicates subtle differences. A brief discussion of this may serve to illuminate the complexities of this problematic phenomenon further.

Firstly, there is the effect of the re- prefix, which implies for all three terms the existence of something that is being seen again. It is interesting to consider how far this can be true. With an object that is an exact copy of a previous version, we know that we are reconstructing with the emphasis upon authenticity. For something for which only partial evidence remains we can only claim to be reconstructing what is known, the remaining reconstruction must in effect be recreation: in some senses 'inventing' again. This is often the case with archaeology where reconstruction takes on something of the elements of hypothesis testing of hunches as to how objects may have been used or 'worked' at a previous time.

In what are often known as 'living history' [1] presentations, we might ask what is being acted out again in the re-enactment being recreated for entertainment and historical presentation? We may assume that the costumes and artifacts are reconstructed or partially created but what of the way in which they are being used, the language being spoken, the relationships which are being acted out through the very people themselves? Are we involved in a re-enactment of a situation which might reasonably be thought to have happened before, or is what we are seeing complete fiction? We can never know how close our educated guesses are to past domestic situations for which no records remain and so we are then in danger of recreating a re-enactment of a past that never really existed.

These potential conclusions, fictions and cases of mistaken identity, especially for the Historian, demand that great care is taken by the re-enactors to achieve as authentic a presentation as possible. This is so that such presentation can be set within an explanation of the factual/fictional elements of the re-enactment and lead to the development of a critically discerning public - one of the aims of History education as envisaged in this book. However, for many visitors such historical presentations may be viewed and judged simply as entertaining spectacles, or interesting or unusual performances, requiring no more consideration of the presentation's authenticity than a play or a TV drama.

## FICTIONALITY IN RECREATING THE PAST

It is interesting here to consider the issue of historical authenticity as it concerns the filmmaker and, similarly, living history exponents and re-enactors. The film Titanic raised the question of the importance of getting the recreation of the disaster 'right'. The relatives and descendants of the ship's captain, however, queried the accuracy of the presentation of this 'character' in the film. Filmmakers have always had a problem with the extent of fictionality in films using historic themes. Establishing accuracy of presentation may take too long and slow down the action. It may be sufficient for the filmmaker just to create an 'impression' of the period or the historical event. Audiences primarily go to the cinema to be entertained and experience certain emotions. It has been argued that the historian is concerned with collecting evidence, evaluating it and presenting a generally informative picture, whereas the filmmaker is more concerned with emotional detail and an entertaining story line.

A useful distinction can be drawn between surface and underlying reality in regard to film and video drama, which may have relevance for the presentations of the past identified as 'living history'. Everything tends to look so real on film. In such dramatisations it may be sufficient for the director to create an 'impression' of the past, by concentrating on getting the most visible elements near enough to ' right' while not losing the plot and sacrificing the underlying 'truthfulness' of the film's interpretation. Perhaps one of the best examples of successfully accomplishing this balance would be the film *Schindler's List*. (BBC Radio 4 Programme in the series *That's History*, 7 March, 1998).

Film is different from 'living history' in many respects not least in the latter's espoused educational function. The film Titanic was made primarily to entertain (and to gross a fortune at the box office) and not to recreate or reconstruct the disaster accurately in order to teach the filmgoer a piece of history. This distinction can further be seen in the use made of film in teaching history packages. Such materials are not designed to publicise a film but rather to illustrate how film is a resource the historian might use to demonstrate how past events can be interpreted through representation. Questions that the classroom learner can be encouraged to ask could be, how do films get made? Whose interest does this particular version of the past serve? Is any archive footage of documented events used and if so, how is it merged with the 'fictional' footage? What is the extent of fictionality in the film? As we will see, parallel questions could be asked of 'living history'.

History and the media of film, TV and video, have been discussed here because to some extent similar problems of reality and authenticity concern all those involved in the presentation of history. The concern being the balance between historical accuracy and maintaining interest and attention. The balance is likely to be very different between those catering to entertain and those whose main mission is to educate: e.g.

- between the theme park with its paying visitors and the school party visiting a historical house where a butler and a housekeeper in Victorian dress demonstrate the activities 'below stairs';
- between costumed stall holders at a medieval fair selling replica armour to re-enactor 'hobbyists' and a costumed interpreter speaking in first person to visitors to an Elizabethan house where it is claimed that it is a specific year in the Queen's reign;
- between a party of primary school children dressed in their own 'home-made' togas, swords and shields visiting a ruined site and a guide dressed as a Roman soldier answering the questions of young visitors between the displays at the Museum of London.

**HOW DOES THINKING ABOUT THE PAST DIFFER FROM HISTORY?**

As the past and history are central concerns of this book, we should try to distinguish between the past and history before going any further. If the past is taken to mean all that has gone before, then history is the exploration and interpretation of that past. Simply, the past is the raw material that the historian mines to construct his or her explanations. It is the traces of past times which form sources of evidence which Historians can then use to support their interpretations and to demolish other versions of what happened put forward by other Historians. These traces are preserved by archivists and curators in archives and museums for scholars to use and consult.

At least that is one way, an elitist position from which to view historical activity. The 'populist' might say that the past is all that has gone before, some of which is remembered and some forgotten. The traces that are left behind are not just preserved in museums, archives and historical sites but in our everyday conventions and activities. In attempting to understand ourselves and the world in which we live, we are all involved in the historical activity of interpretation. The desire of many to understand and of many to teach (from a variety of motivations as we shall see later) led to museums being seen not just as places of conservation and preservation but places of public learning and cultural entertainment.

It is more from this popular educational tradition that the notion of 'reliving' the past or 'bringing the past to life', seems to have emerged.

## PRESENTATION OF THE PAST

Examples of how the past is not only recreated but, in the process, becomes a representation of the past, can be found in:

- museums with their displays and exhibitions;
- historic houses and their furnishings;
- heritage sites which can take a number of forms - battle sites, castles, forts, dockyards, markets, villages and towns - preserved or recreated.

In all these examples, choices have been made as to what and how to display items from the past, and whether information of an interpretive nature is to be provided for those who visit. This can be done by means of:

- labelling and notices ;
- employing persons to act as guides or interpreters;
- providing written publications and multimedia materials such as explanatory films or videos, which may or may not be used to prepare visitors to play the role which the museum expects of them.

## BRINGING THE PAST TO LIFE

This is essentially a paradoxical activity. It is a method of exploring past ways of life to endow them with some sense of completeness. Whereas analytical, critical history has traditionally attempted to maintain some degree of scholarly objectivity, an attempt to bring 'history to life' is likely to be seen by historians as essentially subjective. Exploring the past with the aim of bringing it to 'life' implies that we should see, feel, hear, smell and taste the past so that we can ultimately 'experience' life as it was led by our forebears. The limitations and abuses of this approach have long been the subject of critical debate (Hewison, 1987) but it remains resilient and popular. This is possibly because of the immediacy of experience that it offers and the escapist potential, seldom found to such a degree in other forms of historical inquiry.

However, it is a basic tenet of this book that such subjective exploration has an educational validity dependent on three elements;

1. a critical understanding of the process being engaged with;
2. the evidence on which it is based;
3. the interpretative starting point on which the reliving is founded.

This brings us to the other major element in the book as represented in the title: Education.

## EDUCATION IN THE BOOK'S TITLE

The word appears because we are concerned with the educational implications of living history as an increasingly popular form of historical interpretation and presentation. We hope the book will be of interest to teachers and educationists as well as historians and museum educators and those concerned with heritage sites and tourism. Since we are ourselves educators, we are deeply interested in how people learn - particularly children and young people. As we explained in the introduction, we have been involved in teacher education and have been primary school teachers. We share an interest in how people use language; GB (the history educator) for how the past is preserved through written description, record and explanation and BG (the literacy educator) in how areas of knowledge use and value various text types, thereby making different literacy demands on learners. Also, we have a common interest in how interpretations in school and museum education can present to learners forms of identity which influence how they see themselves as well as how they conceive of others.

This then is the audience we had in mind - not just teachers, but also museum educators, historians, visitors and families spending a day at Heritage sites or historical houses or recreated pioneer villages, as well as those re-enactors and interpreters who 'people' such places.

## 'LIVING HISTORY'

The subjective exploration of the past which we have described above, is generally known as 'living history'. Practitioners of this form of recreating the past usually distinguish it from re-enactment. For instance, the editor of *The Living History Newsletter* (Spring 1994, p.1) described the distinction in this way:

> For me it is the culmination of re-enactment, when hobby turns to passion. Watch the audience at a good living history - they fire up, the intelligence is engaged, it is NOT passive. Quintessential to Living History is the effect of real time, it tends to portray the small manageable and domestic scale, where re-enactment tends to the grand and has to curtail real time to recount the epic story.

In considering the defining characteristics of re-enactment the notion of real time seems to be crucial. The reconstructed epics of the battle of Marston Moor or the Battle of Hastings are recreated spectacles that, by their sheer scale and potential danger, can only be observed by an audience behind some type of barrier. In terms of authenticity they can be seriously flawed because of the distortion of time. In a re-enactment of the battle of Hastings a cavalry charge had to be cancelled as timings had overrun.

The domestic scale of many relivings of the past enables the audience to relate to fairly familiar activities which can be easily understood, whereas when enacted on a large scale they may require greater explanation in terms of technology and political significance. The way in which the audience is personally involved with the costumed characters in a re-enactment and how information about the period and its people is communicated, will depend on the type of interpretation that the re-enactors are using. Visitors will immediately be affected by a living history exponent's decision to use what is known as first or third person interpretation.

Table 1.1 below explains the linguistic difference between these two forms of interaction.

| Interpretation | Tense | Person | Techniques | Characters |
|---|---|---|---|---|
| First-person | present | I, mine, me | various – tells stories demonstrates question and answer | keeps in character at all times |
| Third-person | past present future | they, their them he/she his/her | informs demonstrates shows and tells | doesn't assume a character |
| Red T-shirting  Third-person Robertshaw (1992) | past present future | they, their them he/she his/her | introduces idea of first person to visitors; shows and tells explains how to interact | doesn't assume a character |

## DEFINING 'LIVING HISTORY'

To return to the more subjective conceptualising of the past, a major difficulty in exploring the notion of 'living history' is how it is defined and by whom. Definitions seem to vary as to whether they are being used by groups to define themselves or attributed to groups by others. Users define the notion in their choice of 'label' or 'naming' - whether they primarily conceive of living history as being:

- an **approach, method or medium** for 'doing historical work' or
- the **groups or organisations of people** who share a common interest in using the living history approach.

We are suggesting that there are different usages of 'living history' as a term (in single quotes or written with each word as a proper noun. e.g. Living History). Differences in definitions or explanations of the term can suggest different priorities and emphasis based on the users' beliefs and perceptions. Indeed, some exponents find it easier to define themselves by saying what they are not, since this then enables them to distinguish themselves from other groups. Often such groups will have the same 'label' or involve those differentiating words beginning with the prefix re-, which focus on the process adopted or the 'doing of historical work'; e.g. whether they 're-enact', 'recreate' or 'reconstruct'.

Where all groups seem to have some agreement is in relation to acknowledging that they are involved in interpretation and presentation of the past. Let's look at some of these usages.

## Approach, method or medium

In 1984, Jay Anderson wrote what has become probably the most frequently quoted book about living history. He called it *Time Machines*. He claimed that living history was a **medium** of historical research, interpretation, and celebration which he considered was absolutely right for the period in which he was writing and was about something in which he had been deeply involved for many years. He believed that as a medium, living history had three characteristics that would insure its historical significance as an effective way of 'doing' history. These were living history's :

1. ability to involve all the senses;
2. existence outside the boundary of established academic and public history and therefore its exponents' ability to set their own critical standards for recreating history;
3. rejection of a linear view of the past and preference for studying, interpreting and experiencing the everyday reality of ordinary people.

The result of holding such beliefs was that Anderson could then not only identify the main attributes of such an approach but also indicate how it differed from traditional approaches in having:

> an emphasis on new primary sources, especially material culture, and
> a willingness to try out novel techniques of research and
> interpretation..... Their goal (living historians) is not to discern a grand
> pattern of relationships but to steep themselves in the historical re-
> enactment context of a particular place and time and come to
> understand, appreciate, and feel the life of the people who once lived,
> there and then. (Anderson, 1984, p.192)

Fifteen years later Bill Hubbard, living in Sheffield, England used the advances of information technology to answer the same question - 'What is Living History?'. His answer to the question appeared on a web page he has compiled that is to be found on the Internet. Such pages can be changed frequently. They are more difficult to reference in the standard way in which references appear in published books. However they can be quickly updated and provide evidence of the greater ease with which their author or compiler can change or refine views and ideas being made available for interested readers.

Hubbard on his web page described living history as an **approach** which was used for 'trying to bring the past to life again by reconstructing the clothes, equipment, weapons, armour and tools of the past; wearing the clothes; fighting with the weapons and following the craftsmen's skills with the tools.' He saw it as an approach which could have the features of a pastime or obsession, encompassing all sorts of activities such as crafts, skills and types of knowledge.

> Within it you can take part in shows in front of thousands of people or talk one to one in explaining your craft or go on private weekends to sit wrapped in a cloak by a camp fire , miles from a town and the twentieth century.
> (http: www2.shef.ac.uk/personal/csljwh/living-history.html)

His definition brings out the range of activities which 'living history' techniques can encompass and that differences in definition will be related to the choices exponents make from the variety of activities accepted as being characteristic of living history as an approach.

Other commentators on the use of 'living history' have referred to it as providing an impression of historical events or conditions and as such exponents inevitably tend to be presenting generalisations about the past. (For some, it is only a short step from this to stereotyping) For instance, Robertshaw (1997) has suggested the living history technique offers:

> the opportunity to replicate aspects of the past, not its total simulation. As such we should view living history projects as generalisations about the past. As in any historical account they are based on incomplete evidence. A living history project is only as good as the evidence used to produce it. Like any form of museum interpretation what is central to the achievement of high standards is the quality of research and critical judgement applied to the project by those controlling it. (1997, p.7)

Hubbard acknowledged that there is considerable divergence of opinion as to what the public rather than the exponents understand by living history. He conjectured that the public most often see living history as re-enactment in the form of large shows held on holiday weekends, or spectacular recreations of Civil War battles or demonstrations by smaller societies at village fetes - all functions which emphasise the **public performance** element. The impression gained by members of the audience for living history performances and the approaches used to create the past, may be very different from those of the exponents themselves. They are likely to be immersed in experiencing, learning and developing their interpretation of living history.

## Groups of people and organisations

Although Jay Anderson was able to identify living history as a medium or approach, he also made a point of distinguishing three major **groups** of exponents who, he claimed, differed from one another on the basis of their purpose for simulating life in other times, in what at first might appear to be apparently similar ways. He described these three groups in the preface of *Time Machines* as those who were primarily interested in using simulation as:

1. **a way of interpreting** the realities of life in the past more effectively, and they were usually connected with institutions such as living museums or re-enactments taking place on historical sites. He wrote of these interpreters wanting to 'animate' a restored fort or farm, or village by inviting visitors to involve themselves in the daily activities of the period of time being presented.[2] He considered the goal of this group was essentially educational and that these interpreters often considered themselves as being 'master teachers'.

2. **a research tool**, since many of these exponents tended to have backgrounds in the disciplines of social science and were involved in trying to develop sites as 'outdoor laboratories' through which ethnological theories might be tested or new data collected about the material and cultural existence of specific groups of people living at some time in the past.

3. **escapism by 'time travelling'** for personal reasons being motivated to get away from the present and enjoy themselves, playing at being in another time or being another person. These were the enthusiasts who identified with particular, real or composite individuals of the past and 'fabricate' them into existence in the present. Anderson thought of them as being sticklers for 'authenticity' - especially for reproducing the correct clothing, grooming, and speech characteristic of the period. From his experience with these exponents he likened them to 'method actors' who steep themselves in a role in such a way that they can claim to improvise the character's 'demeanour and behaviour' with great effect. They called this creating a 'persona'. Anderson named such enthusiasts, 'history buffs'. (Anderson,1984 , pp.12-13)

Anderson concluded his book by asking what was the historical significance of these forms of interpretation - of these 'time machines' ? What was their function in the present, and indeed were they likely to have a future?

From his experience of talking to exponents he had identified three reasons for carrying out this activity:

1. a need to escape from what he called 'the tyranny of abstract time';
2. a nostalgic preference for the past - usually for a particular period;
3. a curiosity about the 'nitty-gritty of everyday life' in a specific time. (p.183)

He concluded in his last chapter that many living history exponents actually seemed to prefer the past to the present. They often claimed that they were born in the wrong century. People couldn't control where or when they were born but 'time travel gives them the opportunity to practice a kind of reverse re-incarnation. Living History is a means of being born again in a more congenial time and place.' (p.186)

He also claimed that ' ... all serious historians have a deep curiosity about the texture of life in the past. They want to know what it actually felt like to live, for example, on a Celtic farm and watch, as a Roman commander marched his company of foot soldiers north to man Hadrian's Wall.' He acknowledged that such leaps of the imagination were a dream that had 'the characteristics of a secular mystical experience, and that few living historians talk about it willingly.' (p.188)

Anderson believed that it was possible to 'walk around the bend and into the past' but in the fifteen years since he wrote this, although *Time Machines* is still considered a ground-breaking book on the medium of living history, his style of writing with its almost mystical tone, seems to claim too much for the approach and its exponents. Indeed there have been articles such as the response by the American curator David Peterson which condemned Anderson's claim that living history was 'the best way of teaching history', considering that 'Historical recreations are imperfect interpretations of the past itself.' (Peterson, 1988)

Hubbard also distinguished three main groups on the basis of his experience, although he granted that there would be considerable overlap. His tripartite division was as follows:

- re-enactment: Groups which **re-enact** occasions in history such as a Civil War battle or an Edwardian House Party. They put on shows for an audience;

- Living History : Groups which **research** their period of history very carefully and who try to live for a brief time, just as their historical counterparts did. They practice the crafts and skills;

- combat : Groups that **specialise in historic combat** and try to rediscover the skills needed to handle replica weapons. They too put on shows though these are generally on a smaller scale, so that individual skills and prowess can be demonstrated. (Our use of bold)

  (www2.shef.ac.uk/misc/personal/cs1/wh/definition.html; as at 5 July, 1997)

Hubbard noted that there were other groups but these involved themselves in what he saw as 'pure fantasy' - taking roles as wizards and goblins, or aliens and Starship Troopers. Or they fabricated a medieval period based more on fiction than history, or rewrote the middle ages not as they were but as what they felt they *should* have been. These were obviously **fantasy** groups.

David Lowenthal (1985) who wrote the book *The Past is a Foreign Country* included a section on re-enactments, commenting on the variety of **motivations** within re-enactors as a group:

> Some re-enactors simply seek to entertain, some to convince themselves or others of the reality of the past, some to heighten history's revelatory significance, some for a sense of purpose or excitement lacking in the present. Live actors repeat what was supposedly done in the past, and restored or replica houses are staffed with 'replica people' or 'human artifacts'. Like restorers, re-enactors start with known elements and fill in the gaps with the typical, the probable, or the invented. (1985, p. 295)

He too referred to how the re-enactors' activities can enliven history for 'millions who turn a blind or bored eye on ancient monuments, not to mention history books.' Although he cautioned that they risk turning venerable places into 'jokey or self-conscious replicas of themselves, or worse, persuading participants and even spectators that one can escape to the past.' For Lowenthal this was transportation into 'a fictitious yesterday purged of historical guilt' where members of these groups would be acting out fantasies denied to them in their contemporary lives. This is what might be called the 'escapist' view of the motivation of re-enactors and living history exponents - clearly seen as nostalgia for a time that might have been, but not as extreme a form as the fantasy groups referred to by Hubbard.

Some groups come together combining into larger groups or **organisations**. For instance, ALHFAM stands for the Association for Living Historical Farms and Agricultural Museums, which sees itself as 'An organization of People who bring History to Life' - the Association's banner heading on its web page. Within ALHFAM, living history is taken to mean just that:

> the efforts of history museums, historical societies, and other
> educational organizations to truly engage the public with the impact
> of history on their lives today. This is accomplished using historic
> objects and environs and appropriate recreations to tell the stories of
> the people who used those objects. In the effort to 'contextualize',
> some sites try to recreate a particular time and place in the past,
> ignoring the intrusions of the present.

The Association's statement claims that 'the effort to bring history to life is evident in the use of living animals and plants, in staff performing historic work or trades, and in the effort to be made to provide an environment rich in artifacts that focus attention on life in past times.'

The statement also refers to how some people may think of living history, equating it with:

> costumed role-players portraying life in a different time. Some think
> that it is only the group of folks who put on uniforms of past wars and
> have a good time re-enacting battles. While the Past can not change,
> history - which is an interpretation of the past - is always changing.
> What we call 'Living History' is a relatively recent development in
> the interpretation of history.
> (ALHFAM web page)

## Using information technology to define a group identity

There were and are groups of individuals portraying the past for a variety of reasons and using different methods, which include living history techniques. How do they think of themselves? More often than not as societies or organisations; that is, as definable entities with an existence over time. This can be illustrated by quoting from some of the groups that have created and affirmed an existence through individual web pages on the Internet.

These web home pages are a means of recruiting new members as well as keeping in touch with existing ones. The home page usually provides a 'mission' type statement, outlining the aims of the group as well as the methods they use to achieve their goals. A group's web site also makes use of photos and images, links to other groups' sites or sites of likely interest. Sometimes a bibliography is provided, details of any newsletter regularly produced and always an e-mail address for contact. We regularly searched some sixty relevant sites on the net from 1995 onwards, and an analysis of the type of information provided by such web pages proved useful background data for the framework developed in Part 2.

The examples which follow show the various ways in which some groups defined themselves in organisational terms, and then their aims and references to living history as a method or technique. Thus presenting themselves as groups, in which the members have a shared entity and identity in their shared beliefs and motivations about the significance of living history as an approach to the presentation of history.

Although we have been selective we feel that accessing the text of the home pages of some groups can provide the reader with an opportunity to understand how the compilers of these locations in cyber space realise, through **textual choices**, the group's identity and values. Whether they named themselves as societies, organisations, associations, companies or corporations and their references to using 'living history', appear in bold in the statements quoted from the home page texts on the Internet.

### Brigantia

'is an historical re-enactment **society** dedicated to the pagan Celts of southern Britain of the first century BC... travel around the south of England and Wales performing public displays of combat and **living history** for fairs, museums, schools, local councils and nation heritage organizations.'

'**Living history** displays are usually performed at locations where an iron age Celtic roundhouse has been constructed, such as open air museums or historical farms. Our hosts are usually museums.'

### Angelcynn (English people - period 400-700AD)

'is a **living history** society which aims to recreate, as authentically as possible, the richness of the birth of a nation which has passed into legend and into lore. We seek to create all aspects of life in the period; food, crafts, warfare, pastimes, in fact, everything that made up the life of these English people. Angelcynn lays great stress on all manner of details that comprise the clothing, artifacts and most importantly, the culture of this distant age.'

'We are a **society** that attracts people from all walks of life, young and old, who come together in a spirit of historical recreation.'

'Unlike some Societies, Angelcynn is not just about combat - we are not a "re-enactment" society, but a **"living history"** society - the arts, crafts and everyday "civilian" activities form a major part of Angelcynn's activity.'

'Membership primarily intended for people living in the British Isles, but those from other parts of the world are welcome also.'

The next example although a re-enactment group is included because it demonstrates how a group can continue to use its original name while in fact changing its methods and increasing the scope of its presentation.

### English Civil War Society (ECWS)

'A 17th Century History Re-enactment **Group**.... is a UK based history re-enactment group that portrays events of the period 1642-51 for the entertainment and education of the audience at public displays.'

'... although our spectacular battle re-enactments remain as popular as ever with the public there is a growing interest in smaller events at which the audience can experience close contact with the participants, asking questions and examining the clothing, weapons and artifacts. These **living history** displays often portray soldiers in garrison or under siege, and many now have a "civilian" element so that aspects of everyday life in the 17th century can be demonstrated as well as military skills. These events ideally take place in an appropriate location, such as a castle or other ancient buildings, but 17th century "villages" have been built from scratch where necessary!'

The next example, also a re-enactment group, considers re-enacting the physical presence of persons from the past.

### The 14th Brooklyn New York State Militia International

'Re-enactment **organization** exists to honor the lives and deeds of those men of the original 14th Brooklyn (84th NY Vol. INF). We do this by creating an exact appearance in uniform as a process which brings history to life even to the extent of its members becoming and recreating the persona of individual men and women. We participate in living histories and battle re-enactments throughout the US and Canada. We endeavor to be authentic in our re-enacting but we also try to have fun and educate the public and make them aware of their history.'

'Re-enacting is **Living History**.'

**Living History** is an interpretive tool and process which uses techniques derived from theater and translates data from the historical documents into multi-sensory experience. Basically that means we become the physical presence of those people who made history.

**Living history** has the potential to create an atmosphere of greater depth than the written word and can appeal to the broader range of interests.'

The last two examples are of very different 'corporate' groups.

### Ghost Riders (USA)

'This band of rabble is known as Ghost Riders, a nonprofit **Living History/stunt company** composed of re-enactors with ongoing experience in Civil War and Old West re-enacting.

We do **Living History** interpretations based on either first-person or generic approximations of frontier people and events spanning the years prior to the American Civil War up to the turn of the century.

The Ghost Riders provide slices of history for public consumption. That means the encampment, street scene, or some similar representation of daily life in the Old West.'

### The Living History Foundation (USA)

'is a tax exempt, non-profit corporation that promotes the use of living history as a method of interpreting historic sites and events to the public. The Foundation seeks to help the public become more aware of their kinship with the people of earlier time, and to understand their fears, hopes and attitudes. In this way, we seek to shine a bright light on the present.

The Foundation promotes the use of first-person interpretation. Players take on the roles of historic characters (actual, composite or hypothetical) and project themselves into the time frame and situation being interpreted.'

## 'LIVING HISTORY' AS TRIVIALISATION OF THE PAST

We should now mention that there is a criticism applied to living history which not only conceives of it as fantastical but as a deliberate form of the trivialisation of the past and for which the term 'Disneyfication' has been devised. This has basis in fact to the extent that there was considerable furor when Walt Disney Studios announced plans to develop a 'historic amusement park' near the Manassas (Virginia) National Battlefield Park in the United States. The public debate which ensued about the appropriateness of this action in a region of revered battlefields with their monuments and burial sites, was largely a debate over the popular understanding of history and reflected an ongoing tension between what might be called the academic historians and the purveyors of popular history. (Guest, 1994)

Mike Wallace's book *Mickey Mouse History and Other Essays on American Memory* delves into more examples of this struggle over public memory and the trivialisation of history that seems to pervade the American culture of the recent past. Whether his subject is multimillion dollar theme parks, urban museums or television drama series, Wallace has demonstrated how depictions of history are shaped by assumptions about which pasts are worthy of being preserved and whose stories should be told, as well as what gets left out in the telling and who makes these decisions.

The association of the word 'Disneyfication' with living history has brought a pejorative colouration to the use of the term and an implication that the approach of those who use it is primarily concerned with 'edutainment' and making money, than the practice of serious history scholarship. Something of this 'high' culture valuation of the role of museums might be detected in the words of Robert Anderson, the director of the British Museum when the Museum was threatened with having to charge visitors for entry:

> Museums are a part of our cultural landscape, to be consulted, to
> impart knowledge and to inspire curiosity. In this they are akin to
> great reference libraries, surpassing by far subordinate roles such as
> that of tourist attraction, heritage experience or entertainment centre.
> Charging changes the relationship between the museum and its
> public, encouraging these latter roles over the former.

(*The Daily Telegraph*, 27 November, 1997)

By the early 1980's more than 800 museums and sites in the United States were using the living history method (Shafernich, 1993), an indication of how the institution of the museum is undergoing change. It is only late within this century, that museums have begun to broaden their outlook, to creatively experiment with alternative, more interactive methods, and to accept that there are many ways of presenting both artifacts and ideas. Increasingly some museums and galleries are now focusing on being entertaining as well as educational. The effect of traditional displays in cases can be restrictive to the visitor - the glass comes between the object and the viewer. Where specially trained and costumed staff can demonstrate how the object was used, answer questions about it, and the visitor can handle the artifact - even use it - real learning can result. As Jane Malcolm-Davis has suggested 'the power of human interaction, in what have long been regarded as stuffy institutions, is such that even poor attempts have been heralded as 'breakthroughs' and some visitors believe that the role-playing actors just add to 'the entertainment, which is what people are coming for.' (Shafernich, 1996)

**CONCLUSION**

The starting point of this chapter was the creating and reconstruction of history through enactment and re-enactment and the extent to which this involved replication and concerns regarding the importance of authenticity. There seemed to be largely an emphasis on recreating the past through being able to see and even use the objects and artifacts of the past. However where there was an interest not just in how these were used but also why, when and where, there seemed to be greater emphasis upon a subjective exploration that valued **human** motivation, thinking and reasoning. It appeared to find expression in what has become known as 'living history'. We then explored the variety of definitions and uses of the term.

We would like to conclude this chapter by presenting four vignettes. There are several dictionary meanings for the word 'vignette': it can mean an ornamental pattern or drawing without a border, set into a book especially at the beginning or end of a chapter. Well our vignettes do not have borders but we do place them here at the end of this chapter. An alternative meaning of the word is a short, effective, written description of a character or scene, and this is how we intend to use them here. They are descriptions of four re-enactment and living history experiences taken from our notes of visits. They are scenes that we saw at different times and different places. We would like them to provide you with a 'taster' of 'living the past'.

Two examples were written individually - one as an experience of visiting a living history museum in the United States and one a battle re-enactment in the north of England.

The other two are our descriptions of the same heritage living history site in NSW, Australia, which we visited individually at different times, some eighteen months apart.

## Vignette 1

### Plimoth Plantation: Where history repeats itself. GB's account.

'In the village, people portray residents of the community of Pilgrims. Odd-looking visitors consider themselves as guests transported back in time by modern technology. Not far from where we sit is the 1627 Pilgrim Village, a recreation of the coastal farming community built by the English settlers. Colonists here with stories to tell.'

*So the orientation film set the scene.*

*Leaving the cinema and the museum behind the visitor enters the world of re-enacted Plimoth Plantation to be greeted by a Pilgrim leaning on his hoe.*

*"Good day to you"*

*"Good day to you," replies the visitor. "What crops are you planting?"*

*Welcoming the distraction from his backbreaking, seventeenth century work the Pilgrim pauses, rests on his hoe and explains the types of crops that he is growing, the methods he uses and the experiences of his family. We exchange farewells and he returns to his work.*

*From the top of the hill, the plantation stretches down to the river. The main street, a dusty road with wooden houses either side. The whole village is surrounded by a stockade. At this time on a quiet, bright April morning visitors are few and the pilgrims seldom interrupted in their work.*

*Conversations are beginning to take place all around, some between Pilgrims in seventeenth century speech and some between Pilgrims and visitors; the visitors trying to make Pilgrims understand their twentieth century questions and deciphering the seventeenth century answers.*

*A woman confides, as she repairs the wattle and daub of her house, that she had only recently arrived in Plimoth having committed herself into the hand of God. A man, building his house, explains how a board house is made. He talks about the friendliness of the 'naturals' [Indians] "of faith would they convert."*

*A Pilgrim cutting wood from a tree trunk discusses his carpentry and his reasons for moving to the New World.*

*"Land, aye, there's little else this place has to offer. Yeh? For 'tis but wilderness," he explains.*

*"And not freedom?" The visitor pursues her point. "Mm? Not freedom? To believe what you want to believe?"*

*"Ah your speaking of some of this church here what has separated from the King's church. But truly 'tis not freedom they seek, for such is the chaos of Holland there are all manner of sorts there that do not know what they want. I think that the congregation were well settled when they were there but... I think what has brought them here is much the same as what's brought me here, the opportunities of*

*the place, the land. Well, when you are living in exile...from some of the tales I have heard of their life in Holland 't were very hard and many of their children at a fair early age set to a very hard labour, fearing the years coming on and very fast."*

*At this moment, another visitor interrupts "Excuse me Sir. Did I hear you mentioning the house the Whites lived in? "*

*The first visitor turns away to seek out many other opportunities for conversation with the Pilgrims.*

*(GB's notes)*

## Vignette 2

## Battle of Marston Moor, the Sealed Knot. BG's account.

*It is the 350th anniversary of the Battle of Marston Moor being re-enacted by the Sealed Knot Society (Civil War group) in the grounds of Ripley Castle, North Yorkshire. This was the largest battle fought on English soil and is being commemorated on the exact date of the original battle in what is claimed to be the largest re-enactment ever staged in the United Kingdom.*

*The Allied army of English Parliamentarians and Scots Coventanters faced the combined Royalist forces on July 2 1644. Although lasting a mere two hours, 4,000 Royalist troops were slain. The outcome is known. History will repeat itself.*

*The troops assemble under the trees down by the lake. On the other side of the lake through the trees can be seen the parked caravans of the re-enactors and their huge mess tent. The horsemen, musketeers, pikemen, drummers, women followers, and the groups pushing and pulling the cannon begin moving up the dirt road which leads to the large roped-off area of the battle, passing an ambulance parked under the trees. It is said that some 8,000 re-enactors will take to the field today.*

*Visitors and tourists keep clear of the roped area, some taking up viewpoints on the rising ground above. Costumed characters patrol the roped perimeter cautioning the growing crowd to stand back and think of their safety.*

*The battle commences at 3.00 p.m. There is a broadcast commentary from a parked caravan near the red and white ropes of protective barrier. A male voice loudly identifies the different forces arriving on site. As the cannons and muskets are fired, smoke rises and obscures the groups of men now locked in battle. Horsemen charge and swerve to avoid the grouped pikemen lowering their weapons from the vertical to the horizontal and now tightly packed together in a defensive circle. There is the clashing sound of pike striking pike. The cannon fire is surprisingly loud, and very near as half a dozen mounted royalists clatter to a halt and shout for water for their steaming horses. Women re-enactors in costume duck beneath the roped barricade to offer pails of refreshment to man and beast. At close quarters, it can be seen that some of the 'horsemen' are women, as also are some of the musketeers and the drummer 'boys'. Outside the battle area, there are women, children and babies in costume. A young lad in breeches and shirt sprawls on the grass in the warm July sunshine, eyes closed apparently ignoring the skirmishes beyond the red and white ropes that mark off the battle area. A large mastiff lies beside him, head resting on its paws. Are they sleeping as the smoke drifts out of the battle area and the air resounds to the clash of steel as these historic forces take the field?*

*Near me a woman and several children, all in costume observe the re-enactment with nonchalance. The smallest child looks up at the woman to ask,*

*"are they really pretending Mummy?" The woman doesn't look down or take here eyes off the scene before merely replying*

*"Yes they certainly are! Look over there, there's your father being killed."*

*(BG's notes)*

## Vignette 3

### Old Sydney Town, Australia. BG's account

*(Staying with friends before going on to Melbourne Conference)*

*Lovely morning, no wind now (after gales that did damage the day before in Sydney) and a clear blue sky as we drove to Old Sydney Town - Recreating the birth of a nation 1788-1810 ... The Biggest Heritage Park in N.S.W. Australia" (pamphlet information). North of Sydney (the real one) along the F3 Expressway, take Gosford Exit.*

*We parked the car and went straight into the entrance, passing gift shop and greeted by large gentleman in gold braided uniform indicating entrance to site - so taken with his visual appearance unclear what he said and whether he was acting as someone from the created past. The girl in the ticket office very much part of the present.*

*Passed from brilliant sunlight into darkness of a 'time tunnel' and then windows showing how people would have travelled to NSW by sailing ship - berths for passengers, convicts in the hold. Then out into the open, to see dirt streets and a windmill - sails turning slowly, the mill built of quarried and shaped sandstone, golden in the morning sun.*

*While inspecting the building, heard the sound of a drum and shouts - commotion as someone cried out 'a convict being arrested'. Joined other visitors and a procession of costumed characters or interpreters - ' to the court house'. Diverted by seeing a funeral procession near the half-built church. Stopped to see what was going on. Funeral service not completed. Minister abandoned it to go and see to his 'grog', one of the soldiers having told him it had just arrived and was being unloaded.*

*Joined the crowd seated on benches in the courthouse. Decided that both the burial and the trial were being played for laughs. Woman on trial. Judge made reference to how her fine could be paid by a member of the public. Reference that I didn't understand to bribery ... friends said it was a joke about a local, state* politician! Children and adults made up the audience, interpreters playing to 'the gallery' (to the adults) using mock seriousness and evoking the feeling of a melodrama performance. Or when attempting to include the audience of visitors, more like the verbal exchanges between players and audience in pantomime. Very much a 'happening' that was a timed performance, stage managed and controlled by the performers.

After the court proceedings, the next happening was a public flogging outside the goal. Young children and toddlers present. Flogging brief but 'bloody', but the same strange mixture of joking and authenticity with the prisoner pleading in a high treble for 'just one more stroke, mister' to the gaoler character.

Walked down to the quay and buildings (King's Dockyard) by lake (Sydney Cove) and watched the harnessing of bullocks by elderly man in tricorn hat and checked shirt (later identified from booklet on sale, mainly made up of pictures of characters and happenings, as 'Joseph Dunnage'). Saw a farrier demonstrate how to shoe a horse in the stables.

Had our picnic lunch in the area by the frigate (replica?) tied up at the wharf. Sun now hot and the lake glinting in the sunlight. Across the other side we could see sheep and kangaroos penned in a yard, children having donkey rides.

Went back up the main street to see other places or programmed events. In amongst the trees caught sight of a humpy (Aboriginal hut) made of branches, notice pinned to it said that Bungeree (Aborigine) and his family had gone shopping.

Rode in the horse drawn wagon that 'transports visitors through the colony' (booklet). The driver was young and made no attempt to act 'in character'. He had only been doing it for a week. 'How do you like the job?' asked my friend. 'It's OK. Better than being at the abattoir.'

Is there a difference between the 'service' staff on the site and the costumed recreators as to whether they talk to visitors in character or not?

We visited the King's Head Tavern and had an excellent demonstration by a young soldier, standing on a table, of the problems of musket loading and the potential dangers of the weapon for its user. A chatty, in character, performance which kept the visitors' interest but there was little interchange between recreator and his audience. Then to the printers and to the candle shop of 'Jane Russell' (booklet). Glimpsed some of the 'red coats' (soldiers) chatting to a woman in a long fawn skirt and wide brimmed straw hat. All were drinking tea standing round an open fire. The smoke drifted up through the gum trees, and the scene looked authentic and evocative of a past time, possibly because of the costumes and their colour against the grey tones of the bush - except of course, for the paper cups they were holding.

As the sun lowered in the sky, we passed once again the Government Windmill (booklet), this time in partial shade and out to the car park through a picnic area, leaving Old Sydney Town to its cast of costumed re-enactors.

(BG's notes. This was my first visit to a living history site.)

## Vignette 4

### Old Sydney Town. GB's account, visit some eighteen months after that made by BG.

*You are invited to leave your car and the Twentieth Century here. So says the sign in the Car park. I walk over to the entrance where there is a welcoming board surrounded by life sized cut outs of drawn figures; the characters are colourful. The notice board reads*

Old Sydney Town is the world's first faithful (previously 'authentic' has been painted out) re-enactment of the Birth of a Nation. The period is our early history 1788 - 1810 and the area represented is today bounded by Macquarie, Hunter York and Argyle streets. The people who inhabit the Town are living out the lives of the colourful early settlers. Feel free to question them about their lives. Please value Old Sydney town as part of our heritage and that of future generations.

*I am in luck for*

The battle of old Sydney town is taking place today, the biggest re-enactment of its type is a convict rebellion leading to a full scale military cannon battle, followed by hand to hand combat supported by the Black powder gun clubs from all over Australia.

*The introductory exhibition includes a timeline, some social context and an account of the construction 'after much research' of the site 'as an authentic replica.' The entrance can be through the Time tunnel,*

to share with us something of that 6 to 8 month experience which brought convicts to this land. Magically the ship will take you back in time to around 1808.

*Dimly lit: a rat on a table, hammocks, someone who has been flogged lying as if half dead over a table. There is an alternative entry with barbecues and picnic area.*

*From the start, it is clear that this is not a recreation like Williamsburg or Plimoth. There are information boards on brown wood, manikins with grinning or grimacing faces in contorted or tortured positions and poorly kept interiors viewed through a metal grill. The Bonded warehouse is offering wine tasting.*

*There is one character in costume and glasses tilling the soil and an old beggar with a sign round his neck saying 'kiss me'. The Milliner's cottage*

A pretty cottage this, suited to a lady making items of fashion for the more well-to-do ladies of Sydney...pretty merchandise indicate an establishment of taste and fashion. Sarah Parry was a milliner in England transported for assault and robbery." (There follows further information about her life in Sydney)

*The Observatory: a model drawing of the solar system a soldier's uniform hanging on a peg and a bottle of mineral water on the table. A drinks can is crushed into the floor.*

*The gaoler's story is about torture and punishment. - You're gonna love it!' Or so we are told. The torture instruments are explained and punishments related with great verve and relish by the gaoler who delights in the more bloodthirsty details including details of what happens when a man is flogged exposing his lungs and other organs pulsating inside. Afterwards rock salt is rubbed in to avoid infection 'so we can do it again tomorrow misses.'*

*A technical demonstration of how a musket worked includes jokes and explanations of the phrases 'flash in the Macavoy, one of the Irish rebels. People are excited by this...... 'see that Dad.'*

*The result of his trial is announced and Macavoy will hang by the neck until dead. God Save the King. An Irish rebel hopes he rots in hell. Macavoy is brought out to a muffled drum. Sprung by the rebels, among general confusion he is rushed away through the town, the guards in hot pursuit.*

*We, the visitors are addressed as the people of Sydney, and told that the Irish rebels have made off to the Rocks, 'where you may hear a rabble rousing speech.'*

*'Who will join the freedom fighters to overthrow the tyranny of England?'*

*A man is flogged to the cheers and laughter of the crowd. Volunteers in the crowd are prepared humorously for battle. Martial law and a curfew are imposed. The Reverend is invited to speak but far too drunk to make much sense.*

*It all ends with a full cannon battle complete with dummies blown apart and their blood spattered limbs falling from the sky. It's noticeable that you can see the explosives and dummies before they are blown up. There is a great deal of noise and a very enthusiastic crowd.*

---

## Footnotes

1   We have chosen to use the term 'living history' as a shorthand way of referring to all the forms of historical presentation that use costumed interpreters. We are aware that some exponents make distinctions between 'living history' and 're-enactment' and between being in role or not, and between using first or third person when speaking. These crucial distinctions are analysed in Part 2.

2   From 'animate' the term 'animateur' is derived which is used by some living history exponents. Visiting the Australian gold mining township of Sovereign Hill in the state of Victoria, one of the costumed guides used the term. However, Michael Evans in his paper 'Historical Interpretation at Sovereign Hill' in Rickard and Sperritt (1991) has a photograph of the main street at Sovereign Hill with a caption referring to costumed 'activators'.

*Chapter two*

❧

# HISTORY EDUCATION IN SCHOOLS, MUSEUMS AND AT HISTORIC SITES

In this chapter, we examine ways in which History education can be achieved in three specific institutions; those of the school, the museum and the historic site. The parameters of possibility are defined by the **context of culture**, i.e. the way in which History education can be conceived as a legitimate activity in the western world. The specific realities of this form of education are defined by the **context of situation** within such institutions. That is, what is considered to be appropriate behaviour, values, attitudes, organisation and management within those places identified by the society and culture as schools, museums, and historic sites where the past and History can be represented and studied. Together, the contexts of culture and situation help to determine specific physical settings dedicated to the presentation of the past. These are not only the museums but also the houses, farm buildings, mills, factories, and mines of the past no longer in use but preserved as being representative of another time. There are also the recreated and reconstructed villages and the replica ships. These are all **settings** in which History education may be seen as an appropriate and effective activity.

First, we consider the nature of History education and its manifestation in the school curriculum. A distinction can and should be made between formal and informal education. In a similar fashion, to understand the time dimension, it is necessary to clarify the difference between the past and how we establish a critical relationship with it and what has become constituted as an area of knowledge known as History. (Section 1). We will then briefly consider how History education in the school develops these conceptions of time and the past to enable the teaching of the subject of school History and to develop the skills necessary to critically access historical resources. (Section 2). We will then turn our attention to changes in museums and consider the future of History education . (Section 3). Before leaving this discussion, we consider two educational methods - the adoption by museums of the 'hands on' approach and 'discovery methods', and the role of literacy in History education. (Section 4). This brings us back to a consideration of the power of the' living history' approach as one of the more recent History education methods, to establish a critical relationship with the past. (Section 5). We end by considering the hidden curriculum of museum education.(Section 6).

**SECTION 1: HISTORY EDUCATION**

Chris Husbands in his book *What is History Teaching?* (1996) has distinguished three uses of the word 'history' which may be helpful at this stage of our discussion.

History as:

- the **academic discipline** undertaken by historians who construct intellectually coherent accounts of the past consistent with collected evidence;
- the **subject or area of knowledge** taught by teachers in schools to pupils of different ages and intellectual ability, the value of the subject being reflected in the time devoted to its teaching within the curriculum;
- **information, activities and narratives about the past** which have interest for a wide range of people in different communities within a society.

History as a curriculum 'subject' will differ in different countries. Differences are likely to be related to such issues as:

- the content and scope of the subject;
- the role that the subject plays in the school system in the sense of the value attributed to it in comparison with other subjects;
- the focus at state, national or society level as, for instance, an 'examinable' subject or conferring access to higher education;
- the teaching and how the subject is conceived, particularly in passing on valued knowledge, demonstrating usable or marketable skills, or inculcating empathic attitudes.

In this section, we are referring to school History and History education and its contribution to developing a critical relationship to the past. It is suggested here, and pursued fully in Chapter nine, that such a conception of History education is of great benefit when considering issues of identity exploration

Teachers in schools work within the constraints of the form of curriculum development taking place in the school system at any given time. Chris Husbands (1996) discussed the controversy over how history should be taught in United Kingdom (UK) schools. He suggested that it involved a number of overlapping disagreements, with debates about what was appropriate content for history as a school subject and particularly the balance between 'content' and 'skills' in teaching it. Husbands concluded that all these debates in the UK arose from fundamental disagreements about the nature and place of history in the school curriculum.

**Informal and formal History education**

The controversy inevitably involved implicit assumptions about 'education' and confusions as to the difference between 'educating' and 'learning'. It may be useful to distinguish between informal and formal education. Generally, it is on the latter that controversies tend to focus - what should go on in schools. Informal education on the other hand can best be described as the process of taking our experiences, grouping and ordering them into frameworks or schemas that help us to make sense of our lives. These are expanded and revised in the light of new experiences and can be seen as a developing relationship between 'the world out there' and our internal, personal ways of making experience meaningful.

These informal understandings are likely to be structured and changed by the 'subject' teaching that takes place in the situation of specific schools. Through formal education, the society and its culture organise such personal understandings into forms of knowledge; the 'disciplines' - such as 'Mathematics', 'Science' and 'History'. (We have adopted the convention that when we are talking about history as a discipline or school subject we use the capital letter).

This distinction between informal and formal education is not always clear, especially in educational settings other than the school, such as the museum and the historical site. Moreover, the process of shifting from informal to formal understanding is not straightforward or uncontested.

To illuminate the process it may be useful to consider Guy Claxton's idea of minitheories which, although developed in the field of science education, can be applied successfully to other subjects. (Claxton, 1993). These minitheories consist of three types: the gut, the lay and the school formulation. Although Claxton is concerned specifically with school learning, a similar process may be undergone in any educational situation at any time in life. A carefully designed museum display or living history re-enactment may challenge and restructure our gut and lay conceptions, as readily as a lesson in the classroom and perhaps to greater effect.

Such minitheories function as 'working' schemas that can be discarded, changed or stubbornly retained unaltered by the individual. They correspond to informal education. Formal education takes such minitheories, which are often fragmentary and contradictory, and modifies and attempts to extend them through carefully designed learning experiences into conforming conceptions of school knowledge.

### Understanding the time dimension

History education is also the process by which we come to understand the time dimension of the world and more specifically the relationship between the 'past', the 'present' and perhaps the 'future'. Informal History education is the construction of minitheories based on our daily experiences of the traces of the past with which we come into contact. It is the process of making sense of living in an historical environment surrounded by objects, buildings, people and ideas that are derived from the past. Through the stories we hear, the television we watch, the music we listen to, the books we read, we are bombarded with images and references to the past.

To investigate the television aspect of this idea GB conducted a small-scale study with some first year undergraduates. He and the students analysed the output of children's television for one week. Of 500 minutes of viewing of BBC children's television, almost a quarter, 118 minutes (23.6 per cent) of time included references to the past. On Independent Television, the amount of time was 63 minutes (12.6 per cent of the total time). References to the past appeared in stories, cartoons, and news items.[1]

Although the study's methodology was unsophisticated, it enabled the students, as future teachers, to become aware that children have amassed a huge amount of informal information about the past. Some of it may be relatively accurate and some verging on total fantasy. The incorporation of this information into a person's developing minitheories, depends on what is meaningful to the learner at their particular stage of development. Sensitive and intuitive teachers tend to understand the logic of the child's reasoning from what the learner can verbalise and communicate. Clues are there to be interpreted and become part of the teacher's informal professional knowledge and development.

## Establishing a relationship with the past

We make sense of our historical environment and construct a relationship with the past, which, through memory, influences our thoughts and actions. This relationship has enormous power to influence both our views of ourselves and others, and our understanding of the creation and clarification of our identities. The version of history on which it is based might be akin to myth: a narrative of real psychological 'truth' which may be at variance with, and certainly more powerful than, historical 'truth'. In the process of identity formation it is what the individual or societies choose to believe to have occurred that may be more important than what actually happened (Baldwin, 1996). If this is true, it is crucial that this relationship with the past is established and examined critically. This must therefore become one of the chief aims of formal History education, both in schools and in museums and at historic sites.

These everyday experiences of the past, the minitheories that are derived from them and the consequent relationship that develops with the past, all correspond to informal History education. Formal History education structures them into the knowledge and skills incorporated in History the academic subject.

## What is History?

There has been much debate recently about the nature of History and its claims to truth. Whereas once History was simply a search for the truth about the past, we are now much more aware of our own, individual role in constructing that past. However it is Historians, operating as products of their own time, who explain the 'past' to their own 'present'. They select evidence from the traces of the past that remain in order to construct their version of the past that relates to their particular perspective. There is no 'correct' interpretation as such but rather a number of competing or complementary versions.

Hayden White, a particularly lucid and perceptive critic of historical thinking, expressed the value of entertaining a variety of views, explanations and interpretations. If Historians were to:

> recognise that there is no such thing as a single correct view... This would allow us to entertain seriously those creative distortions offered by minds capable of looking at the past with the same seriousness as ourselves but with different orientations.
>
> (Cited in Husbands, 1996, pp.57-8)

This doesn't mean that 'anything goes.' Historians still operate with honest regard for their sources but they are increasingly aware of the partial nature of those sources, the assumptions that they make, and the imagination that they use in interpreting them.

White also wrote 'how else can any past, which by definition comprises events, processes, structures and so forth which are no longer perceivable, be represented...except in an imaginary way?' This introduces the notion of **historical imagination**, which can be seen as the controlled use of the creative intellect. It can be used for two main purposes: first to fill in the gaps of an historical account which are left by the partiality of the evidence; second to attempt to understand why historical characters acted in the ways in which they did and what they intended by those actions.

It was the historian R.G. Collingwood, who first seriously analysed the contribution of historical imagination to developing historical understanding. He saw it as central to the process of history: a re-enactment of past experience or a rethinking of past thoughts. Historical reconstruction is conceived as a work of the imagination and historical understanding yields self knowledge. (Dray, 1995, p.5)

So we come to a view of History as an act of the imagination reflecting the perspectives of the Historian which contributes to self-knowledge and therefore our understanding of identity.

## SECTION 2: HISTORY EDUCATION IN SCHOOLS

On returning to History education, it can now be seen that History educators have a complex task. They must take students' minitheories and, by modification and the introduction of new ideas, encourage them to become imaginatively involved in the past in order to examine critically their relationship with it. Learners may be helped to articulate their own identities, while being aware of, and critical of, identities imposed on them by others.

This more usually takes place in school but can also be tackled in museums and at historic sites; that is, in different settings with different cultural backgrounds and educational expectations than the school. The problems are therefore different. In the school, the teacher has the time and opportunity to expose gut and lay minitheories and work with them. In museums, where people may only visit once, misunderstandings will need to be predicted. The message of the exhibition needs to be made very clear and convincing so that modification can take place. This is clearly a less certain outcome than it might be in school. There is a danger that lay minitheories will be reinforced by museum visitors selecting what already fits their framework of understanding, rather than modifying that framework to fit the new information confronting them. It is therefore important that museum visitors are encouraged to view their perceptions in new ways. (Sword, 1994)

We want now to provide an example from History education to illustrate how an understanding of the derivation of historical accounts may be developed, not only in the context of the school setting but also in that of museums and historical sites, by examining the use of **historical sources**.

Much use is made of historical sources from the earliest stages of formal History education in the United Kingdom. Three-year-olds are introduced to old things and five-year-olds may look at old pictures of themselves and their families. As the History curriculum becomes more content specific and units are designed for the study of separate periods, so sources are used to develop a picture of an era to stimulate questions and to structure an historical inquiry. As children proceed through school, the use of source material becomes more complex and closer to the practice of the Historian working in the archive. Husbands (1996) has reminded us however, that it is naive to equate the child's use of sources with the Historian's. The teacher uses sources in school to develop children's thinking skills through the ways in which the sources are interrogated and deployed, the child's understandings being essentially personal and private. The Historian has already developed those skills and is focused on constructing an interpretation of the past that will contribute to public knowledge and understanding. (Husbands, 1996, pp.13-29).

The use of sources in school does, however, alert children to the process through which historical accounts are constructed by Historians. Contextualising sources, verifying them with others, considering how other Historians have made use of the information and applying their historical imaginations, can develop a critical awareness in children. They are learning how the past is constructed and turned into History.

## SECTION 3: HISTORY EDUCATION AND MUSEUMS

Museums also engage in the process of constructing historical understanding from sources, indicating through their displays the different meanings that have been attributed to artifacts in differing interpretations at different times. They can make clear the reasoning behind the construction of an exhibition and indicate perspectives that are missing or voices that are unheard. They can produce displays, organise events over a period of time and marshal their resources providing this as a service to the schools, visiting adults, and family parties. The following account of such an exhibition is taken from GB's field notes of April 1994 , written text (*History*) indicating his notes and print (History) text material.

> *The Valentine Museum in Richmond, Virginia, USA mounted an exhibition entitled "Creating the Valentine Family: a museum history" and showed how the*

> *interpretations had reinforced cultural norms. I quote from the museum's*
> *information boards (Visit April 1995).*

History is an interpretation of the past. We all create individual and unique
histories in:

> our own minds according to our own needs by combining our personal
> versions of history with interpretations of other's: expert or otherwise.
> It is our own individual histories, our understandings of the past on
> which we act and effect the present. 'Creating History' presents three
> generations of the Valentine family as a case study to explore how the
> emerging social values of the 19th century middle class influenced
> their beliefs and actions. These values were often projected into the
> community through the creation of an institution, in this case the
> Valentine museum, that was perceived to have authority.

The exhibition traces the family's history and presents four interpretative
periods at the Valentine:

> The museum's collecting and interpreting artifacts and ideas more
> often reflects and validates cultural norms than it challenges and
> reshapes them. In each of these periods the Valentines, through their
> museum, explicitly and implicitly collected and presented a different
> view of culture and history. These changing views reflected changes
> in social assumptions, evolving scholarly understandings of culture
> and the past and the finding of new evidence... Over the years
> histories that were once advocated by experts were replaced with
> more pertinent views of new sources and authority. Today many
> former icons in the collection have been reinterpreted. The reactions
> by visitors to these changes both positive and negative have affected
> their roles as their own historians as they view exhibitions at the
> Valentine.

This exhibition was an outstanding example of how museums can make
explicit to visitors the process whereby they construct and communicate
their view of History through their use of original source material,
encouraging the visitor to develop a critical relationship with the past. It also
draws attention to the museum as a shaping cultural force. We must
therefore now consider what a museum might be.

## What is a museum? Settings for the conceptualisation of the past

In the context of the culture of the western world, the museum fulfils the
function of a specific place and institution, which visitors usually enter for
the purpose of considering and thinking about the past. Collections of
objects from the past have been used for many years to evoke the past but
through changing value systems, as well as technological developments,
there is less consensus as to what museums should 'house'. The choice of
objects and the medium of their presentation can provide very different
situations in which the objectification of the past may be achieved.

Technological advances also make possible a greater exploitation of different media for determining how the past should be presented and we describe some of these in the next chapter. Indeed, there has even been acceptance of the notion that the presentation of the past in museums should be determined by a wider range of interests - not necessarily by one powerful individual or group. This has been referred to as the 'democratisation' of the museum.

There are in existence, therefore, different conceptions of what a museum is or should be. Indeed this is related to the cultural values and beliefs of the society. The idea of a specific building dedicated to the physical representation of the past through collections of objects selected for their historical significance may not even exist. One thinks of the Australian aborigines who in their tribal culture would seem to conceptualise the past through their myths of a time (the 'Dreaming') before their ancestors had peopled the continent. 'Among the Unda Gnoora tribe of the Cooper region in Central Australia they talk of a time when the dry lake systems were once well watered and fertile'. (Cowan, 1992, p.14). An environmentally different past is conceptualised in orally handed down myths and rock paintings. A specific, dedicated building is not required when myth and imagery permeate physical features of the landscape with meaning that creates not just a past but a whole cosmology for its people, a nomadic people with no need for buildings, let alone one to house their past. Such ideas and values have of course undergone change as the culture of these indigenous people has been, and continues to be, 'invaded' by explorers and settlers from lands beyond the continent, where the concept of museum as building has a long 'history'.

In western society, history and versions of the past are presented in a number of ways. We worked together for two years (1993-95) on a funded project *The Presentation of History* that considered various means by which the past is presented. We found it useful to do this under the three categories of institutions and sites, texts, and multimedia. We have come to think of these as ways in which the culture of a society can formalise how the past should be conceived, preserved and studied. Through institutions and sites such as the museum, heritage site, historic house, fort and castle the past can be located and controlled within a physical entity. The past can be described, analysed and contested through the texts of books, journals, newspapers, handbills, advertisements, etc. The past can become the content of new technologies and multimedia such as film, video, CD-ROM and the Internet. The virtual museum can be made to exist in cyber space. There are now many settings and situations in which the past can be localised and commodified.

If we include the living history approach and re-enactment groups, we expand the concept of **settings** in which the past is presented. For example, medieval fairs may take place in historical houses but a town square, market place or even an open field may be considered as an appropriate setting for such recreation. Battle re-enactments may be performed on the actual site of the original battle or demonstrations of the fighting techniques performed in a school playground. In Chapter five we discuss further the importance of setting both in regard to the range of performance venues and how the conception of the past can escape not only the confines of the glass case but also the 'warehouse for dead items'.

## The changing concept of the museum and museum education

Just as the settings for conceptualising the past vary, depending on cultural variation, so they will change over time depending on culturally determined priorities. Two examples follow which illustrate something of how the conception of the museum is changing.

The first, **The Fiji Museum**, might be thought of as a **transitional** example in that people as well as objects should be included. Kaye Hindle, the Museum's curator opposed the view that museums are 'warehouses for dead items from the past'. She saw them as places where the visitor could view the objects in terms of the ways in which they have shaped the present and her mission 'to make the museum less a place of glass cases and static displays and more somewhere that people can interact with the artifacts and ideas of other ages.' (May, 1998) This is the type of museum in which live people are present but subservient to the objects in the sense that they are local artists and crafts people displaying their skills and the use of traditional cultural objects. Their opportunities to interact with visitors would, however, be limited and to some extent they were 'on show' as much as the artifacts.

The second example, Daniel Liebeskind's new **Jewish Museum in Berlin** is even more revolutionary in conception. It has been constructed to provide a physical setting which will impact upon the visitor's experience; to convey metaphorically and dramatically an emotionally overwhelming representation of the past of Berlin's Jewish community. The architect, who comes from a family of Polish Jews devastated by the Holocaust, has designed an extension to the older Berlin Museum, with routes and settings that act as metaphors for the experience of the Jewish people. For instance the space seems to shrink, the slope of the floor becomes steeper, and the roof lowers, so that walking for the visitor gets increasingly uncomfortable. When the visitor emerges at last, there is a void, an emptiness to represent the Holocaust, from which there is no exit. Worsley described how 'a single shaft of light illuminates its beautifully finished concrete walls. From far away, the distant sound of traffic penetrates, just enough to remind one that ordinary life continues despite the shocking horror. It is an extraordinarily powerful, overwhelming space.' (Worsley, 1998)

The visit to the empty museum is powerful and moving but will this experience be changed with the addition and arrangement of exhibits? A museum building can be made to communicate with the visitor architecturally but the addition of people and their valued objects provide a different experience.

Changes in the concept of the museum are not restricted to design and content. Robert Lumley (1988) more than a decade ago concluded that museums were an international growth industry, which was also acquiring new functions in the organisation of cultural activities. He wrote that:

it is through museums that societies represent their relationship to their own history and to that of other cultures and people. Today, there are great differences and conflicts both inside and outside museums about how this should best be done, leading those concerned with running them to question the traditional concepts of what a museum is, what it can offer the public, and how history is conceived and presented.

(Lumley, Preface, 1988)

Lumley had three major concerns about museums:

1. 'commercialisation' in that marketing, retailing and advertising were becoming so crucial to the institution's existence that an educational function was being displaced by an entertainment orientation;
2. their pursuit of 'realism';
3. the impact of the media.

In referring to the impact in the 1980s of the media, Lumley had in mind competition from television as entertainment rather than how museums might be able to use innovatory approaches with film, video and computer images. He mentioned the use museums were making of costumes and period dress, role-play, working exhibits, real locations and settings, and smells, sounds and 'experience' to produce a feeling of 'reality'. For him a 'reality effect' had been substituted for an attempt to reveal historical processes. It was not clear, however, how to represent these processes. He accepted the need to develop this 'object-centred' representation of 'reality', because those without property would still not find a presence in such creations.

This argument is taken a stage further by Kevin Walsh in his book *The Representation of the Past: Museums and Heritage in the Post-modern World* (1992). Walsh claimed that 'as with all processes of modernisation the past became something which emerged as yet another form of institutionalized discourse, often articulated through the museum and the academy.' The past became a thing to be discussed by the professions of the historian and the curator and therefore unrelated to people's daily experience except through heritage centres and popular imagery.

These two writers provide some indication of the criticism focused on museums and the realisation that change was taking place. Change that was powered by the need for museums to be more commercially viable, the 'democratisation' of the museum, and the rapidity of the development of media technology. In this climate of uncertainty and reappraisal, the education role was likely to be among several roles that museums must consider.

## How important is the educational role of museums?

The Department of National Heritage (DNH) carried out a questionnaire survey that was reported in the publication entitled *A Common Wealth: Museums and Learning in the United Kingdom* (Anderson, 1997). Responding museums had been asked to rank their functions in order of priority. Most of them placed education in second place, stating that their *first* priority was that of the management, exhibition and display of their collections. However, the Report concluded that education in the United Kingdom was in transition from a model of predominantly state provision through formal institutions to a broader concept of 'a mixed economy of formal and informal learning in which community participation, training and formal education are mutually enriching processes.' (p.89) At a time when the concept of education is being broadened, museums should be seen as the means whereby the public can access self-education and personal development. Given the current conception of life long learning, museums should undergo fundamental change becoming active 'centres for public learning'. The Report claimed that such a change would give museums a central role in cultural development and public policy. To meet the needs of the public, they would however have to develop what were termed 'cross-sectoral links', particularly to support education.

We have referred to museum education staff several times in suggesting that museums can offer schools specialised facilities and advice, provide appropriate information and teaching material, and organise the loan to schools of historical artifacts and learning packages. The Report confirmed that although the number of specialised education posts in the United Kingdom museum services had almost doubled since the estimation of such posts in the early 1980s, it was difficult to assess whether the nature of such museum education provision had also changed from being simply 'a separate, add-on activity to becoming a core function integral to all museum activities'. (p. 11). There were no national statistics on educational policy and provision available from earlier decades. Nor were there national standards against which such provision could be measured. The Report concluded, therefore, that in many crucial respects the educational function of museums remained 'uncharted territory'. The Report was published while a Conservative government was in power.

Under the Labour government a policy report outlining the strategy for England's museums, by then numbering more than 2,000 institutions, was published in May 2000. Produced by the Department of Culture, Media and Sport and the Department for Education and Training, the document was entitled *The Learning Power of Museums - A Vision for Museum Education*. It emphasised that education was central to the role of museums, acknowledging that many museums were already providing learners with an excellent service, often only with limited resources. The conclusion was, however, that 'the provision of educational services by museums is patchy, ranging from the outstanding to the mediocre.' (*The Learning Power of Museums*,p.7). It was planned that an education audit of existing services would be carried out and research commissioned into staffing levels, visitors numbers, and how people make use of museums. (Slater, 2000)

**Is the future of History education in schools or museums?**

The dynamic of change, which could dramatically revolutionise museum education, is also present in schools. Reference has already been made to the debate over the nature of History education and its curricula in the United Kingdom. A growing issue for schools in England and Wales has been the problem of the 'over crowded timetable'. This has also been a matter for concern in Australia. 'In the past schools didn't have to educate about health, drugs, safe sex or gambling. Today every new social problem is referred by politicians to the classroom.' (Button and Walker, 1997).

In Australia there have been concerns that adults have little historical knowledge. When Agahha Fedrizzi gave an Australian history quiz 'testing' secondary age students' knowledge of their country's past, just one boy was aware that Portuguese and Dutch explorers had reached Australia before the English. He knew this only from having played a CD-ROM game called *Exploration and Discovery*. (Button and Walker, 1997)

This led to nationwide discussions about why young Australians seemed to know so little of their nation's past and whether this really mattered. In 1972, 41 per cent of students in the Australian state of Victoria completing their schooling had studied History. Twenty five years later it was only 6 per cent. This and similar studies raised questions about the extent and nature of the historical knowledge possessed by the country's citizens.

The Australian federal government sought to fill the gap in *public historical knowledge* when it announced the distribution in its primary and secondary schools of an Anzac Day information kit called *Don't Forget Me Cobber*. John Cantwell of the History Teachers' Association (Victoria) although welcoming the Anzac Day Information Kit, was troubled by the extent of the army's role in its compilation. He feared that if History teaching continued to decline, students might be exposed only to 'history' as told by vested interests - 'the people who can afford to generate packages.' (Button and Walker, 1997).

Button and Walker believed that even if Australian youngsters were not being taught so much History in school there were plenty of signs that their *interest* in history (or in the past?) remained high. For instance each year at the living history site of Sovereign Hill - the recreated gold mining town at Ballarat in Victoria - some 70,000 primary school children spent two days in period costume and followed an 1850s curriculum. Dr. Jan Penney, the Sovereign Hill's head of interpretation and research, said that the children during their visits were immersed in gold rush society, learning about everything from blacksmiths to Chinese immigrants. She also expressed the view that primary school teaching of Australian History had become so piecemeal that 'Sovereign Hill has taken over from the schools.' (Button and Walker, 1997) This could be wishful thinking on Dr. Penney's part as a service provider for this tourist and heritage site, but it does question the extent to which there are other interests - cultural, commercial or political - waiting to take over the role of the schools in the teaching of History.

To summarise the position, History education in schools is declining due to pressure from other curriculum subjects and people are becoming more dependent on the museum and historic site as well as mass media and the new technologies, to learn about the past. One final example of History education from America, termed *Heritage Education* , will further expand the possible settings in which History education can legitimately take place. It also introduces the idea of an 'inherited past' - something precious because it belonged to our ancestors. This colours the more 'neutral' notion of History-in-school.

## Heritage education

Heritage education has been described as an approach to teaching and learning about history and culture that makes use of information available from the material culture and the human and built environment as a primary teaching resource. (Hunter, 1988). In the United Kingdom this has often gone under the name of local studies. Heritage education has been integrated into some of the existing curriculum patterns found in United States schools and local studies still has a place in the National curricula of England and Wales. Various kinds of programmes and educational materials about the historic built environment have been produced not just by museums but by educators working in such places as heritage sites, historical houses, replica ships and fortifications. In the United Kingdom much of this work has been developed by English Heritage and the National Trust.

## SECTION 4: LEARNING HISTORY IN MUSEUMS AND SCHOOLS

Having considered History education in schools and museums, we highlight two approaches to learning that are particularly important to this book; first, the practical interaction with historical material which enables the learner to 'experience' the past; second, the emphasis placed on literacy as a means of structuring this experience and assessing learners' historical knowledge.

## Experiential and 'hands on' learning

Sometimes referred to as a 'hands on approach', experiential and discovery learning seems to be linked with assumptions that visitors, especially children, learn from careful observation and handling of objects and possibly experience the past through interaction with costumed characters. There is a strong belief in the value of being able to feel and handle objects as motivating the learner and therefore that discovering things for oneself, is an effective form of learning. Proponents of discovery learning, believe that in order to learn, the learner needs to have experience; they need to do and see for themselves rather than to be merely told or instructed. Rather than organise the subject content based on its logical structure - simplest to the more complex - the educator is likely to organise it so that it can be 'experienced'. The teaching method takes on a practical aspect as well as an intellectual one.

However, the purpose of this 'hands on' approach is still for the learner to understand ideas and concepts that are independent of the learner. Through 'experience' it is assumed that misconceptions will be replaced by more accurate and valid conceptions. Certainly, this experiential quality of learning is more likely to happen with the historical object being made available outside the confines of the glass case. From the point of view of the object's owner, there is of course, the question of the fragility of the object and its value in both monetary and historical terms. Often this concern leads to the handling of replica objects rather than real ones.

Geraldine Brennan (1993) describing a visit to the Weald and Downland Open Air Museum in West Sussex, England started by noting that there were no 'do not touch' signs in the great hall of the Bayleaf Farmhouse, one of a collection of some thirty typical buildings fifteenth to eighteenth century that have been saved from demolition, dismantled and rebuilt on the site. She continued by explaining that the stools were for sitting on, and the pewter dishes and wall hangings could be handled. 'They are meticulously researched replicas, but the scorch-marks that the 15th century candles left on the beams are among the signs that the building itself is the real thing.'

The site's director explained that one of the museum's aims was to:

> use the buildings as triggers for a journey of the imagination into the past rather than to recreate the experience of living in history. 'Disney does recreations : we're more a series of urban and rural galleries without a roof.' The Weald and Downland has no actors in period costume, but well-informed staff and volunteer interpreters: no slick audio-visual centre, but a hands-on exhibition of building materials, where pupils can practise tiling a roof or building an arch and discover how the houses they have visited were put together.

Some analysis of the site director's statement is illuminative because of the comparison being made by the director between their conception of living history and the aims of the museum. For instance, actors can be well-informed and have extensively researched their characters or personas. Is 'slick' a derogatory attribute? Or does the speaker mean verbal fluency from a scripted presentation? Brennan recognised the pupils' experience in the museum as being 'hands on', referring to practising *tiling, building* an arch and *discovering* how a house was built. (italics used to emphasise the actions (verbs) in which the pupils were involved). These were the 'triggers for a journey of the imagination into the past' that she had noted.

Of course, it is not possible to experience the past in the past. The historical objects (real or replica) provide practical contact but this needs contextualising. In schools this is often done by the use of textbooks, work sheets, and multimedia. In museums and historical sites, there are of course, the brochure and the guidebook, which often bring in much needed revenue as well as providing relevant information about displays or sites. Education staff may produce work sheets, quiz material or questionnaires based on exhibits for students or children with their parents to complete during or after visits.

More recently, museums and heritage sites have become aware of the informative nature of the web page on the Internet. Pictures and text can resemble tourist literature and 'sell' the building or site's attractions and services. Web pages can also provide detailed historical information as well as authenticating the prestige and national importance of the site. Even the most pictorial of these resources require reading skills, either to understand the writer or the illustrator's interpretation and framing of the message he or she wishes to convey. This brings us to our second approach to learning.

## Literacy and History-in-school

As they progress through the school system, children and young people are expected to become familiar with language resources that enable them not only to think and talk about groups rather than individuals, but also to gather events together into periods of time and conceptualise the idea of historical eras. The text types that learners encounter at this stage of their schooling move them away from a subjective, personal and emotional way of evaluating the past, as might be provided by practical experiences, towards a more valued language of deduction and judgement expected by History teachers and Historians.

Learners are likely to be required to portray events, people or occasions from a particular perspective other than their own, and collate and organise their 'evidence' to present, for evaluative purposes, a more objective view of the past. History-in-school as curriculum subject may seem to learners to be obsessed with the mastery of the expression of historical knowledge through the medium of written text.

It is only comparatively recently that the role of text types or genres in the teaching of History-in-school, has been highlighted. If students are to be effective readers and writers of History texts, they need both to understand the *purpose* of a text and to acquire the relevant language skills. An understanding of how these social and linguistic resources work to position a reader or a listener, will enable students to critically interrogate both primary and secondary historical sources. Additionally, an understanding of these resources can enable students to construct new or original interpretations of the past. We think that understanding the functions of language is not confined to empowering the reader/writer in school, but can also be applied to what at first appears to be an entirely non literate approach to museum, school or heritage History education - the living history approach. In Chapter eight, BG takes a closer look at how linguistic choices are involved in the interpretations created by the living history approach and the extent to which this approach can contribute to literacy in History-in-school.

## SECTION 5: HISTORY EDUCATION AND THE ESTABLISHMENT OF A CRITICAL RELATIONSHIP WITH THE PAST: THE POWER OF LIVING HISTORY

We turn now to the specific methodology of historical interpretation examined in this book. Much more will be said of this later but whilst considering History education and the critical relationship which it can develop with the past, we pause to consider the efficacy of 'living history' as an educational technique.

The method of living history has been much criticised as appealing to empathic understanding, trivialises history and pays insufficient attention to learning the facts. In order to counter this argument with evidence, Mike Pond and Alan Childs (1995) conducted some research to statistically measure whether there was any advantage for children in the acquisition of factual historical knowledge through living history. They tested groups of children who had taken part in a two and a half day residential evacuees experience at Holt Hall in Norfolk against control groups equally matched by age, sex and ability. They found that

> those children who are able to become immersed in a period by
> playing a role as part of the re-creation of times past acquire a better
> knowledge of the period (as measured by the ability to comment on
> pictures of happenings and activities) than other learners.
> Furthermore, this greater understanding persisted over time and was
> noticeable up to nineteen months after the learning experience.

It was reported that the scores of those attending the living history activity improved by between 45 and 80 percent over the controls.

There are numerous accounts of such work being pursued successfully in museums or at historic sites, but they need to be evaluated carefully as to whether the 'success' was in terms of innovative or 'good' practice on the part of the institution or the achievement of specific learning outcomes with visitors. When museums evaluate the success of their own programmes they often adopt simple visitor statistics as a single criterion.

## SECTION 6: THE 'HIDDEN CURRICULUM' OF MUSEUM AND HERITAGE EDUCATION

To this point, we have considered the nature of History education, its realisation in the institutions of the museum, school and historic site, and then the potential effects upon it of change in terms of setting, content and its relative curricula value. We have suggested that with changes occurring in museums, increasing acceptance of 'hands on' methods might supplement what teachers can do in school. We now conclude the chapter, by considering the 'hidden curriculum' of museum education.

Not all of the messages conveyed by the museum and the historical or heritage site are overt and intentional. The ways in which certain types of knowledge are legitimated, certain histories told and certain classes of visitor welcomed, carry messages that can be seen as constituting a hidden curriculum. Duncan and Wallach (1978) wrote that a 'museum's primary function is ideological, and its task is to impress on visitors society's most revered beliefs and values.' They then proceeded to analyse the Louvre and identify a ritual, experiential agenda that incorporates the unaware visitor as an ideal citizen of the state.

Closer to our own concerns, Williamsburg, the reconstructed colonial capital of Virginia in the United States has been seen as a presentation which, at its inception, commemorated the colonial elite, 'in whom were seen to reside the timeless virtues of "Americanism", the social order was harmonious, there was no class conflict and no reference to the fact that half the population were slaves.' By 1981, the interpretation had been revised and conflict was nominally recognised. This was only done superficially by concentrating on productive techniques rather than processes such as capitalism and trade unionism. Leone (1973) has described Williamsburg as the empirical substantiation of national mythology: 'the reinforcement of modern American values like those surrounding the myth of our own origin as a nation that comes out of today, not two centuries ago'. This message is 'communicated with unusual effectiveness because of the environmental niche of extraordinary reality imposed on the artifacts.'

### Is the visitor taken in by what they see?

The problem with these analyses is that they assume that the visitor is a totally passive recipient of 'the message'. (Hooper-Greenhill, 1994). The research summarised in Falk and Dierking (1992) showed how active visitors are in constructing their own meanings and interpretations from what they choose to attend to and observe. Merriman's survey (1991) of people's attitudes to history shows that the rosy and sanitised view of the past, which critics such as Hewison (1987) claim are portrayed in advertisements, films and at heritage sites (often through living history), is not absorbed uncritically. Respondents were overwhelmingly aware of the physical toil, disease and violence of the past although they did cite some benefits such as family closeness, little pollution and a slower pace of life. Interestingly in relating the past to the present younger people seem more likely to note the absence of material advantages whereas the elderly are more likely to note poverty, lack of food and social exploitation. ( Merriman, 1991, p.28) If these are indicative of the attitudes and the minitheories about the past that visitors bring to museums and historic sites, and if visitors do construct their own meanings, then it is unlikely that they will absorb uncritically any ideologically based message. It is certainly unlikely they will all leave the site having the same account of that message.

In this chapter, we have used the concept of minitheories to emphasise the individual, progressive nature of learners' development of a historic perspective on the past. Varied experiences modify and extend the gut and lay minitheories about the past. This can be facilitated so that a view of the past, which accords with the academic view of History with all its complexities, can be achieved. This is part of creating a critical perspective on our individual and group relationships with the past.

In the next chapter we consider some of the methods which museums use to communicate their conceptions of the past to us to enable us to form some relationship with the past. Whether that relationship is critical or not will depend on the nature of the interpretation. In terms of living history, this is considered in Chapter nine.

## Footnotes

1   In the week of BBC children's television studied, in the time referring to the past, there were no specific documentaries but (times rounded to the nearest minute):

44 minutes was taken up by historical drama,
8 minutes with specific reference to past memories,
31 minutes of history related news and
35 minutes of cartoon with a historical setting but usually no historical content.

Such a cartoon might feature animals on a mystery adventure set in ancient Egypt where the wall paintings come alive and dance.

On the Independent television channel, of the total time, there were:
23 minutes of specific documentary,
16 minutes of drama,
14 minutes of reference to memories and
10 minutes of cartoon with an historical setting.

*Chapter three*

❧

# PEOPLING HISTORICAL SPACE: THE CONTEXTS
# OF THE LIVING HISTORY APPROACH

In the last chapter, we considered the possibilities for museum education in which living history might play a part, in a variety of institutions undergoing change. We suggested what might happen to History education in general and in schools, and then considered implications for museums and historic sites. We concluded by discussing some aspects of the 'hidden curriculum' that might be learnt in such settings.

In this chapter, we consider the contexts for living history. We are using 'context' in two ways. First, we examine the historical context of living history; i.e. its place in the development over time of methods of presenting the past. Second, we consider its methodological context as a position on a continuum of communicative action; i.e. as a form of developing the illusion of a two-way dialogue with the past. The more obvious consideration of physical context will be dealt with in Chapter Five where a thorough consideration of setting is given.

This chapter is divided into two distinct parts to establish that assumptions about settings and the appropriate behaviour associated with them are related to social and cultural values. For instance, the museum can be viewed as a cultural means of conveying an idea of the past to those who visit it. However as cultural values change, so may the function and aims of the museum.

The first part briefly and selectively traces the way in which the function of museums in western society has been changing and demonstrates how the roots of living history interpretation are to be found in various phases of that change. Then in the second part we examine some of the techniques used by museums and historical sites to represent human presence in the past and facilitate the formation of a critical relationship with that past, as discussed in chapter two. We have called this technique 'peopling historical space'. Technological advances and the changing aims of museums are affecting the range and nature of such techniques.

## SECTION ONE: THE PRESENCE OF THE PAST IN A
## RECONSTRUCTED SETTING

The history of museums has been skillfully examined on a number of occasions. Perhaps the most illuminating accounts are Kenneth Hudson's *Museums of Influence* (1987) and Tony Bennett's *The Birth of the Museum* (1995).

This section will not attempt to trace another history but select key institutions which contribute to the development of museums as appropriate contexts for living history interpretations. Here we will show that living history as a technique has its roots in various aspects of the development of museums over time.

We want to pursue three major themes:

1. presentation of the past in a 'complete' context;
2. presentation of domestic history through artifacts;
3. role of dramatic effect and humour in presenting the museum's message.

## The presentation of the past in a complete context

Here we are concerned with the development in museums, which has led to the display and demonstration of artifacts and activities in a reconstructed setting. Examples would be the schoolteacher at Old Sturbridge Village (United States), the printer at Colonial Williamsburg (United States) or the candlemaker at Blist Hills (England). Their work is demonstrated by using reproductions or refurbishments or original equipment by costumed interpreters in reconstructed buildings from the eighteenth or nineteenth centuries.

The most obvious antecedent for this is Skansen near Stockholm, Sweden opened by Artur Hazelius in 1891 (Bennett, 1995, p.115) and peopled by wax tableau vivant. This collection of Swedish domestic architecture was inspired by the rising Nationalist movement in Sweden in the nineteenth century; a desire to establish a national identity by looking back at life before industrialisation. (This same desire to preserve a way of life in danger of vanishing as a means of reinforcing identity can be seen in open-air and living history museums today.)

This notion of displaying historical interiors and peopling them, either with wax works or costumed guides, seems to have reached America at the 1876 centennial exhibition in Philadelphia which included a number of folk life tableaux. Hazelius had sent six from Sweden; elk hunting, courtship, christening, life among the Laplander, bible reading and the death of a little girl. The use of people rather than manikins can be seen in two further American examples. The first is from the same centennial exhibition, featured a New England Farmer's House occupied by ladies who conducted the visitors through the house. (Hudson, 1987, p.152). The second is from Salem in 1907 when George Francis Dow moved the John Ward House of 1685 to the Essex Institute and interpreted it with costumed guides, original or reproduction furniture and utensils 'giving much of the atmosphere of livableness....' (Hudson, p.153)

This leads into the second theme.

## The presentation of domestic and social history through artifacts

Most living history reconstructions are concerned with everyday life. The English industrial museums of Ironbridge, Beamish and The Black Country Museum aim to preserve the industrial past and represent the lives of 'ordinary' workers. In the United States, Colonial Williamsburg may be primarily concerned with the government of a colony and Plimoth Plantation with the founding of 'European' America, but these themes have more recently been developed to include and present the lives of ordinary people and their artifacts.

The idea that collections of objects can be informative can be traced to seventeenth century collections of curiosities. One of the most famous examples of these is John Tradescent's Closet of Curiosities, some of which is now housed in the Ashmolean Museum, Oxford, England. This collection of 'varieties and oddities' is, according to Hudson (1987, p.21), a reflection of the seventeenth century assumption that everything was potentially interesting, useful and central to the pursuit of knowledge. Tradescent's collection included exotic souvenirs of his travels, North American hunting implements, a collection of ladies' shoes and Cromwell's death mask. The objects arouse curiosity and raise questions but no attempt is made to organise them systematically, explain their use, or use them to interpret the past or other cultures. Those concerns, which are so central to the use of artifacts in a living history presentation, arise later in the history of museums.

The first great systematic collection of social and industrial artifacts to be used to explain a particular interpretation of the past was that of Pitt-Rivers. He amassed more than 14,000 items drawn from around the world and these were arranged according to evolutionary principles of culture. He refined a typology of objects which he believed could be used to throw light on the cultures that created them. (Hudson, 1987, p.31). His aim was to build up a picture of the lives of our ancestors through the collection and methodical recording of the objects they used. The living history museum takes this a stage further and attempts to recreate what it was like to live by the use of these objects. In the presentation of everyday life in Sturbridge (United States) or Ballarat (Victoria, Australia), it is the minute domestic detail that fascinates and usefully informs us of the conditions in which our ancestors lived and the ways in which they materially constructed their lives.

## The role of dramatic effect and humour in presenting the museum's message

Drama and setting are central to the message of the earliest example of a proto-museum: the Renaissance Studioli. A throne was placed in a windowless room with cupboards around the walls in which artifacts were housed. The doors of these cupboards were closed and decorated with symbolic images:

> The sphere of the actually visible (the paintings on the doors) mediated
> the Prince's exclusive access to the, in principle, visible but, in practice,
> invisible contents of those cupboards and thence to the order of the
> cosmos which those contents represented. (Bennet, T. 1995, p.36)

This symbolically represents through the staged setting the absolute authority of the Prince as he sits alone (the only one able to see the 'museum') in the centre of the universe.

Less ritualistic use of dramatic settings can be seen at the Sir John Soane Museum in Lincoln's Inn Fields in London. This delightful juxtaposition of architectural models, curious rock formations, paintings, the tomb of Setti I and a recreated monk's cell are set out still as Sir John intended. His aim was to educate and to amuse. He used the artifacts and models to teach his students and played with lighting and display to dramatic effect. Art is revealed and hidden in a dramatic spectacle as the hinged panels, displaying Soane's own designs for London, are thrown open to reveal 'a view... of the upper part of the monk's room and the recess therein, in the back of which is a large window glazed with painted glass.' Soane was aware of the power of the **setting** to influence the mind of his visitors to his fancifully reconstructed monk's cell:

> the ruins of a monastery arrest the attention. The interest created in
> the mind of the spectator, on visiting the abode of the monk will not
> be weakened by wandering among the ruins of his once noble
> monastery. The rich canopy and other decorations of this venerable
> spot are objects which cannot fail to produce the most powerful
> sensations in the minds of the admirers of the piety of our forefathers,
> who raised such structures for the worship of the almighty disposer of
> events.

A stone structure at the head of the monks grave contains the remains of Fanny 'the faithful companion, the delight, the solace of his leisure hours'.Fanny was Mrs Soane's pet dog.

(Quotations are from Soane's catalogue to the collection edited and expanded by Thornton, 1990)

This combination of drama, humour and instruction is often present in living history interpretations, (as are the spurious recreations of historic settings!) The dramatic staging, lighting and action are designed to recreate the atmosphere of the past. Interpreters often use humour and repartee to involve visitors, for example the schoolmistress's gentle teasing at Old Sturbridge Village (quoted in chapter nine). At times the humour is unhistorical and to some, offensive. There are examples from Australia where the sado-masochistic jokes of the gaoler at Old Sydney Town and his sexist asides are aimed at amusing the spectators. (See Vignette 4, Chapter One)

Pitt-Rivers did not use dramatic effect to get across the message of his collection but he did understand that to attract people to the museum so they might learn, he should provide amusements for them. Consequently as well as the museum, a bandstand, open air theatre, wild animals, golf links and a race course were all built to provide the working man with a good day out on the Pitt-Rivers county estate. For he had a serious educational intention: the avoidance of revolution.

He saw the voting masses as largely ignorant.

> The knowledge they lack is the knowledge of history. This lays them open to the designs of demagogues and agitators who strive to make them break with the past and seek remedies of existing evils, or the means of future progress in drastic changes that have not the sanctions of experience. It is by knowledge of history that such experience can be supplied.
>
> (Journal Society of Arts 18 December 1891, p. 115, in Hudson 1987 p. 34)

Through demonstrating the slow evolution and inevitability of social progress through the organisation of his exhibits Pitt-Rivers hoped to convince ordinary people to be patient and allow time to grant them improvements to their lives.

Education, enjoyment and amusement are all factors important to living history and heritage interpretation. Critics are rightly concerned when the enjoyment and attraction of the interpretation lead to a distortion of the 'heritage' that is presented.

The examples of recreations we have selected from the past have people as their central concern. The focus of the historical presentation tends to be domestic and industrial - events are told through the exploration of ordinary objects in ordinary people's lives. The artifacts collected are every day and of social rather than political or artistic interest. However, we would acknowledge that the people involved are also central to their presentations of history: the Prince, Tradescent, Soane and Pitt-Rivers reflect their personalities through their collections and the forms of their presentation. Each of them has a crucial, if not critical, relationship with the past. Even today when visiting these collections, their owners' personalities, their dialogues with the past, and their relationships with the pasts they forged, are still apparent.

## SECTION TWO: PEOPLING HISTORICAL SPACE

In this section, we explore the techniques museums use to 'people historical space', so that living history can be seen in the context of the other methods available to establish and explore a critical relationship with the past. We outline the range of methods used by museums and historical sites for representing people in the past.

What is important at this point is the historical meaning conveyed by museums and sites, not an aesthetic appreciation of the spaces or artifacts as they appear today. A museum or site may offer a variety of attractions to a visitor, some of which relate more to its beauty, than its historical importance: for example, Rievaulx Abbey and the Greek vases of the British Museum can be enjoyed for their aesthetic qualities without regard to their historical significance. This is not to infer that there is not a certain 'beauty' in the pleasing effect of discovering and imposing a pattern of meaning upon the perceived evidence of the past.

As we argued in the previous chapter, History education can be the critical exploration of our relationship to the historical environment in which we live. In this section we explicitly explore ways in which that relationship with people in the past can be explored in museums and historical sites. This discussion is based on four assumptions:

1. that the establishment of a relationship with the past is most realised when there is a representation of people in the past to be related to;
2. that the fabric of a building or a collection of artifacts cannot be fully understood unless the people who inhabited the space in the past and created, used and disposed of the artifacts are considered;
3. that as more people visit museums and historical sites as leisure activities and may not benefit from a formal history education, the peopling dimension becomes increasingly important as an effective method of interpretation and communication;
4. that there are a host of issues relating to choice, both on the part of the visitor and the curator which must be critically examined. This becomes increasingly important as the 'reconstruction' becomes more complete and the relationship, between visitor and the representations of people in the past, more involving.

## How do we communicate our representations of people in the past?

As teacher educators, we are interested in the process of communication. It is often divided simply into one-way communication and two-way communication. (Stanton, 1986) The former is usually related to the situation where there is no opportunity for immediate feedback. This type of personal communication would include any face-to-face communication where there is no real opportunity for the receivers to question the communicator verbally or clarify their understanding. One-way communication would also include practically all forms of written communication in that although such writing may be intended to evoke some meaningful response, it may not take place immediately.

Two-way communication is generally seen as allowing for constant feedback. Probably a two-person, face-to-face conversation where both participants are free and able to contribute as much as they want to the interaction would be suggested as the purest example. Each person would take it in turn to be the communicator or the receiver of the messages being sent, and both therefore would be expected to get instant and relevant feedback. But this would not necessarily insure continuous communication and mutual understanding, as throughout the interaction interpretation of the language used and the other's motivation and values would be involved. Sufficient here to acknowledge that the process is not without difficulties and frustrations, and that advantages and disadvantages in using personal interaction can be listed. The efficiency of using one or two person communication can be related to the situation and the purposes of the participants.

However, the choice of one or two way communication can be used for examining how museums and historical places choose to communicate and therefore control the visitor's experiences of the museum's construction of the past.

## The range of methods used by museums and historical sites

What follows is a survey of methods collected from our visits and personal experiences, organised on a continuum ranging from free, 'romantic imagination' to a fully reconstructed environment and setting by the institution. The first section deals with methods in which the interaction is *largely one way*. The visitor sees, hears, feels and smells, can question and by experiencing the representation may receive answers, but any discussion will be about the exhibit rather than a communication with it. The second section deals with techniques of living history where the interaction is two-way and discussion can take place between a visitor and another person who represents a character from the past.

Each stage of the continuum raises different issues about the presentation of the human past, the reliability or truthfulness of the interpretation, the thinking behind choices made by the curator, the identities and perspectives represented and therefore validated, and the freedom that visitors have to construct interpretations for themselves.

### *The Romantic Imagination*

By this we mean the use of mental images stimulated by an historical site in a variety of ways, which a visitor might use to imagine what the people who occupied the site at sometime in the past, might have been like. GB has been reminded that his imagination is particularly prone to visual imaging and he make's no claims that this 'technique' is widely used! Nevertheless to illustrate this extreme of the continuum we offer three examples from GB's personal experience.

> *Sitting on a hillside overlooking Rievaulx Abbey in Yorkshire, England, on a warm summer evening with the sound of sheep grazing in the background, the medieval monks carry out their daily tasks, stopping only for prayer, food and sleep.*

This is the most extreme form of romantic imagination relying on a considerable amount of prior knowledge, acquired from formal study or the media, about the nature of medieval monasticism and its presence in the north of England and a willingness and ability to conjure images in order to come into closer contact with the human history of the site.

> *The sun beats down over Ephesus on, what is now, the Turkish coast . 'In there it is like a grill' we are told by a man who wants to save us the effort of walking up the hill by driving us in his horse and cart. The main street is thronging with visitors from all over the world, just as it would have been as a busy metropolis in Graeco-Roman times.*

Here the imagination is helped by the crowds. The site is peopled today: all the imagination has to do is to re-costume them, reconstruct the buildings and introduce the smell. Again we are dependent on prior knowledge of the period - perhaps images from TV and film, a visit to the site museum and a passing acquaintance with classical history and St. Paul's activities in the New Testament.

*The fog is thick, Cashel Abbey stands on a hill, an imposing ruin with buttresses reaching into the grey cloud. The medieval carvings of monks on the walls spark off the imagination and one can almost see them silently slip behind pillars on their way to prayer.*

Here the fabric of the building enters into the process. The images of the past, recorded and surviving, help to conjure up the people who once worshipped here.

These examples of interpretation rely heavily on the atmosphere of a place and rest on prior knowledge, a memory of images, and a predisposition to report in this way. They only contribute to an historical understanding of the site and the people who lived there in a superficial way. The informed visitor has the freedom to make educated guesses but the uninformed can do little more than appreciate the spirit of the place as it is today and move on. The only voice heard and perspective represented is one's own and the only identity explored is oneself.

Of course, each of these sites is interpreted through guidebooks, exhibitions and visual displays that can fuel and inform the imagination. Left to its own devices, however the romantic imagination is an enjoyable but unreliable means of peopling historical space. We will now consider the way in which the institutional setting can be deliberately structured with the intent of influencing the 'experience' of the visitor and providing a perceptual basis for his or her imaginative and, hopefully, critical response.

## One-way communication

### Pictorial Imagery

Pictures have often been used in museums to show people using the artifacts on display. They can provide additional source material and a period feel, if engravings, paintings or contemporary photographs are used. The effect can be dramatic and disturbing. The tower of photographs in the United States Holocaust Memorial Museum, Washington or those simply displayed at the preserved concentration camps of Dachau (Germany) or Le Struhof (France) are poignant and simple examples of the power of the photograph to bring people from the past into a relationship with the visitor in the present.

This process is taken a stage further by the use of life-size cut outs enlarged from contemporary sources. This technique is used to welcome visitors to the reconstructed ship, Mayflower II, at Plimoth, Massachusetts. Monochrome seventeenth century engravings have been blown up and an appropriate contemporary text attached. Enlarged life-size photographs as well as models, text, video, artifact and reconstructed interiors were used to great effect in the Museum of American History, Washington in the 'Field to Factory' exhibition which told the story of African American Migration to the cities, 1915-1940.

### Image and Sound

Life-size images were also used at the House of Detention in Clerkenwell, London. Here the history of eighteenth century prison life was explored through taped commentaries that used primary source material to dramatise the story of an individual prisoner. The visitor listened to these on personal cassette players. She or he being guided from cell to cell, as a different aspect of the penal system was highlighted in the narrative and further explained using enlarged newspaper cuttings and life-size engravings.

Sound and life-size images were combined at the Valentine Museum in Richmond, United States where the domestic slaves were represented by faceless silhouettes and a background tape of overheard, half completed conversations. In the Hyde Park Barracks in Sydney, Australia ghostly grey cut-outs of convicts lined the walls accompanied by the sounds of swinging hammocks and mutterings. In both of these examples the human dimension is marked by absence rather than presence. These museums were dramatising a basic problem of human representation in museums: that those who were faceless and voiceless in the past are difficult to see and hear today.

In representations of more recent history, it is possible to use video or sound recordings of the stories of ordinary people. The Ellis Island Immigration Museum, New York is concerned with migration to the United States and looks at the impact that this had on the lives of individuals, families and the development of modern America. Imaginative use is made of photographs, artifacts, and three-dimensional displays of population statistics to involve the visitor in many different aspects of the migration issue. In addition, the visitor can listen to the oral histories of people recounting their experiences of moving to America. The combination of these sources of information makes for a powerful representation of a variety of people from the past. The process is, however, reliant on the visitor wishing to make contact, to pick up the handset and listen. There is a conflict here between the individual's right to choose which part of the museum's presentation to engage with and the mission of the museum to present a certain interpretation of the past allowing the immigrants' voices to be heard. The visitor may also choose to explore aspects of his or her own identity or that of someone else.

No such choice was given to the visitor to the National Museum of the American Indian, New York which intentionally allowed the Native American interpretation of historical artifacts to dominate. 'Creations Journey' examined objects through the eyes of the art historian, the anthropologist and the Native Americans themselves. In 'All Roads are Good' twenty-three Native Americans were invited to select items from the collection and talk about the significance of these selections. These explanations were played throughout the exhibition. The presentation of the human past, the establishment of a relationship with that past and the methods used to explore it were clearly political issues. In terms of identity exploration this museum presented Native Americans as they interpret themselves and allowed other ethnic groups to relate to those interpretations from their specific perspectives. Rather than the more traditional approach, which presents different identities from a western perspective, this museum encouraged western visitors to explore their own identities in the context of Native America.

When GB visited the Smithsonian Museum, Washington in 1995, he noted that Native American Culture was still represented through displays in the National Museum of Natural History/National Museum of Man. The history of relations between Europeans and the Native Americans of New Mexico was provocatively explored in The National Museum of American History exhibition, 'Encounters', with artifacts, reconstructed interiors, video footage and oral histories. The exhibition ended with a clear statement about the relationship between the visitor and the people from the past which it represents. 'Out of conflict [we] may get survival, self-determination and mutual respect. It is your story and everyone's.'

A similar issue arose in The National Museum of American History exhibition 'A more perfect Union: Japanese Americans and the US Constitution'. These displays examined pre-war prejudice against Japanese Americans, a large number of whom were interned in detention camps although they were American citizens with constitutional rights. These people were represented by photographs, models and video, including an interactive screen that allowed the visitor to select questions to ask those imprisoned in the camps. An illusion of a two-way interaction was created which allowed visitors to believe that they could ask real individuals real questions even though those questions were predetermined by the curator. As at Ellis Island, visitors could choose whether to make contact with these people from the past. What they could not avoid was the video of an interned Japanese American who said, 'If you believe that the constitution is good and protects you, make sure it is actively operating...[be] constantly vigilant!'

These American and Australian examples show ways in which modern technology can be incorporated into displays to help 'people' the historical space. In these ex-colonial countries this process of 'peopling' explicitly raises issues of racial and ethnic identity which are rarely confronted in English museums. A notable exception to this was the 'Peopling of London' exhibition at the Museum of London. Oral histories of people from various ethnic groups who had settled in London were presented alongside artifacts and pictures to trace the development of London as a multiracial city from prehistoric times.

Technology enables the image of a person from the past to move and speak. Once this happens museum presentation moves closer to creating the illusion of a relationship with the past, based on a two-way interaction with a person from the past. The more convincing this illusion becomes the more visitors need to be aware of the ways in which it is constructed. For instance, the editorial decisions made by curators and the historical assumptions underpinning the interpretations.

Before moving on to develop these issues through examples of living history, one further method of peopling historical space needs to be considered: the creation of a context for artifacts and people that involves life-size models.

## Models and Sound

Ever since Philippe Curtis, Madame Tussaud's uncle, first created his wax portraits from life (including the dying Voltaire in 1778) models of historic personages have been used to people historical space even if those spaces are sometimes more akin to the fairground and theme park than an historic site.

The use of life-size models in reconstructed or even original interiors, which can be viewed by foot or at the mercy of an electric car, have been the centre of much controversy in the field of heritage interpretation. The debate has focused around historic authenticity and the supposed dichotomy between scholarship and entertainment. Much the same views have been expressed about historical re-enactment.

For the purposes of this survey we will present a range of examples of models in reconstructed settings which represent human presence in the past. Some of these examples come from places using history to entertain rather than to advance scholarship. These images along with those from advertising and other media form part of the historical environment and so influence the formation of our relationship with the past.

In an extreme example, the London Dungeon, visitors may witness life-size models of humans tortured and mutilated in a number of horrific ways. Although not ostensibly an historical space, the 'attraction' does use rather incongruous, academic sounding texts in display panels throughout to give credence to the voyeuristic nature of the 'entertainment'. This is capped with a series of wall cases featuring original torture instruments. The interesting contribution that this makes to our understanding of the past is that it reinforces any notions that we might have about the past being less civilised and more barbarous than the present. At a more sinister level, it may justify cruelty, insensitivity and violence in the modern era by presenting these characteristics as part of human nature developed over time.

A more serious example of using models to interpret an historical site is Stanstead Mountfichet in Essex, south east England. This uses models in reconstructed buildings to describe life in a Norman Castle. The groaning man whose limbs are amputated by the barber-surgeon and the body swinging on the gibbet may have some of the ghoulish elements of the London Dungeon, but there are also more serious representations of the Nobleman and his entourage at the banquet in the main hall. The site is authentic and the buildings and characters are reconstructed with some historical accuracy but one is left with the impression of having visited a film set rather than an 'authentic' historical experience. The 'human' element of the costumed manikin in these contexts seems less convincing and harder to relate to than the partial representations of pictures and sound used in museums, although the contexts presented at the castle are more complete. Perhaps the visitor is more aware of the artificiality of the plastic model contrasted with the conventional authenticity of museum evidence and that this blocks the development of a relationship with the past in terms of human emotions and motivations.

Much more convincing is the use of models in the Mary Mackillop Place, Sydney, Australia: 'More than a museum its a miraculous journey.' (Publicity leaflet, 1995). This strange combination of museum and shrine tells the story of Mary Mackillop, Australia's first saint who founded a teaching order of nuns. Reconstructed interiors with life-size models and dramatic lighting tell of her life story, death and first miracle.

Why was this experience more convincing to GB than Mountfichet castle? Was it because of the lighting which detracted from the artificiality of the models or did it have more to do with the expectations and attitude of mind of the visitor? Stanstead Mountfichet sets itself up as an historical experience which one may approach with an academically critical mind. Mary Mackillop Place is part museum, part shrine so it is visited with appropriate devotion (some of the other visitors were touching the exhibits with their crucifixes) or scepticism. Whatever the reason, it raises an important element so far ignored in our discussion of peopling; the attitude of mind of visitors that may predispose them to be convinced by the devices used.

The worst example of peopling with models at the sites visited was at Old Sydney Town, Australia. This is largely a living history site but manikins are used as permanent representations of people in the transportation ship, in the gaol, and caring for the milliner's shop where the model of the shop girl grinned inanely at the visitor. The main problem was that the quality of the models was so poor that they detracted from the setting they were peopling. This observation raises an interesting point though. This was something that made a distinct impression when GB visited Old Sydney Town in 1995. When BG had visited the site eighteen months earlier, she had failed to notice any use of models. The milliner was a real, personable young lady conversing with visitors. Discussing our impressions at a later date, raised the question of whether the use of models had anything to do with staffing levels - models are undoubtedly cheaper to use than living history exponents - something we were unable to check. This does not detract from GB's point that the visual quality of the model or manikin may be an important element in the acceptability of the notion of peopling historical space.

### Dark Rides

In the examples above, visitors have been free to view the exhibits at their own pace and, apart from Mary Mackillop Place, in their own order. The examples discussed below control the speed, order and perspective of visitors by moving them through the exhibit in an electric car with a taped commentary.

Jorvik Viking Centre in York, in the north east of England, is built on the exact site of a dig carried out by the York Archaeological Trust:

> A massive range of detailed, often microscopic evidence was
> recovered and has been used to recreate (in intricate detail) every last
> aspect of everyday life. This is no waxworks, this is the closest you'll
> ever get to time travel, the sights, the sounds and even the smells of
> Jorvik in 948 A.D.
>
> (Internet description, 12 September 1996).

Visitors are moved through the reconstruction in a time car and given a taped commentary through speakers at the back of the car. The sounds of Viking York are 'played into the exhibition area through carefully positioned speakers to give the most realistic atmosphere possible.' (Timecars, p.5)

The Tower Hill Pageant in London beside the River Thames, also played with ideas of time travel. Here visitors descended in a lift taking them through the layers of an archaeological dig back to Roman London. A 'time car' then carried visitors past a series of tableaux with sound and smell which reconstruct scenes from London's past. 'Inspired by the Museum of London's work along the waterfront, the Tower Hill Pageant combines archaeology with computer technology, bringing back to life 2,000 years of history.' (Publicity Leaflet, 1994).

These Dark Rides introduce us to the idea of 'time travel'. Not only do we have the illusion of forming a relationship with someone from the past but also we can travel back in time to experience every aspect of their lives with them! The focus shifts from the peopling of the space as a device to strengthen our relationship to the past to physically moving us through a fully reconstructed environment, timing our experiences with the precision of a well directed play and assailing our senses with sight, sound and smell to give the impression that we have travelled through time to somewhere real. Physically moving us may be achieved in ways in which the movement itself may symbolise how visiting the past is conceived. At the Tower Hill Pageant we descend by lift, while at Jorvik the electric car travels back in time - the car facing backwards, but as we reach the date of the reconstruction the car is turned around, so travellers face forward as they pass through the Jorvik of 948 AD.

As mentioned above the more complete the historical experience created for us and the more controlled that becomes, the more critical we need to be of the experience . The interaction is still one-way. We can only be acted upon, we cannot act ourselves.

**Two-way communication**

We will now consider those reconstructions, recreations or re-enactments of the past called living history. Here the technique of peopling switches from representations of human presence to the use of costumed interpreters, people who look as if they lived at the time of the re-enactment. They may be in the role of actual or fictitious historical characters attempting to live life as it was lived in the past by using appropriate technology, admitting appropriate knowledge and espousing contemporary values and attitudes. There are many ways in which this is done and they will be examined in the rest of the book. Here we will introduce three examples which typify the range of living history that can be experienced.

At Blist Hills open air museum, part of the Ironbridge complex in England, the emphasis is on costumed interpreters demonstrating crafts, working in a bank or serving in a shop, as they would have done in what is a recreation of town life at the turn of the last century. It is a fifty acre site of shops, cottages, workshops, steam-powered machines, animals and railway sidings:

> Smell fresh bread, watch candles being made and enjoy the children's streetgames. Costumed staff explain what life was like in those days.
>
> (web site www.vtel.co.uk/igmt/museums/m1-1.htm as of July, 1997)

Demonstrators explain what they are doing, place it in historical context, speak modern English and can make connections with the present day. This is called **third person interpretation** and takes place in a mixture of restored industrial buildings and recreated Victorian shops, workshops and public buildings.

At Plimoth Plantation, Massachusetts, the interpreters take on actual historical characters from 1625. The language that would have been spoken by each person, the attitudes and values that they would have had, and the tools and methods they would have used to build, cook or farm have been thoroughly researched. The characters know nothing of life after 1625 and can only converse with visitors and explain their way of living using concepts and language from the first half of the seventeenth century. This is known as **first person interpretation** and takes place in a carefully recreated village. (See table in Chapter 1 on p 12.)

The third type of living history places the visitor in costume and in role as well as the site interpreters. An example of this is Kentwell Hall at Long Melford, Suffolk, England. Here, a year from Elizabethan times is re-enacted by volunteer interpreters who research and accurately costume generally fictitious characters constructed by type. They carry out crafts, farm, and work in the great house and some re-enact the gentry. They are visited mostly by school parties who are costumed, have been taught some of the relevant historical information and are encouraged to speak an approximation to Tudor English.

Of course, contact with a living past is impossible and these living history presentations in museums or at historic sites are as much illusions as any other form of peopling of historical space. Their chief benefit is that they allow us to explore our relationship with the past through human contact. This is also possible with a guide or expert in a museum. We are able to ask questions of someone whom we presume has greater knowledge of the exhibits than we have. The crucial difference is that in living history the setting, costuming and sometimes sounds and language have been reconstructed to provide a complete historical context as the setting. This is so that we are immersed in an atmosphere that may approximate that of the period in the past.

Obviously, there are huge problems in attempting such ambitious recreations and they are surrounded by much controversy. We can never check the authenticity of an atmosphere: we can never know what life in the past felt like to those who lived then. But the careful juxtaposition of artifacts, sounds, language and perhaps even the attitudes of the costumed interpreters, supported by evidence, may give rise to a 'most likely' atmosphere that parallels the acceptance of a 'most likely' interpretation in modern historical scholarship. Moreover, there are many areas of traditional historical study defying absolute verification, where the controlled use of historical imagination is inevitable.

# PART TWO

———

# THE EXPERIENCE OF LIVING HISTORY

# Chapter four

### ❧

## INTRODUCTION: DESIGN OF THE STUDY
## AND SOURCES OF INFORMATION

Part 2 brings us to the heart of our investigation. Here we examine the phenomena of living history through the information and data that we have collected over a period of approximately four years from a wide range of places and sources spanning three continents. This is restricted, however, to anglophone examples. Inevitably this task led to a large and varied amount of material and to progress, we had to decide on an appropriate form of analysis, which would relate to the nature of our research and would produce some meaningful conclusions.

We begin this chapter by outlining some of the considerations influencing our choice of analytic procedures and list the types of sources we drew on for the study. We then develop an analytical framework derived from a conception of living history as an interaction between setting, visitor and exponent or interpreter. We hope that this successfully captures and demonstrates the phenomena in all its complexity.

Our study was essentially qualitative in its stance. We chose this approach because we wanted to analyse the variety and complexity of living history rather than to measure it. This research approach also seemed most relevant because of the issue of communicating findings in a meaningful way to a varied audience. Our analysis needed to make sense to students of the area of study and participants and practitioners in the experience, both interpreter/re-enactors and visitors; this latter group to include both family members and teachers.

However, we have certain reservations about the generalisability of our statements given the specific contexts in which they occur. This is exacerbated when change - technological, economic and social, is so rapid. Also any interest in language usage and function increasingly underlined for us the way in which discourses of all types involve the social construction and presentation of events, people and processes taking place, uniquely at a point in time. The deconstruction of 'texts' (used here in the broadest of conceptions) may provide insights into individual and institutional attitudes to the topic studied. Such interpretations, presented here in written text, are open to discussion and may be viewed differently by those with alternative experiences and schooled in the precepts of different disciplinary backgrounds. In trying to create order from our diverse sources of information, we are well aware that we may be moving away from the 'ground' in a way unrecognisable to an individual practitioner. Our hope though is that this demonstration of the complexity of the living history approach, both in conception and practice, may be welcome to the many practitioners of this means of viewing the 'past' and help to illuminate their practice.

## OUR 'RAW' MATERIAL

This was derived from five main sources:

1. a telephone survey;
2. newspaper, radio and television material;
3. web sites on the internet;
4. our own data from visits to sites in the United Kingdom; United States and Australia;
5. traditional library search.

### (1) Data from a telephone survey of historical and heritage sites in the United Kingdom

The Times Educational Supplement (TES) in the United Kingdom publishes a section three times a year consisting of a number of pages on ideas for school visits called 'Going Places' containing three types of information:

- articles by named writers on places and events;
- advertisements for a number of sites and centres;
- a listing by which the reader can send for information and details for up to ten places, which is passed on to the advertisers who then send further information by post.

The articles and advertisements as texts may or may not be illustrated by line drawings or photographs, in colour or black and white thus providing written (language) and visual (images) data about the presentation and representation of the 'past' that may include reference to the living history approach.

In 1995, using the Spring term section, 'Going Places', as the basis for contact, a telephone survey was carried out. We asked whether 'people dressed up in costume' were used and if so what activities did they carry out, was first or third person speech used and why did the site make use of people in costume. We avoided the use of terms such as 'costumed interpreter', 'interpreter-educator' or 'actor', unless informants made use of the term themselves. We only contacted places where a reference was made to the use of living history or recreating the past.

As a result of the phone survey, we were sent further information, deemed relevant by the sources contacted, which included brochures. Such information showed considerable variation, from a brief letter or tourist brochure to packs for schools intended as preparation for visiting. The sample of places contacted was of course restricted since the first stage involved the TES publisher's selection of articles (it is not known whether these were commissioned or unsolicited) or bought advertising space in the section. At the second stage, our own selection was based on the possibility that the use of 'costumed people' would provide more data about living history and re-enactment practices.

## (2) Data from newspaper, radio and television

This was not systematically collected. Indeed, finding such information could often be described as accidental. It needs to be mentioned because it was an additional source of data and consisted of news references, particularly about tourism and possible attractions for planned visits or holiday destinations. The main source was the weekend travel section of The Daily Telegraph newspaper.

## (3) Data from an online search of web sites on the Internet[1]

Since the telephone survey mainly produced information about places and sites to be visited by teachers and related to the teaching of the national curriculum, there was little information about re-enactment groups or societies. We had increasingly used the Internet to search for information, so throughout 1995/99 searches were undertaken using terms such as 're-enactor' and 'living history'. As with the library search (see below) difficulties were encountered in selecting the most effective search terms. Information was found which, like that emerging from the TES 'Going Places' articles and advertisements, was in the form of written and visual data which might be analysed.

Our search of Internet sites produced verbal and pictorial information about groups, often of a recruiting nature. These sites provided considerable detail about the aims of a group, its history, its organisation, provision of training, membership numbers, and whether a handbook of guidance was available to members. There were often links to the sites of other groups or to museums, and an individual web site master or e-mail contact for further information. Also there were sometimes links to electronically published versions of society newsletters, which included accounts of re-enactment events, letters and photos.

Another useful but limited Internet source was the discussion or chat group, members of which were interested in living history and recreating the past.

## (4) Data from visits made to sites in the United Kingdom, the United States and Australia

During the research we visited sites in three countries, collecting guide books and pamphlets and we also wrote up field notes, recorded auditory tapes of observations, conversations and interviews,[2] and took photographs.

## (5) The traditional library search

This was mainly undertaken in the British Library in London by GB and by BG in the Institute of Education, University of London from 1994 to

1996. This uncovered magazine accounts of living history sites and staged re-enactments but most fruitfully produced secondary materials, which helped us to conceptualise the 'living history' phenomena and to place it in a number of research contexts.

GB used the British Library, which shed only limited light on 'living history'. It seemed to indicate that an established body of knowledge relating to the phenomenon was hard to track down and not expressed in the categorical terms, those 'key words' used to search any catalogue that would make it accessible through common sense inquiry. The key words, terms which are often used in association with 'living history' and discussed in the introduction to this book, threw up many interesting and often amusing references but rarely material directly concerned with this research.

More fruitful inquiries have resulted from following threads through bibliographies and footnotes and scanning relevant (and not so relevant) journals.

This material can be divided into six broad categories:

1. Descriptive accounts;
2. Practitioner produced information on how to relive the past;
3. Critique, often negative and scornful;
4. Heritage management material which takes the activities more seriously;
5. Archaeological writing on the interpretation of artifacts;
6. Museum studies material on presentation, interpretation, accessibility and education.

### BRINGING ORDER, STRUCTURE AND MEANING TO THE MASS OF DATA

In qualitative research this is usually done by generating categories of data to be collected either before the research is undertaken as a focusing device for the study, or after the data has been collected to search for possible emerging categories. As Schatzman and Strauss (1973) pointed out some time ago, 'probably the most fundamental operation in the analysis of qualitative data is that of discovering significant classes of things, persons and events and the *properties* which characterise them.' Analysis they suggested, was complete 'when the critical variables are defined, the relationships among them are established, and they are integrated into a *grounded theory*.' (our italics).

The main aims, however, of the process of analysis inevitably need to be the *reduction of data* as the mass of collected material is brought into manageable chunks and '*interpretation* as the research brings meaning and insight to the words and acts of the participants in the study' as Marshall and Rossman stated. (their italics, p.114). In our analysis we are conscious that such interpretation will be influenced by our disciplinary thinking and interests. In many ways the categories we have utilised have been 'working' ones that we have tried to 'flesh out' with illustrative examples. As Marshall and Rossman point out 'raw data have no inherent meaning; the interpretive act brings meaning to those data and displays the meaning to the reader through the written report' or as in this case, the structure of the jointly composed text of this book.

We have organised our material under the various circumstances (settings) and participants (visitors and interpreters) and draw conclusions from the interplay of these elements. To do this we start by considering the Setting (Chapter Five) followed by the **Visitor** - where least data exists (Chapter Six) and the **Interpreter** that draws on considerably more information (Chapter Seven). In each chapter we start by identifying types and then illustrate the features or 'properties' of each.

---

Footnotes

1   It is difficult to provide reliable web page addresses or urls because of the ever-changing nature of the Internet. Some web sites are constantly being updated whereas others may stay the same or languish as the web site master changes or enthusiasm for this form of communication flags.

2   The conversations and field notes were taped and then transcribed. Some of the conversations were barely audible. The conversations are therefore reported rather than quoted. There has been no distortion of meaning.

# Chapter five

❧

# THE SETTING OF LIVING HISTORY

## WHERE DO WE FIND THE LIVING HISTORY APPROACH BEING USED?

The Association for Living Historical Farms and Agricultural Museums, which is generally known by its acronym ALHFAM, 'has been instrumental in establishing a philosophy, terminology and methodology for living history.' (Robertshaw, 1997, p.2) This is an international organisation linking individuals and institutions concerned with the preservation of rural and agricultural history. Most of the Association's members are involved in living history demonstrations, costumed interpretations and hands-on activities for visitors. The member organisations 'include restored villages, historic houses, agricultural and industrial museums, and ships and military establishments in the United States, Canada and fifteen other nations around the world.' (Doon Heritage Crossroads web site 1996).

This list is only of institutions but with the inclusion of re-enactment groups and their performers the concept of setting can be extended to locations such as battle sites and castle ruins, and public areas within cities and towns such as parks, show grounds and market squares - often open air spaces rather than buildings - where the re-enactment groups perform. The ALHFAM listing might be thought of as those institutions which are an integral part of the 'built environment' presenting the past in its cultural setting in contrast to the re-enactment groups recreating the past predominantly through costumes and weapons. However, even among the latter, some groups enthusiastically erect tents or temporary buildings to provide a more appropriate setting for their performance than the town square or grounds of a historic house.

Inevitably in living history, the setting may appear as ephemeral. The tent is taken down and packed away and the rooms of the historic house appear deserted when its cast of costumed guides have disrobed and gone home. As with a stage set, when the cast have made their bows and departed, the setting in which the living history approach is used, must have people in costume with their 'props' to provide any semblance of 'living history'. When GB got off the bus at Williamsburg, the recreated weather board houses appeared quiet, and in his notes, he commented that it was beautiful, but this first impression soon gave way to a feeling that he had alighted in a 'ghost town'; (Williamsburg observation notes)

Having considered where we might find living history settings and their ephemeral and ghostly nature when human interaction is absent, we explore three aspects of the setting of museums, centres, houses or heritage sites using the living history approach:

1. total site;
2. individual locations within the site;
3. influence of the time of day and the weather on interpreters' and visitors' perceptions.

## 1. The total site

The overall size of the site and the number of buildings it contains make up the **total site**. The Black Country Living Museum (England) occupies twenty-six acres and is almost half a mile from north to south. It is an open-air museum where historic buildings and transport have been brought together to recreate the living and working conditions of 'that region of industrial activity, originally based on the mining of coal and the working of iron, which lies to the west of the City of Birmingham and straddles the ridge of hills running south east from Wolverhampton.' (*The Black Country Museum* 1991, published by Pitkin Pictorials).

Costumed guides tell visitors about the Black Country and demonstrate traditional skills. In the Entrance Building there is a *What's On Board* to inform visitors of activities and demonstrations taking place on the day of their visit and they receive a pamphlet that opens out to show a detailed, coloured drawing of the site and the various locations such as the Cast Iron Houses, the Tilted Cottage, St James's School, or the Pawnbroker's Shop as well as facilities such as Refreshments, Picnic Area, and Gift Shop. This pictorial map is also produced as a signboard near the entrance. Visitors standing on the higher ground where the entrance is located not only see the extensive nature of the site in front of them but by consulting the map they can identify the various **individual locations** within the site's totality.

## 2. Individual locations

Together the overall site and its individual locations are the environment for the visitor's encounters with the costumed guides and living history exponents. Both aspects form the Black Country Living Museum's setting for its living history activities. The individual locations are linked by a combination of period, story and theme to make up the site. The following examples, Beamish (England) and Old Sturbridge Village (United States) illustrate the way in which the variety of settings illustrate different aspects of rural and industrial life in the nineteenth and early twentieth centuries. Each one is therefore linked into a site by common period and theme. There is no story to develop so the visitor is free to explore the locations in any order they desire.

*Beamish*

The North of England Open Air Museum at Beamish is a large and extensive site set in over 300 acres of countryside. It recreates life in the nineteenth and early twentieth centuries showing the social, agricultural and industrial history of the region in what is referred to as a 'living way' - a phrase used in the site's web page. In such an extensive site, travel by tram or period bus is provided to take the visitor to the Colliery Village with its school, chapel, pit cottages and pit head buildings. Costumed staff welcome visitors into various types of shop, homes, a sweet factory, motor works, a public house, railway station and other work places typical of industrial town life of the early nineteen hundreds in the north of England. At Home Farm traditional breeds of animals and poultry are penned in the farmyard and in the large farmhouse kitchen, the farmer's wife carries out her daily chores. Extensive sites such as Beamish provide a number of different individual locations, not all of which will be seen by visitors, unless they are prepared and able to spend considerable time exploring all the locations such a site has to offer.

## Old Sturbridge Village

The largest historical theme museum in the north east of the United States is located at Sturbridge in the state of Massachusetts. 'The museum recreates the daily work activities and community celebrations of a rural 19th -century town in authentic – living history – fashion. It's fun to dwell in the past!' (http: www.osv.org/Welcome. html ) There are people every where in costumes. Even the animals have been 'back-bred' to resemble those that would have grazed here in the nineteenth century. The Herb Garden has preserved plants the early New Englanders cultivated for fragrances, flavourings and medicines. 'The Village is alive with *sights and sounds* – of farming activities, of militia musters, and of music and merriment.' (Our italics). (http://www.osv.org/pages/ss.html)

The site includes more than forty staffed 'exhibits' such as historic homes, craft shops, mills, and farm buildings, created on more than 200 acres of fields and farmland. The particular functions of these individual locations are emphasised by special events such as:

> haying contests, music and dance demonstrations, garden days, a
> celebration of crafts, an 1830s wedding, and visits from such special
> guests as Daniel Webster and P. T. Barnum.... Costumed
> "interpreters" plow the fields, stitch leather into shoes, and keep
> strict discipline in the one-room schoolhouse.
>
> (Welcome to the Village! Web site)

## Jamestown and Mystic Seaport

The following two examples, also from the United States, use a variety of locations for different purposes each, in different ways, bringing coherence to the visitor's experience of the totality of the site.

At Jamestown, the individual locations are linked chronologically. The visitor moves from a Powatan Village to three replica ships and then to a recreated fort. This gives different perspectives on the sequential stages of the story of the first European settlement in America. At Mystic Seaport, however, the variety of locations are used to illustrate different aspects of America's seafaring past. Hence they are linked solely by theme.

*Jamestown*

Not only is the setting here divided into three chronological locations but each of these contains a number of smaller settings. In the Powhatan Indian village costumed interpreters 'discuss and demonstrate the Powhatan way of life.' This Indian village is made up of several dwellings, a garden and a ceremonial dance circle. Its recreation is based on eyewitness drawings of the period and on archeological findings from sites in other parts of the state. A path leads from the Indian village to the pier where the three ships - the *Susan Constant*, the *Godspeed* and the *Discovery* are docked. On board visitors can converse with appropriately costumed interpreters about the voyage from England - the crew and passengers were at sea for four and a half months. Finally, James Fort is a recreation of the one built by the colonists. It has a wooden stockade inside of which are wattle-and-daub structures with thatched roofs that represent the earliest buildings - homes, a church, a store-house and an armoury.

*Mystic Seaport*

This is the Museum of America and the Sea, located in Mystic, Connecticut. It was started in 1929 to preserve the rapidly disappearing remnants of America's maritime past, being built on the banks of the Mystic River on land formerly part of a shipyard. Now the home of 'America's largest watercraft collection', Mystic Seaport comprises more than sixty buildings covering an area of some thirty-seven acres.
(http : //www.mystic.org/public/visiting.mem/history.html)
There is a common theme on this site - the importance of the sea in American history, and to illustrate this, a whole range of settings are used by the Museum's staff who interpret the exhibits, present special programmes, and demonstrate traditional maritime skills. As the institution's web site claims, it is more than just a museum of different buildings. It is a 'spectacular waterfront collection of ships, buildings, crafts, trades, music, food and art that brings the story of America and the sea to life.

### 3. The influence of the time of day and the weather

The third aspect of the setting we should mention is how the site is perceived differently by interpreters and visitors in different weather conditions and at different times of the day. BG and her daughter found that they had stayed at the Black Country Living Museum until closing time. Most of the visitors with children had already gone home by the time they made their way back to the entrance building. BG noticed that several of the costumed guides had moved from their 'stations' in the various houses. They were standing in the street near the canal talking together - the topic of conversation appeared to be duty rosters for the next day.

The setting must take on a different feeling for the interpreters when the visitor has gone, if for no other reason than the site is no longer 'peopled' by strangers. Living history exponents have also commented about the differences the seasons make and certainly both visitors' and interpreters' impressions are affected by the weather.

We both visited Sovereign Hill in Victoria, Australia that recreates the Gold Rush days and the first ten years of the city of Ballarat's existence after the discovery of gold in 1851, a site:

> where Australia's History comes to life! The streets are bustling with people dressed in costume of the period. The Diggings are alive with miners panning for real gold. And you can take a ride through the streets in a horse-driven carriage. There are shops, hotels, schools, a theatre, crafts, steam-driven machinery and working plant all known to have existed in Ballarat in the 1850s......you'll experience life as it was ... It's just like stepping back in time.
>
> (Web page http://www.ida.com.au/vic/sovereign/ as of August, 1998)

Although visiting Sovereign Hill at different times, we both experienced similar weather conditions - wet and stormy - since we were in Australia during the country's winter months. When BG was there the horse-drawn coach driven by a costumed interpreter, careered down the town street splashing through the large puddles that had formed after an hour-long downpour. She took shelter in one of the recreated buildings, somewhat frustrated at her exploration having been so suddenly interrupted. Our negative impressions of the setting at Sovereign Hill might have been different if we had experienced the site under blue skies and in bright sunshine.

Chris Fautley (1997) describing a school visit to Battle Abbey, East Sussex, England and a recreation of the Battle of Hastings wrote of battling with the elements - thunder, lightning and for good measure, a cloudburst which appropriately renewed the boggy conditions that historically were said to have hindered William the Conqueror's cavalry. In this example, the weather conditions did not put a damper on the tented Saxon village recreated on the battlefield. Fautley described the 'Saxons' as casually squelching barefoot in the mud as they still managed to explain to the visiting children what they ate and demonstrated their means of fire-lighting and cooking. As he commented, telling the children to treat the experience 'like a time warp' was hardly necessary - 'they were absorbed from the start and mingled freely with the re-enactors playing the Saxons.'

Having examined the variety of locations which go to make up the site, the various ways in which they are linked and the host of factors that influence our experiences of them, we turn our attention to a common consideration in the construction and interpretation of all settings - the issue of authenticity and accuracy.

**CONSTRUCTING THE SETTING: ISSUES OF AUTHENTICITY**

## Original or reconstructed buildings

The buildings in open-air museums may be the restored originals, as at Williamsburg, or fabricated or replicated. They may be located on the original site or a totally different one. At Beamish and at Sturbridge, buildings from the region were brought to the site, rebuilt and furnished to look as they might have appeared in the time period depicted, whereas at Plimoth replicas of houses and furnishings were used.

An interesting example of the problems of authenticity is Old Sturbridge Village. Set up to recreate an early nineteenth century rural town, the Village is a composite made up of buildings brought from all over New England and the occasional 'reconstructed' inventions. GB was told that:

> The Layout of village, is purely fictional, based on an archetype New England Town. Most of the buildings are real in one way or another either moved from other sites or built here from plans. We couldn't get a sawmill to move in here so we based it on a mill in New Hampshire, documented with drawings (post Period) and from the 1930's and pieced together. This we feel is a very accurate building.

> The Grist Mill on the other hand, we don't tend to talk very much about. It's fantasy, used for demonstrations but not staffed regularly and no signs say that it is a fake. (Ironically) In the 40's and 50's it was the symbol for the museum.

> The Shift to authenticity came in the 1960's . We're pretty good about where the missing pieces are.

> (Sturbridge Conversation 1.)

These missing pieces in the material culture obviously influence the nature of the interpretation. If the institution wants to interpret a vanished or partially absent past, then it must either reconstruct settings from similar evidence or create imaginary buildings and therefore imaginary environments. The same problem exists, as we shall see later, when giving characters to the interpreters. On a more general theme, if the material culture of a whole section of society is absent, how can it be interpreted with any degree of accuracy? If a part is absent, how can the overall interpretation be said to have any claim to authenticity?

> The missing pieces that we are working on now are what people on the fringes of society did. The material life is not there and the written material is limited. We are in the process of doing archaeological digs.

> (Sturbridge conversation 1)

Various compromises are, therefore necessary. The problem comes in communicating these to the visitor. In the bank in Old Sturbridge Village there is a book of photographs which shows where the bank came from and how it was moved. The Grist Mill however is ignored, rather like an embarrassing elderly relative, in the hope that no one will notice it. No one on the other hand has the heart to throw it away!

Attempts are made at Sturbridge to make the nature of the composite site and the limits of authenticity clear to visitors through an orientation film. This method is, however, dependent on the visitors attending. GB overheard the following inquiry from a visitor

> Visitor:        Was the village....was it here?
> Interpreter:    Sturbridge itself is down the road.
> Visitor:        Does this...have... any proximity to it?
>
> Interpreter explains that it is a conglomerate.
>
> (Sturbridge Observation)

A different problem of authenticity exists at Plimoth Plantation. The plantation is built on a site with similar geographical features to the original settlement. The site of the original fort can still be visited on the burial mound in the centre of the modern town. The buildings are, however, all reconstructions and the layout of the village based on contemporary accounts although smaller than the original. The furniture was original in the early days of the interpretation but for curatorial reasons it was removed and replaced by reproductions. The site is in two parts. The visitor firstly visits the pilgrims' village and then the Native American area. When GB visited the village, the interpreters were very much in role, speaking in language reconstructed from the seventeenth century. The Native American section certainly felt less influenced by the material setting, the interpreters were not in role but explained what they were doing dressed in modern uniforms like park rangers. The juxtaposition was unfortunate as the Native American interpretation felt like an afterthought on which much less care had been lavished. This feeling may well be related to the lack of a constructed setting as much as the change in interpretative style.

## Compromising authenticity: an issue of safety

The Tilted Cottage at the Black Country Living Museum is an interesting example of a building that has been dismantled and relocated at the Museum site. As the costumed guide explained to BG, this small building was carefully ' built back on the same tilt as we found it ... and of course made safe...'

Her explanation raises the whole question of authenticity and safety. The fabric of the cottage is the same in its rebuilt state, the tilt recreated, but the cause of it - the mine shaft below the original house - is not there. Visitors may experience the physical sensation and consequently ask questions about the reasons for it, but they are unlikely to experience feelings of fear about the building's safety.

So the setting, however 'authentic' will never evoke extreme emotional reactions in visitors. They will never, on a visit to the Black Country Living

Museum, fear the total collapse due to subsidence of the tilted house. The visitor is in no danger. For employees who stay longer in the 'authentic' surroundings, working conditions might, however, be difficult, even hazardous.

Lumley (1988) in his book *The Museum Time-Machine: Putting cultures on display* quoted Bob West's concern when visiting Ironbridge Gorge Museum in Shropshire (England) for the purpose of seeing what it really felt like to be involved in candle-making. West was affected by the smallness of the space in which the work was carried out and the 'gagging vapour' of melted wax that provided authenticity but brought home to him 'the potentially unacceptable consequences of actually reproducing a hazardous environment.' (Lumley, pp.12-13).

Managers must ensure that buildings on the site meet present day health and safety standards for visitors and for employees without distracting too much from an authentic experience. In an example from Sovereign Hill, Evans (1991) explains that buildings are occasionally added to the site. When this happens visitors see the modern drainage systems being installed. On completion, such evidence of present day requirements, is invisible to the visitor.

Historical and heritage theme parks have been criticised for, in Evans's words, 'sanitising the past'. Graeme Davison commented that Sovereign Hill's recreated gold mining township was a 'necessarily quieter, cleaner and more orderly' place than the original and that there were more 'middle-class matrons in crinolines and bonnets, than young male miners and certainly there was an absence of prostitutes on the authentic looking streets.' (Evans, 1991, p.142)

So modern drainpipes may have to be hidden to ensure health standards, while preserving or recreating the 'look' of the past. Although, elements of that past may be omitted because of current social beliefs and difficulties dealing with less acceptable or problematic aspects of that past.

## Compromising authenticity: what feels 'right'

### Sovereign Hill, Ballarat, Victoria, Australia

Evans's paper from which we have quoted, is an interesting examination of the kinds of reductions and integrations which have determined the eventual form of historical representation at Sovereign Hill. It is also about how the history presented there in the first twenty years of the site's existence focused less on 'antiquarian reconstruction' and in the main, more on myth creation and preservation. This is well illustrated by the story of the miner's cottage and its 'dunny' - Australian term for a toilet or lavatory.

The miner's cottage, a building on the main street, was not the recreation of a specific building with appropriate visual features. The local branch of the Country Women's Association was responsible for the decoration and furnishing of the cottage's interior, based on their assumptions of what they believed would have been familiar to the district's pioneer women .

Behind the miner's cottage stands a small timber outhouse; the dunny, an:

afterthought, added because it looked appropriate. At the last minute
a hurriedly called committee meeting discussed this dunny in some
detail as no one was happy with its appearance. On the morning
before Sovereign Hill first opened a bulldozer was made to 'nudge' it,
producing a distinct lean: it then *looked right*. (Our italics; Evans,
p.144).

In somewhat similar fashion, a landscape architect was brought in as a
consultant to make the artificial creek look more 'natural' - his solution was
to bring in water-worn rocks from different areas of the state.

## Changing approaches to authenticity: developing policy

During this initial phase of the establishment of Sovereign Hill, when the
'diggings' part of the site was being created, great care was taken to recreate
a variety of mining technologies and practices. Various types of mine
timbering and several sorts of shaft were put in place. 'Processing of alluvial
material was shown through re-created puddling machines, long terms and
cradles.' Evans suggested that at that initial stage there was a commitment
by the Ballarat Historical Park Association to depicting as accurately as
possible a particular township and goldfield at a specific period of its history
while at the same time recreating:

> the Ballarat of the goldfields - as they believed it had been, and as the
> local community remembered that historical period. Thus the
> pioneering families could be represented by a 'typical' house or
> houses brought in from outlying districts. The myth of the diggings
> could be represented by the landscape creek, and the Chinese
> presence by a symbol of the orient, a brick joss house.
>
> (Evans, 1991, p.144)

Evans's account traces the tension that existed in the development of
Sovereign Hill between the 'mythologising folk museum concept' and
'adherence to the concept of historical accuracy'. During the development of
the site, there was a distinct shift away from presenting the history of the
city's growth to a more general history of the discovery and mining of gold in
the state of Victoria. The intention was to appeal to a wider audience. By the
1980s, it was felt that Sovereign Hill also needed to differentiate itself from
other theme parks and this was brought about by the site's management
focusing more on the social history of the period being represented. A
volunteer organisation was created called the Friends of Sovereign Hill that
provided 'a pool of costumed people' who could 'activate' Sovereign Hill by
means of 'historically accurate activities.' (Evans, 1991, p.149) The group
quickly grew to over 300 and the adoption of a living history approach, soon
distinguished Sovereign Hill from small historical sites or the larger theme
parks such as Seaworld and Dreamworld.

Michael Evans had become curator at Sovereign Hill in 1986 and
considered that it was his training in ethnohistory which led to his awareness
of how the presentation of history at this historical theme park was not just

a presentation of research findings but rather 'a constructed representation of that history, highly loaded with the ideology of the present.' Under his direction the aim of Sovereign Hill's historians became that of engaging visitors, 'however fleetingly, in some discourse with our representation of the past, to converse with visitors rather than talk at them.' (Evans, pp.150-151). In the early 1990s at Sovereign Hill emphasis was upon 'the creation of opportunities for visitors to experience some involvement in re-created historical situations - an attempt at living ethnographical history.' (Evans, p.152).

## Reconstructing the setting: 'authentic' Williamsburg

Unlike the examples cited so far in this chapter, Williamsburg is a reconstructed town where the buildings are restored to their eighteenth century 'original' appearance on the original site, faithful to the street plan of the original settlement. The issues of authenticity and accuracy here are therefore of a different order to those encountered at a composite site. Unlike many reconstructed sites there is a huge variety of restored buildings. Weather boarded domestic homes and shops, taverns, a church, and a gaol house contrast with grander buildings redolent of the civic pride of the eighteenth century (and mythology about America's 'greatness' from the time of the cold war), the Capitol, the Governor's house, and the court room.

Just as at Ballarat, the construction of a myth has also taken place. When visiting in Spring one of the most striking features is the tranquility of the gardens. There is a feeling at Williamsburg that it must appear more beautiful and more pristine than could ever have been the case when it was a thriving commercial and administrative centre. The dominant politics of the era in which the interpretation was developed influence the physical setting as much as the content of the historical interpretation. Williamsburg is, after all, the home of American Democracy and the American dream. In the 40s and 50s when the reconstruction was undertaken, democracy was challenged by fascism and the cold war tensions were growing. GB was told that a lot had changed since then:

> The attitude was 'right- let's make it look the best we can.' Now
> concessions are made to authenticity, the grass is allowed to grow
> higher and some of the paint left to crumble. They now place sand in
> the streets on top of the asphalt. The costumes were made of
> crimpolene because washing was easier but now they are made of
> natural materials as they would have been.
>
> (Williamsburg Conversation 1)

The question of creating an 'authentic' experience for visitors is obviously contentious and compromise has been reached. Again GB was told that 'Williamsburg is a twentieth century museum bringing the visitor *in touch*' (our italics) with the eighteenth century town.

This attitude is important. To be brought in touch with something does not imply an immersed, truly authentic eighteenth century experience where every aspect of life is as the way it was. Immediately the aim is recognised as being to bring the visitor in touch then compromise is possible, indeed necessary, as the museum would not wish to alienate its visitors or endanger them:

> Some would throw an air conditioned dome over the lot. Others create
> an eighteenth century town where they'd bring in squalor, tear up the
> asphalt and dirty it up a little. You have to accept a medium balance.
> You have to accept the realities of getting people here and keeping
> them comfortable. You have to keep the trees. You can't see the
> uniform facade of grand avenue as it was designed but it's as hot as
> hell in summer.
>
> (Williamsburg Conversation, 1 )

There is one interesting anachronism in this lovingly restored setting and that is the nineteenth century house. Whilst this is somewhat incongruous being neither of the visitor's time or the interpreter's, it serves to remind the visitor of intermediate historical events and the *process* of change which can often be absent from historical reconstruction. Visitors can make comparisons between then and now but rarely have the opportunity to explore why things are different from the past and how they have come to be so.

So in conceiving of these settings, we have the realisation of the overall site and its individual locations, the issue of authenticity and compromises for reasons of safety, the impact of the institution's policy for living history activities and how they are actually carried out in the interactions taking place in the site's locations.

## THEMED SITES IN SINGLE SETTINGS

Up to this point in our survey of living history settings we have concentrated on large complex sites in which the individual locations combine into one site linked by period, theme or story. We now turn our attention to those smaller sites where one theme or story is pursued and, as examples, will consider replica ships, penal heritage sites, the schoolroom and 'below stairs'.

### Replica ships

There are a number of replica ships in existence, some tied up at wharves and jetties (as already mentioned at the Jamestown Settlement) - moored museums -whereas others are venturing across vast areas of ocean to recreate voyages of the past. The HM Bark *Endeavour* is a copy of the ship in which Captain James Cook set sail from Whitby in England in 1768 for his epic voyage of discovery and exploration of present day Australia and New Zealand. It is claimed by her skipper Chris Blake to be 'the most accurate replica 18th-century sailing ship in existence - a living, working and moving museum' (Grosset, S. 1997, pp.24-25) The *Endeavour* was built in Fremantle, Western Australia and has been sailed to New Zealand, Britain and the United States. When she is in port the ship becomes a floating museum, the lower deck hammocks in place and tables set with wooden bowls and spoons, the officers' cabins with writing tables, quill pens and uniforms, so the ship gives the appearance of the officers and men having only recently gone ashore.[1]

The replica of John Cabot's flagship, the *Matthew* left Bristol in the west of England on 4 May 1997 to retrace the explorer's 2,000 mile voyage to Newfoundland 500 years earlier. It was noticeable in the TV news coverage of the ship's departure that the eighteen man crew were in medieval costume but it is unlikely that they retained this authenticity of dress for the whole of the voyage across the north Atlantic.

There are however replica ships which are used as the setting for visitors to pay to experience sea board conditions where costumed characters add to the realism of the experience. Strictly speaking a reconstructed ship, Sir Francis Drake's the *Golden Hinde* has, since its launch in 1973 circumnavigated the world but has also been berthed in London Docks where it has hosted overnight living history sessions for primary school children. (Neumark, 1997, p.26)   As Victoria Neumark, a mother accompanying her seven-year-old son, commented in her account of the night's experience, 'despite noticing the modern surroundings (*of the ship's location*) confinement to the vessel very soon creates the feeling of a close little world'.

On the other side of the world, in Sydney, school children can experience 'Tried and Transported' which recreates being charged and convicted for various misdeeds, followed by being marched to the transport ship *Solway Lass* moored at Man O'War Steps. Although being 'the oldest tall ship on Sydney Harbour, its initial launch in 1902 made it at least seventy years too young to play its part in the historical reconstruction'. (Richmond, 1994). As the notes for teachers explain, the re-enacted voyage to Australia commences with incidents which may involve renegade convicts, stowaways or marooned escapees. Returning to Man O' War Steps, the convicted are met by more costumed re-enactors and marched the short distance up the hill to Hyde Park Convict Barracks (present day Hyde Park Barracks Museum, Sydney). There they are led to their hammocks in the reconstructed dormitories of the third level of the building and stay the night until the early morning when they are awakened - if they have been able to sleep (teachers are required to sleep in the hammock room with their charges, although the concession of being able to bring an air-bed is allowed) the experience concluding with a mean, convict-style breakfast.

Simon Richmond ,who underwent the 'Tried and Transported' experience as a tourist, described how, as they settled down for the night in their truncated hammocks (the original convicts were much shorter than present day visitors), 'strange murmuring and noise echoed through the draughty hall ... the soundscape created by the museum to give an aural sense of the past.'

Both BG and GB visited this Museum in Sydney - a solid brick block of a building with pitched roof originally built to house 600 convicts but in which at times were crammed as many as 1,400. In the sleeping area, dark and shadowy even in the middle of the day, we saw the canvas hammocks and heard the 'soundscape' of mutterings and groans - really not needed as this room with its ghostly hammocks, occasionally moving in a non existent breeze, was a strange and eerie enough dormitory with its shadows and rafted roof.

As Simon Richmond found himself released from the Barracks after a night there, he commented that:

> unlike the prisoners of old we were not expected to go off to build the
> city's roads or grand buildings, such as the nearby St James Church. In
> this fine fresh dawn we were free men again. It felt good to be back in
> 20th-century Sydney.

### Other penal heritage sites

The 'Tried and Transported' experience is available to both school children, and adults and children as tourists and brings us to consider what has come to be known in tourism as 'penal heritage'. This is the existence of themed museums set up on the remains of old jails in which visitors can experience what the conditions were like for those incarcerated in them in the past. Two such sites recently developed in London as tourist attractions are the Clink in Southwark and the House of Detention in Clerkenwell. The latter was a working jail until the end of the nineteenth century and the former closed a century earlier. 'Now its inmates are tourists gasping at the horrors of incarceration past.' (Bennett, 1995, p.22). Bennett quotes Neil Taylor of Regent Holidays as noting that 'the number of penal attractions is growing steadily. How long will it be, he asks with tongue only slightly in cheek, before the Gulags are welcoming coaches?'

The Galleries of Justice in Nottingham (England) now promise visitors 'a romp through 600 years of prison history by letting them "experience" jail by assuming the identities of the lags of ages.' (Bennett, 1995, p.22). This 'Crime and Punishment Experience' is located in the city's nineteenth century Shire Hall and adjoining County Goal:

> Visitors assume the identity of real 19th century criminals, experience
> the nerve tingly clamour of a public trial and next the site of the
> hangman's gibbet where some of the region's most notorious
> murderers met their death. (Advertisement *Times Educational
> Supplement* Going Places supplement, 3 February, 1995, p.36)

At Old Sydney Town in NSW visitors are offered a number of different buildings. An important element on this extensive site are the court and gaol where visitors will have experiences that it is claimed, they will always remember. They can be 'part of a typical trial of the day as colonial justice takes it's (sic) course in the Magistrate's Court. See convicts tried and punished.' (pamphlet *The Greatest Adventure In Living History* advertising Old Sydney Town).

What follows is a description of such a trial taken from BG's notes when she visited Old Sydney Town. Visitors were seated on rough benches as the event unfolded:

> Decided that both the burial (just seen outside the church) and the trial
> were being played for laughs. Woman on trial. Judge made reference to
> how her fine could be paid by a member of the public. Reference that I
> didn't understand .... friends I was with said it was a joke about a local,
> state politician! Children and adults made up the audience ..
> interpreter/characters 'playing to the gallery'... to the adults, they were
> assuming mock seriousness and evoking feeling of a melodrama
> performance, or with attempts to include the audience of visitors - the
> verbal exchanges of pantomime. Very much a 'happening' that was a
> timed performance, stage managed and controlled by the performers.

We have quoted these examples, including Old Sydney Town's 'happenings'
that were staged at particular buildings on the site, since the choice of
locations and buildings as settings can involve the depiction of specific
aspects of the past that represent a view of human nature that 'colours' the
whole interaction between interpreters and visitors and is encapsulated in
the term 'dark tourism'.[2]

The term encompasses the representation in various media such as
newsreels, books, television, and films, of inhuman acts such as the
Holocaust and concentration camps or past social institutions such as the
identification and treatment of the 'criminal' and how these are interpreted
for those who may go on to visit the actual sites. Many tourists and visitors
feel an interest in visiting the actual places, the images of which have been
seen and possibly become familiar from mass media, to experience the
reality of the situation for themselves. As suggested in Chapter Two, the
living history approach could be a particularly effective form of teaching
children versions of history. In dealing with the kinds of issues which are
becoming the focus of 'dark tourism' we feel that schools and their teachers
and parents have a specific responsibility. This is to consider and discuss the
way in which sites 'bring to life' the social practices and events of the past,
which are no longer tolerable today. The example of Williamsburg which has
made a point of portraying slavery amongst much controversy will be
considered in the following sections on visitors and interpreters. The
educational potential of such visits, if handled sensitively, is huge since they
relate a version of history to issues of morality, social justice and citizenship
all of which are current concerns for educational policy makers particularly
in the United Kingdom.

### The school room and 'below stairs'

In considering the educational resources provided by sites in England or
Wales we became aware of the current tendency to create two particular
settings: the school room and 'below stairs'. These appeared to be related to
the curriculum changes taking place in schools during the past decade and
to assumptions about what might interest children.

For instance, classrooms with a costumed teacher using the living history
approach seem to be a popular 'attraction' in which the practice of the past

assumes importance not only because the 'Victorians' are a topic of study but also because it is assumed that children are aware of the features of their schooling and can make comparisons between past and current practice. Reva Klein reporting on a Welsh school museum (Klein, 1997, p.17) which she believed presented a simulation of Victorian school life that was realistic rather than nostalgic, expressed this view that a comparative approach is effective because 'there's no better way of trying to understand the past than by *delving into the way things were for people of your own age.*' (our italics).

Usually the teacher in role is portrayed as 'strict' and control is maintained through harsh language and the use of the cane. Inevitably this representation of educational methods is likely to make present practice appear superior.

Another example, the Ragged School Museum is situated in a Victorian canal side warehouse which was part of the largest Ragged (free) School in London – the Copperfield Road Ragged School. During the period 1877-1908, thousands of poor local children received a free education with free meals in the winter and help towards finding their first job. The Museum has a special interest in the development of education in London and pre-booked parties of primary aged school children can take part in a re-enacted Victorian lesson, which is 'a unique and popular resource.' (Museum pamphlet information).

The classroom is furnished with wooden desks with attached benches set in rows facing the teacher's desk, with blackboards, abacus and a store cupboard for slates and ink trays. (Jerman, 1998, p.22). Children in costume attend an hour-long session which starts with an introduction to what 'life was like for ragged school children.' The female teacher wears an authentic bustled costume and launches into role-play which concentrates on the 'three Rs', the children rote learn, copy on their slates elaborate style lettering from the blackboard, and as they do sums, delete work with their dusters to make room for the next lot of calculations:

> By chanting sing-song fashion after the teacher they learned spelling,
> a bit of grammar and a bit of geography of Great Britain, part of the
> British empire under Queen Victoria, 'our Queen'. The crash of the
> cane on a desk and the order 'to sit up straight!' were entirely
> accepted. (Jerman, 1998)

In historic houses it is often the rooms 'below stairs' which can most easily be utilised for the living history approach since there are few items likely to be easily damaged or valuable furnishings about which to be concerned. Again it is assumed that children will be more familiar with cooking and food preparation and can grasp the technological difference and improvements between the equipment of the Victorian kitchen and today's labour saving gadgets.

Gunnersbury Park Museum, London is housed in a Victorian period mansion once the residence of the Rothschild family and provides a 'Victorian Kitchen Experience' for schools, designed "to support key stage 1 'Then and Now' and key stage 2 'Victorian Britain' ". (Cooley, 1997, p.18). Monsieur Athlone was, according to the 1881 Census, the cook in the mansion and is now recreated in 'the Experience' by the Museum's assistant education officer. As many children as possible are given a part to play and the chance to wear costume. As well as working in the kitchen, they have the 'below stairs' social hierarchy explained to them 'with everyone learning to address the cook as Sir or Monsieur with a bob or a nod.' (Cooley, 1997). They are also shown the scullery, the laundry and the cold room and 'how the heavy old-fashioned broom, the cumbersome cold-cupboard and the three-legged washing 'dolly' in an iron tub have been replaced by vacuum cleaners, refrigerators and washing machines.'

So far we have concerned ourselves with the large scale permanent settings but living history can also be carried out by those groups of interpreters and re-enactors that might be described as 'peripatetic' in that they travel to different places and establish their own settings, usually on a temporary basis. As we shall see these settings may be in 'authentic' places as on battle fields or in stately homes but they may be in less relevant settings such as the school hall. What follows is a survey of some of the most interesting groups who illustrate different attitudes to temporary settings.

## RE-ENACTORS WHO CREATE THEIR OWN SETTINGS

**Brigantia** is the name of a Re-enactment Society in Britain whose members research 'all aspects of late iron-age Celtic life (usually referred to as the late La Tene period), including history, myth, religion and archaeology.' (http : //www.loop.com/-madpoet/brigantia/ ). They travel around the south of England and Wales 'performing public displays of combat and living history for fairs, museums, schools, local councils and national heritage organisations' - a wide range of settings in which to perform. However on their web page they explain that usually the living history displays are put on at locations where an iron age Celtic roundhouse has been built. Locations then are likely to be open-air museums or historical farms. Invited to such places, the Society's members being relatively small in number, can live in the roundhouse during the day when visitors are on the site, hanging their swords and shields on the walls, cooking on the fire, and generally making the place look 'lived-in'. In this created setting they talk to visitors, recreating for them the visual images of what an iron age family would have looked like. If their host will allow it, after the public have left for home, they will stay on in the roundhouse, sleeping there over night and for that time making it their 'home' and experiencing the setting for their own education and enjoyment.

The **Ermine Street Guard** is also a re-enactment society but this group carries out research into the Roman army and the reconstruction of Roman armour and equipment, mainly in respect to the latter half of the first century A.D. They like to perform their displays, which include 'aspects of the Roman soldier's training and firing of the artillery', at the major Roman sites in Britain. (http://www.ncl.ac.uk/-nmcb3/groups/esguard.html). At displays, the Guard members answer questions from visitors about the life of a Roman soldier. In consultation with archeological experts the group made what they claim is the 'first ever hand stitched reconstruction of an eight man goat tent'. So even here, where the group may be performing on an actual site dating from Roman times, they have wanted to provide an appropriate and authentic tent and carry out their own research into the practical experience of this specific setting.

**The Vikings**, who claim to be the oldest and largest Dark Age society in Britain with some five hundred members, stage battle displays and set up encampments, which include the erection of a full-sized Saxon Hall. (http://www.biochem.ucl.ac.uk/~davis/vikings.html)

In just these three examples we have living history groups who are skilled and knowledgeable enough to live 'authentically' in a Celtic round house, build a Roman army tent, or a full-sized Saxon Hall, and in so doing provide not only accurate artifacts and costumes but also create their own historically authentic setting within the more prosaic location in which they have been asked or hired to perform.

Many re-enactment groups will of course organise occasions on which they are not performing for an audience and there are references on their web pages to the way in which creating the 'past' is a different experience where the 'public' are absent and the authentic setting is in an appropriate location. For instance, the Pike and Musket Society of New South Wales in Australia each winter hold a living history long weekend in the state's Southern Highlands:

> Setting up an authentic soldiers' campsite, we live in period-style
> tents, eat and drink appropriate food (which we prepare and cook
> ourselves) and fire our muskets on the range. If we are really lucky, it
> snows heavily – and we get full value from our authentic clothing and
> later, our wool blankets and straw beds. (Home page on the Net)

## THE SCHOOL AS A SETTING

Many re-enacting groups, societies and individuals have an educational aim and are willing and interested in visiting schools in costume. On the Internet, they often refer to their desire to 'teach' (rather than inform) the public about the country's history and so for them, their interest is in bringing the past 'to life' for school children. They often express the desire to counter balance an assumption that history-in-school is dull and only to be found in the pages of difficult to read textbooks.

Regia Anglorum is a society with some 500 members who aim to recreate the life of the British people in the late Dark Ages and early Medieval period, dressing as Celts, Saxons, Vikings, or Normans. They own a large quantity of 'props' which, like the three groups described above, enable them to create their own setting. These 'props' include large-scale tents, looms, coin-striking equipment, cooking equipment, and other museum-quality artifacts' and it is from the tented structures that the 'members teach and demonstrate some twenty different craft activities.' Visits to schools are an important part of the Society's work, a typical school visit taking up a full morning or afternoon session and including 'a brief talk, followed by interactive demonstrations using reconstructed artifacts'.

(http://alethea.ukc.ac.uk/SU/Societies/deBec/regia.html).

A local branch of the Society known as **Sancte Albantes Stow** in February, 1996 set up camp on the playing field of Chauncy School (Ware, Hertfordshire, England) . One of the Society's members came to the school a few days before the rest of the re-enactors to talk to one of the History classes. The school's students who produce the school newspaper *The Chauncy Challenger* wrote up the Viking re-enactment for the local newspaper. (*Mercury*, 16 February, 1996, p.31). The school was in fact a good site for this particular re-enactment as it is located on the banks of the River Lea, the border for the Viking realm of East Anglia. Viking war parties would cross the Lea to raid the country beyond, either to demand Dane Geld, a form of protection money, or to abduct local villagers and hold them for ransom.

The re-enactment Viking group arrived at Chauncey school in authentic clothing and included men, women and children. The warriors in authentic chain mail and helmets performed several battles, one of which was thought to have originally taken place in the Ware village of Dane End. The group also erected a large replica tent from which 'Viking methods of fire making, cooking, drop spinning, jewelry and weapon making were demonstrated' to the school children. With tent, equipment and costumed characters, the members of this society endeavoured to transform the familiar playing field or playground to another time. One wonders whether, for many of the school children who experienced this re-enactment and learnt more about the past of the school's location, the grassed playing field would ever be quite the same again!

Sometimes it is an individual in authentic costume with a selection of relevant artifacts who will visit a school. In this case they usually come into the school and visit the children in their classroom. This latter type of school visit has become popular in the United Kingdom not only because of the re-enactor's communication skills and historical knowledge, but also because the cost to the school is likely to be less than the expense of taking children to visit museums or historic houses, which usually involves transport as well as admission costs.[3]

Where schools continue to visit museums, they may encounter the costumed guide or character who adds a more human touch to the formality of the museum rooms and exhibition spaces. Increasingly in the 1990s in the United Kingdom, museums and galleries have introduced the practice of costumed guides who will converse with visitors and possibly demonstrate artifacts and weapons. For instance in 1996 the Museum of London introduced the use of actors for the first time in their new Roman Gallery with its reconstructed street of interiors of artisans' workshops, showing commodities such as shoes, glass and furniture. These room settings provide a stage for the 'actor/interpreters' who assume the parts of typical characters from Roman London : 'Marcus the veteran soldier who has gained his citizenship and turned trader: and the maid Martia Martina, a one-time slave who has been given her freedom.' (Norrie, 1996, p.16) Teachers who accompanied children to the Gallery thought that the actor clearly fired the children's imagination, on the evidence that the children studied the displays and answered questions. Their conclusion was that 'the encounter had brought the visit to life.' (Norrie, 1996). One of the primary teachers commented that 'While my pupils tend to focus on the Romans as soldiers, the actor reminded them that they were civilised people, who brought us good things' and another teacher summed up the museum gallery visit as 'a good interactive session, a reflexive exercise.' (Norrie, 1996) These comments suggested that such results might not always be achieved by the more formal and conventional school visit to a Museum.

## VIRTUAL SETTINGS

Advances in technology have already revolutionised the setting of living history which can now be experienced in the classroom with the help of cyberspace. Many of the larger and adventurous living history museums not only provide a range of forms of interactions with schools but experiment with the usage of electronic educational resources.

Williamsburg hosts some 130,000 school children and more than three million other visitors each year but 'we realized that economic and geographic considerations will prevent most of our nation's students from actually visiting the museum in person.' (web site) The museum has therefore created **Electronic Field Trips** to make use of new technologies which allow students to 'travel' without having to leave home or school.

The Electronic Field Trips are described as having three components:

1. a teacher's guide, containing historical background, suggested lesson plans and copies of original documents and prints;
2. a one hour live, interactive television programme;
3. special Internet activities.

Several weeks before the televised programme is to be shown, schools receive the teacher's guide and its preparation material for their classes. The interactive television programme is offered twice on the date of broadcast.

Important to our interest is that the televised programme offers eighteenth century historical dramas, opportunities to vote on issues presented in the programme, and opportunities *to speak directly with historical interpreters at Williamsburg* (our italics):

> Once the televised portion ends, Colonial Williamsburg's historians continue to answer question that could not be answered on air, and students use the Internet to discuss issues with each other and with Colonial Williamsburg's staff. Students also continue to 'visit' Colonial Williamsburg electronically by participating in several Internet-related activities.
>
> (http://www.history.org/other/teaching/tchinfo.htm)

Williamsburg claims that it offers a multitude of opportunities for educators and their students, visitors being able to 'visit our living history museum, in your classroom, at home.' Technological advances offer a unique exploitation of the living history approach but as yet we know very little if any thing about how the approach is likely to be adapted to this different medium and how it will influence the interaction between setting, visitor and interpreter. Indeed we have only a somewhat limited conception of the interaction in the varied settings in which the approach has been developed so far and certainly little about the role and function of language in the interaction.

It is the aim of this part of the book to develop some idea of the complexity and interactivity of the living history approach in its present variety of forms. As far as we know, no systematic research is being undertaken on the development and evaluation of electronic field trips and the living history approach.

Before turning our attention to visitors and interpreters and their interactions with each other and the setting we must mention some of the more unusual settings for living history.

## THE SETTING OF THE FAIR

The settings for living history are not confined to historical or educational sites as the following example demonstrates.

### Renaissance and Medieval Fairs

Lists of these events are available on different web sites on the Internet; usually for a variety of locations in the United States. All of such events tend to have things to buy and food to eat, and most have additional entertainment such as short plays, musical performances and battle pageants or re-enactments. The things on sale - food, toys and tableware etc. - may be appropriate to the period and aimed at the public to purchase, or clothing, weapons and armour intended for the hobbyist or re-enactor to buy. Listings of these fairs sometimes involve an element of evaluation and personal opinion. The following is an example which includes references to the effect of the setting. It comes from Blars' Renaissance Fairs Page on the Internet and is information about the Long Beach Renaissance Arts Festival in California held in August in 1996:

> Easy to get to faire benifiting (sic) "Travellers Aid." The pay parking
> does not, find on the street if you can. The battle closes a chunk of
> the faire site and is difficult to figure out what is going on. Good faire,
> but the buildings can be distracting. (Our italics)

A distinction can be made between the 'historical' fair and the 'fantasy faire'; although in practice elements of both types can be identified at an individual event. An article by Elizabeth Gilbert (1996) illustrates this point. When she visited the New York Renaissance Fayre (NYRF) it was supposed to be taking place on an English Summer's Day in 1589 but she thought the organisers had 'taken some liberties with that date' since they had included Robin Hood (a medieval character) and Leonardo da Vinci appearing along with William Shakespeare! What's more, the reigning monarch was not Queen Elizabeth but 'an Elizabethan-clone, whom the Fayre's organisers have named Queen Winifred.' The organisers appeared to be selective in the areas in which they sought to provide an element of authenticity. For instance, four days before the Fayre officially opened, all the vendors on the site had to assemble for 'a mandatory Olde English dialect class.' Most of the sales staff were local people who had been hired on a part-time basis to man the stalls and booths selling food:

> They would be making low wages, selling Steak-on-a stake, Royal Baked potatoes and Ye Olde Spicy Cheese Fryes. They were having trouble understanding why they needed to speak as if it was 1589 in order to perform their tasks. (Gilbert, 1996)

Gilbert described the friendly Artistic Director of the Fayre as explaining to the vendors that they were 'helping the visitors *to experience a fantasy*' and 'from this moment on, you must deny all knowledge of the modern world.' (Our italics)

Of course, being historically accurate may not be desirable for those who live in the area where medieval fairs or markets become established or for that matter, for local tourism. Totnes in south Devon, England is a delightful town, whose sixteenth century wool merchants were the basis of its wealth and still has the appropriate medieval architecture to be the suitable location for recreating a period market. The Elizabethan Society's costumed charity market is held outside the Civic Hall every Tuesday as much for the tourists as the local citizenry. Seen by some though as something of a 'kitschy heritage romp' several years ago:

> group of students from near by Dartington[4] crashed it dressed as lepers. Though historically accurate - Totnes did indeed have leper colonies - it didn't do much for local understanding.
>
> (Bennett, 1996)

The type of fair which caters in the main for the needs of re-enactors, is more often called a **Living History Trade Fair** and is usually held inside. In the United States such fairs can often include at least a hundred tables of traders as well as tables or booths set up by volunteer organisations to provide information. Traders may measure for coats or corsets ordered by re-enactors or be showing ready made clothes, or materials such as wool and linen on sale for individuals to cut and sew their own costumes. There may be a special selection of books and replica artifacts and weapons on sale. Such trade fairs can be a chance for re-enactors to meet and share interests, but they are not really a setting in which the living history approach is actually performed.

**CONCLUSION**

In this chapter we have been considering the huge variety of settings as the location for re-enactments and the use of the living history approach. The influence of the setting on the living history experience is not confined to its physicality (the constraints and limitations of such bricks and stones and replica or actual artifacts) but is modified by the situation encountered there. The setting, must be such that visitors are not endangered and have confidence in the historical exactness of the site. However within the constraints of the physical realisation of a historical site, visitors can be challenged by **situations** planned to provide them with a particular 'experience'. This may reinforce or challenge their first impressions of the setting derived from a variety of factors - what was learnt at school and the advertising and tourist information about the site. What may be remembered though, is the total experience brought about by the physical surroundings and an interaction with costumed 'characters'.

Evans gives as an example:

> visitors entering a re-created cottage and commenting on its
> attractions may suddenly find themselves embroiled in a domestic
> dispute between costumed interpreters over the advantages and
> disadvantages of living in Ballarat in 1857. Here the situation
> counterbalances the physical surroundings and the visitor's experience
> of the cottage is modified.
>
> (Evans, p.151)

The setting then, as a collection of images, evokes assumptions about the life styles and social values of its inhabitants in the past, which influence the behaviour and perceptions of interpreters and visitors alike, and can modify experiences of the physical setting.

Both individual re-enactors and re-enactment groups intervene to create the setting in which they perform with varying emphasis upon physical authenticity and the social and cultural values of the period of their interest. This mixture is then perceived by the visitor as a version of the past presented as history, further modified by their own assumptions and expectations. It is to the human elements of this interaction that we now turn.

We now consider the visitor in Chapter Six and then the interpreter in Chapter Seven, as elements in the interactive situation that the 'living history' approach seeks to create.

---

Footnotes

1   Private communication by BG with an Australian friend who acted as a costumed guide on the Endeavour. BG asked what sort of questions the younger children asked when visiting the ship. She wrote that many wanted to know 'where the plank was' but she always replied that the Endeavour hadn't been a pirate ship and captain Cook was a fair disciplinarian so no one was sentenced to 'walk the plank'. She had told children that 'several marines got twelve lashes and there were three who got twenty four lashes from the cat-o-nine tails... but that that was it. One man had committed suicide by jumping overboard, it was in response to him being caught stealing.' She was amused by the fact that the children also thought that the crew (fifty six in number who sail the replica ship) did not sleep in the hammocks but that there must be 'proper beds hidden somewhere' on the ship.

2   Dark Tourism by Malcolm Foley and John Lennon, lecturers at Glasgow Caledonian University published by Cassell in their series 'The Cutting Edge of Tourism' 1998 explores the concepts including how many acts of inhumanity are celebrated at heritage sites.

3   Diane Spencer Times Educational Supplement 4 September 1999. Museums and Galleries Commission

- the national advisory body for Britain's 2,500 museums - reported that since funds had been delegated to schools in 1993 as part of the introduction of local management, school visits to museums had declined in many areas. For instance in Manchester, schools were passing on charges to parents, despite having been given the delegated funding for museum education. 'The number of visits from poorer areas dropped, adding to the problems of social exclusion the children already faced.' The Commission's Director, Timothy Mason, expressed the belief that museum education services were not 'simply add-on' experiences, but play a crucial role in supporting the National Curriculum, developing literacy and in motivating pupils.

4    Dartington Hall, a progressive art college, school and foundation established by the rich idealists Leonard and Dorothy Elmhirst.

*Chapter six*

❧

# THE VISITORS

In this chapter, we consider the role of visitors in the 'living history' interaction. We must emphasise at the start that the term visitor is often short hand for a whole range of groups or types of person attending living history events or activities. They can be in the role of an observer or a participator but crucially they have not organised and do not control the event. They may not even be aware that such an approach is going to be used. When we talk of visitors we are, therefore, aware that we are not talking about a homogenous group but a disparate collection of individuals united by the fact that they are witnessing, or at least are physically present at, an event in a particular setting.

Information about the reactions and contributions of visitors to the living history approach is limited. Before considering our own reactions as visitors and our observations of others we will explain how the types of sources listed at the beginning of Chapter Four can help develop understanding of the approach. We pay particular attention to the way in which they can be read to indicate exponents' and institutions' expectations of visitors to sites where the living history approach is in use.

## SOURCES OF INFORMATION

### Literature

In the literature on living history there are references to visitors and their role but limited information on types of visitors, their understanding of the approach, or how it compares with other methods associated with museums and heritage sites. There are taxonomies of tourist types but little that specifically relates to living history. There have been surveys of museum visitors but these are usually evaluating the visitor's reactions to what the institution provides in the way of facilities and services. As so many institutions are commercial organisations much emphasis is placed upon attendance figures as an indicator of **visitor satisfaction**.

However, in 1992 there was a study at Hampton Court Palace, one of the English Royal Palaces, which attempted to investigate visitors' reactions to live interpretation. (Cummings, 1993; Malcolm-Davis, 1995; Department of National Heritage, 1996). This survey showed that 87 per cent of visitors considered there were no disadvantages to live interpretation and 64 per cent thought the live interpreters were the most informative method of the techniques being used. The methods assessed were those used in the Tudor Kitchens and Tudor Apartments of the Palace.

Many of the writers of books and articles about the living history technique draw upon their own experience of visiting sites and conversations and discussions with interested colleagues as well as more systematic interviewing of exponents of the approach. There is a delightful example in Jay Anderson's book *Time Machines*. In the late 1960s and 1970s many museums in the United States had decided to go for a more 'earthy realism' and in Plimoth Plantation it was the long hair and dirty feet of the Pilgrim interpreters that shocked tourists. They found it hard to accept an authentically sweaty Pilgrim. Jay Anderson continued:

> I vividly remember the words of a well-known professor of American Civilisation who visited Plimoth and, asked what he thought of it, tersely said "I found it vulgar, tasteless, and dirty. It will give the museum field a bad name if it gets any more popular."
>
> (Anderson, 1984 pp. 60-61)

The collation of material in the literature on visitors is made more difficult because of the speed and the manner in which practice in museums and heritage sites changes. What was true even a year ago may not be true now. Valid information about the visitor is less easily obtained than that about interpreters. We found further relevant information about visitors in articles which were published in the *Times Educational Supplement's* section called 'Going Places'. These were usually accounts written by teachers describing their reactions and those of their pupils when visiting an institution or site using the living history approach. Far less frequently, we sometimes came across visitors' reactions in articles published in the 'Tourism' sections of the national press such as those in the Saturday edition of the British newspaper the *Daily Telegraph*.

## Internet

Reading the web pages of re-enactment groups and sites using the living history approach, we noticed a difference between groups and sites in the extent to which reference was likely to be made to the visitor and to their anticipated role. For instance, the word 'visitor' was used but also 'the public', 'spectator', 'audience' and 'client' each indicating a different type of participation in re-enactments. The English Civil War Society (ECWS) on its web site described itself as follows:

> The English Civil War Society (ECWS) is a UK based history re-enactment group that portrays events of the period 1642-51 for the entertainment and education of the audience at public displays.

Here the visitor is identified by the terms 'audience' and also 'public'. We found that the former term was usually only used by re-enactment groups whereas 'public' was more often found in the text of institutions. There was a difference also in the type of visitors mentioned. Institutions referred specifically to children and their teachers (on school visits) but less frequently to parents/adults and children and families, possibly because they are more aware of their distinctly educational function.

Analysing the text of web sites for any reference to the visitor led us to the realisation that such linguistic references might not provide any information about how visitors thought about themselves or their role, in the sort of interaction implicit in the living history approach. Such textual references by the re-enactment and museum interpreters are more likely to provide information about living history exponents' *expectations* of the 'visitor'. These can be detected in the strategy used by some sites of directly addressing the potential visitor reading the text of the web site. In outlining the activities available to the visitor, the composer of the web site indicated the conceptualisation of the role expected of the visitor, by the linguistic choices made in the writing of the text.

The web site of Sovereign Hill in Australia illustrates this. Here you are likely to see this strategy operating in the choice of verbs used in the text:

> *Imagine going* back over a century to Victoria's Gold Rush days and *reliving* the history and the excitement of the era. ... In Sovereign Hill you'll *experience* life as it was in the 1850s. It's just like *stepping* back in time. ....
> *Try* your luck at panning for real gold on the Red Hill Gully Diggings. *See* and *experience* the lifestyle of the early diggers... *Learn* about the influence of the Chinese. .... In the main street you'll *meet* people in period costume and *see* business typical of the era. (Verbs in italics)

The verbs used in the text realise the actions and activities available to the visitor - the processes in which they are expected to take part, while the nouns and noun groups which follow, often provide the places and people, the participants involved in the processes available to the visitor in the context of the particular site being visited.

Of course, the texts used on web sites do change. The textual information of the home pages of societies and sites can be analysed to provide insights into how groups and institutions *expect* visitors to behave but such views may be transient.

## Materials supplied by museums, heritage sites and historical houses

These institutions often provide information in the form of **brochures or packs** which can be obtained before a visit, and these too can be analysed for the way in which the text realises interpreters' expectations about the roles and functions respectively of living history exponents and their visitors. For instance the London Transport Museum brochure has illustrations accompanied by a block of text which exhorts '*Travel* through time at the London Transport Museum.....' and lists a programme of activities which includes 'Actors playing characters from the past (daily).' In the pack available to schools an information sheet outlines preparation (by their teachers) for children's experience of the 'Time Bus'. In this part of their visit children are '*transported* back to different periods in history where they *meet*' a road crossing sweeper from 1870, a 1920 cleaner of an early motor bus, a 1939 tram passenger, and a 1940 wartime bus conductor.

Analysing text for the choices made by the writer in the language used, we have been referring to the verbs and nouns used, but equally we could examine the adjectives that realise the qualities attributed to the visitor. Where the interpreter/ re-enactor's web page or the site's brochure uses terms for the visitor do they also use adjectives ascribing specific qualities or characteristics to the visitor? Do any of their linguistic choices reveal their expectations of, or attitudes towards, the visitor?

The language model which underlies this form of such analysis is described and explained in detail in Chapter Eight, but sufficient at this point to note that the text of web pages or brochures intended for interested readers may provide not only information about how those using the living history approach believe they do this, but can also reveal their expectations of the visitor. This can be in terms of what it is thought the visitor will want to see and do. These expectations of the visitor on the part of the interpreter may of course differ greatly from what the visitors themselves want, or expect, to happen. There may be little or no consistency between visitors' expectations. This may create tensions within the visit: the interpreters' expectations may or may not act as a restraint on the visitor's behaviour. Visitors may fail to have a clear idea of what their visit is likely to involve. Their expectations may be derived more from other forms of media and socialisation processes in general than information from a site's printed and published material.

## HOW THE VISITOR MAY BE PORTRAYED

Accepting the possible limitations of the various sources outlined above and in spite of the imbalance of information about the interpreter and visitor, our collected data may still be used to suggest some ways in which the 'visitor' is conceptualised in the interaction between interpreters and their visitors through the medium of language. Interpreters know the site, are familiar with their role, and have much practice in it compared to the visitor. This may constrain the actions available to the visitor and provide evidence for **controlling mechanisms** practised by interpreters. For instance, in the majority of interactions, the interpreter makes the approach to the visitor. From their experience, they may have developed or been trained to launch into a rehearsed routine, to take the initiative to start and maintain a conversation.

The interpreters' expectations are likely to influence the provision made for visitors and the way in which they interact with any visitors they meet. We can illustrate this by quoting from the Medieval Combat Society's web page. This is a group interested in medieval foot combat from the middle ages. Originally formed in 1970, they claim to be one of the oldest tournament groups appearing in the 'United Kingdom today.' The Society claimed on its web site that its object was:

> to entertain the public and generate an interest in our English history.
> We recreate a 14th Century tournament complete with all it's (sic)

pomp, pageantry, and Knights testing each others skill in the art of combat... None of the fights are staged and each combatant must rely upon their own skills and training to survive the contests - bringing you one of the most exciting shows in the country.

(http://www.smy.com/soc/mcs.html in 1996)

Visitors need to be entertained, they want 'exciting shows' and they won't have an interest in English history - it has to be 'generated' by the interpreters.

## IDENTIFYING TYPES OF VISITORS

Some sites on their web pages deliberately suggest the breadth of their **appeal to a wide variety of people**. Ironbridge Gorge Museum, a World Heritage Site of only fourteen such sites in Britain, announces that 'the Gorge is ideal for a weekend break, or a day's visit, offering activities and interest for all ages and tastes.' Indeed the information about Ironbridge and other museums and historical sites refers to the 'special venue' appeal that the site may have for certain purposes such as club outings, ' business events, treasure hunts, birthday or anniversary celebrations'. Often special rates are made available to groups such as 'children and students, senior citizens and families, booked groups, and the less able.'

There are what might be called the 'ordinary' groups and those most often singled out for specific mention, the family groups - parents and children.

Depending upon the extent and nature of the educational services provided, school parties of children and their teachers will be visitors. On some sites such parties are encouraged to take part in the re-enactment of the past. Participation by these groups may be in costume (possibly made by their parents with help from the school) or provided on the site so they can 'dress up'. From accounts of visits, it is not always clear whether the teachers have chosen to wear costume as well. When GB went with a London primary school to Kentwell, it was expected that he would be in a costume appropriate to the Elizabethan period as were the other accompanying adults and the teachers.

We will specifically analyse groups of school visitors, adults, and the less able; each group having different expectations and needs. We will then consider common factors affecting visitors' experience of living history.

### School children

We start our consideration of types of visitors and their varying experiences by considering school parties. We looked at the educational benefits and limitations of the living history approach in Chapter Two and in the next chapter on interpreters we consider the ways in which interpretations are approached with children in mind. However, in this chapter we are interested in school children's experience of living history, especially when they are invited to dress up and explore historical themes through role-play.

School children can be provided with the 'hands-on' experience of artifacts and equipment of the period but they can also 'dress up' and have some knowledge of what it 'may have felt like then'. This is seen as a way of 'bringing the past to life' for young learners. The strategy involves importance being attached to the idea that young children's interest is more likely to be captured by such physical contact and sensual experience and therefore, that learning will be more effective.

Museums or historic properties may choose only to supply the simplest of costumes for children, such as mop caps for the girls and caps for the boys whereas others may take the risk of allowing individual children to try on expensive and elaborate costumes of the period. An important factor in the provision of complete costumes for child visitors is that the size is appropriate for a youngster and in keeping with the fashion or conventions of children's dress for the period.

Dunham Massey is a red-brick country house owned by the National Trust in England built on the flatlands of Cheshire. Funding provided by Grand Metropolitan Estates has enabled groups of children from inner city schools to visit what is a grand country house. The groups are allowed into the building before the public visitors to dress up as Victorian servants in caps and hats provided at the house. The children are then met by a costumed butler and his assistants, mostly volunteers, who take small groups away to try their hand at activities such as 'baking bread, laundry work, and making soap, scent and cheese.' (Berry, 1995, p.32)

> The stated task for all the servants is to prepare the house for mealtime and periodically their progress is checked by "Her Ladyship" who uses Dunham Massey's ancient internal telephone system to communicate with them. They work in a domestic wing dominated by a huge, mouth-watering kitchen with green tables and huge pots and pans. When all has been prepared and sampled they tour the house and Pauline Mills (Dunham's educational officer) explains how they would have fitted into the social hierarchy when the estate was active.

It is interesting that this experience for school children is planned to move from providing the physical sensations of dressing up, being aware of the almost intimidating size of the working environment, and using the kitchen equipment of the period before the school children are told of the more theoretical concept of social classification. The living history approach, by which they experience what was meant by working 'below stairs' and being acquainted with the physical and exhausting demands made on those who fulfilled the position of 'servant', is used to ensure that the children are initially learning by 'doing' before being introduced to the more abstract social concept underlying the experience.

Another interesting example of this practice appeared in a BBC TV news item showing staff at the Royal Palace of Hampton Court dressing up two young visitors from a school party, a boy and girl, in replica costumes of the historical period. There was considerable giggling among the children when the Palace member of staff named and described the extremely large cod piece which was part of the male costume. The young lad seemed to take trying on and wearing this costume with considerable panache. Perhaps he had been chosen for his ability to be unembarrassed by the unexpected!

However it would have been interesting to know what the children made of this particular 'dressing up' experience and its emphasis upon accuracy of historical detail.

This seems to be an example of the possible 'clash' between Museum and school 'cultures' as to how gender differences are treated and reflect the cultural values, not only of past and present, but also the physical features emphasised to contrast the genders. The member of staff may see the 'experience' being created for a school party visiting the Palace as a means by which the children could experience the feel of the rich cloth and the restrictions of the costumes worn by children of noble families of the period. Historically there was little distinction between the costume of adult and child but more marked differences between the fashions of men and women. A Palace staff member in the context of imparting historical knowledge to a school party may deal with gender differences in a way which would be quite different to how the same details might be introduced in the classroom. The giggling of those children who were not modelling the costumes, might be viewed as evidence of their understanding of the social and cultural values of context, not only for different historical periods but also for what is appropriate talk in the school classroom or the situation of a museum visit.

As we have seen in an earlier chapter the living history experience is not without its critics. The major rationale for using the living history approach is usually that it:

> enhances historical understanding: that children dressed in costume
> and playing in role somehow understand more about the life of
> medieval monks through the experience, for example, of gardening in
> a monk's habit than they would do without the advantage of taking
> part in such an event.
>
> (Peter Stone, 1988, pp.21-23}

Peter Stone thought it was more likely that what the children were experiencing was the difficulty of wearing unfamiliar clothing and carrying out tasks usually not in children's experience. His conclusion was that such experiences were 'more of an exercise (extremely valid in itself) in social interaction and drama.'

He also raised the question of the extent to which children being 'in role' could be maintained, considering it was 'difficult enough for adult actors or teachers to pretend to be in character from the past - even given a deep understanding of the period under study.' (Stone 1988, p.22) Such a discussion is interesting as it reminds us that the experiences which visitors have of living history may not have the effects for which they are designed. In fact, the feeling that a visitor is acting in something historical may be no more than an illusion.

## Adults

Children dress up with gusto and enter into the 'experience' usually with little or no anxiety, as far as we could gather from reading accounts and talking to teacher colleagues. It is a different matter in relation to adults visiting sites, who may feel self conscious about changing their dress. GB visiting Kentwell in the role of a monk, wearing an itchy habit, experienced a peculiar, dislocating effect. He was pretending to be someone he was not - wearing a costume that created unfamiliar feelings for him. The experience was not altogether pleasant.

We came across only one account on the Internet of living history exponents who chose to visit a site (Colonial Williamsburg) in their own period costume. The previous day they had visited in 'regular 20th century attire and brought the brochures, sun glasses and cameras.' (*Living Historian Quarterly*, Spring 1987) The day that they visited in costume other visitors thought they were employed by the site and didn't identify them as visitors like themselves. The costumed visitors found the professional interpreters 'very cordial' and they felt it was 'comforting to know that, in conversation with them about living history, they experience the same problems, such as acquiring period shoes, that we do.' They did however find their ride on the bus in period dress 'rather awkward.' Costume is a very easily identified, initial feature of difference between people which influences their expectations of interactions between themselves and others.

Adult visitors are often only given the chance to 'dress up' as attendees at some revelry! Christopher Middleton wrote about what he called 'a strange time-warp experience' in an article 'Once more unto the breeches' when he stayed as a paying guest at Old Coulhurst Manor in Shropshire (England) (Middleton, 1997, p. 23). The manor house is furnished to provide a '17th century Experience', although concessions are made to the modern visitor with under floor heating in the bedrooms, electric blankets on the beds, and shaver sockets discreetly hidden in the wall panelling. However what interested us was Middleton's comments about the unease of guests, not on meeting each other for the first time as strangers but at being 'clad from head to toe in Elizabethan costume.' The costumes are kept in a storeroom in the house from which visitors make their own choice of clothing to dress up for dinner with glowing candles and open fire. The food is authentic; dishes adapted from 400-year-old English cookery books. But Middleton noted that the conversation was uncertain, less than sparkling since as he explained 'none of us is really sure how we're meant to behave' since their host, the proprietor 'has made it clear that this is not your average down-market, wench-fondling Tudor Nite Out':

> "We don't throw chicken bones over our shoulders here," he says,
> launching into an interesting little discourse on the evolution of
> English eating implements. It appears that the nobility originally
> resisted the introduction of two-pronged forks because they looked
> too like peasant pitchforks - it was not until the addition of a third
> prong that they were rendered gentry-friendly.

Middleton describes this part of the meal as an effective transition from Manchester City's best-ever players (the visitors' choice of conversation) to a 'history lecture' and that this was followed by 'another mental leap' when the costumed minstrel insisted on addressing all the guests as 'Master' or 'Mistress' and 'determinedly talks in Elizabethan English.'

We have quoted quite extensively from this example as it illustrates some of the problems that the visitor who consents to dressing up may have in an interaction with a costumed interpreter who has studied the period and has extensive knowledge and much practice and interest in re-enactment. Visitors are more likely to be rendered 'uncomfortable' - a word that often appears in the accounts of re-enactors and in museum material. Concern for evoking such feelings in the visitor, seems to exert considerable influence on the extent and nature of the activities and interactive experiences provided by institutions and groups for their visitors. On the practical level, provision of costumes for large numbers of visitors would not be feasible and institutions would want to be able to distinguish between their interpreters and paying visitors. Providers have an interest in visitors' feelings being aroused by their experiences on site since these influence the likelihood of a return visit or the recommendation of sites to friends. Providers are justifiably concerned about any identifiable, apparent causal relationship between presentation methods and visitors' perceived affective reactions.

We return to this issue of 'comfort' when considering general issues that relate to the visitor's experience.

## The less able

Our third group for consideration are the less able who may require specialist facilities or additional provision and whose experience of living history might be severely limited by attempts to make the site historically accurate. One historic site had some problems with such provision and the accuracy of site recreation with the building of a ramp to provide access by wheel chair to a period building. The solution adopted was to cover the ramp with leaves to render it less an anachronism although of course it tended to make it less visible to those who might have used it!

Even ground is likely to be a requirement of both handicapped visitors and re-enactors. Although obviously not always possible, less uneven ground, or arranging the site so that activity locations are on the more even ground is usually possible. Ease with which to use a wheel chair is important to the physically handicapped but the condition of the ground surface is equally important to those with young children that need to be wheeled around in buggies or push chairs.

As to interpreting for the disabled public, we found only limited advice in the web search but Horne-Jaruk (1996) in making suggestions for how to do this, thought one of the most valuable things which would make it easier for people with a wide variety of different conditions was likely to be to learn how to talk more clearly. Of obvious use to hearing-impaired visitors, our tape recordings of interpreters brought home to us how often snatches of conversation were lost as the re-enactor turned away to indicate something or addressed a different member of the group of visitors. Transcribing the tapes we realised how often the meaning could be affected, particularly when interpreters were describing processes or common practices, and how quickly such loss of understanding could affect one's interest and motivation to attend to or take part in the interaction.

We would support Horne-Jaruk's conclusion regarding the living history exponent's responsibility to the public who 'cannot easily overcome the impediments we never notice' to ensure that they can visit and participate to the limit of their abilities:

> Fulfilling both of these responsibilities makes our hobby (as a re-enactor) better, richer, and more valuable for use and for all those we hope to reach. It requires far less work than researching the buttons of the underdress uniforms of some obscure regiment, and yet its impact is so much greater and so much more precious.
>
> (Paper written by Honour Horne-Jaruk reprinted from Issue 7 September, 1996 of *Reading History* at http://www. recreating-history.com/Evenground.html)

These three groupings of people, the school visitors, adults and the less able all have different needs and expectations. If the living history displays are to be inclusive, either for educational or economic reasons, then interpreters need to consider the needs of these groups. In the following section we consider how these needs are perceived and may in fact modify and contribute to the versions of the past exponents choose to portray.

## VISITORS' IMPACT ON THE LIVING HISTORY EXPERIENCE

We now consider aspects of the impact of visitor expectation and need on living history. Our analysis is largely based on material presented from the interpreters' perspective. Although the data is therefore 'second hand' it does give us the opportunity to see the visitor from the interpreters' point of view. Presumably, this viewpoint influences the interpreters' approach to the visitors and it is from this perspective that interpretations and presentations are modified.

There are a number of ways in which visitors may differ in how their past experiences, attitudes and interests are likely to effect their willingness to respond and participate in dialogic activity with interpreters. From our material the following factors emerge:

1. visitors' comfort;
2. visitors' attitudes and expectations that they bring with them in terms of
   a) attitudes to History as a subject and
   b) prior historical knowledge,
3. visitors' approach to museums and sites
   a) previous experience of museums
   b) attention span
   c) curiosity, willingness and ability to ask questions

We conclude with a timely reminder that the experience of visitors to the same setting might be perceived differently depending on the interpreter's perceptions of the visitor's purposes.

## 1. Visitors' comfort

In the example quoted above of Christopher Middleton's experiences in Elizabethan costume we have seen that the comfort of the visitor might be both physical and psychological. The likelihood of an adult visitor being asked to dress up is rare, but the living history approach can create a situation in which the visitor is uncomfortable because they do not know how to behave; what is being asked of them is unfamiliar. They find themselves in an unexpected role. Michael Evans, writing as curator of Sovereign Hill, Ballarat (Australia) has described two examples which illustrate how, having made the decision to use the dynamic process of peopling the site, it will be necessary to 'consider visitors' reaction to, and interaction with, the re-creation.' (Evans,1991 p.150). Both of these examples show how perceptions of visitor comfort influence the design and planning of a living history interaction.

The Criterion Store, a recreated and carefully researched drapery store, was opened on the site in 1985. The accuracy of the physical setting (based on the study of still existing buildings, illustrations and written descriptions) was brought to life by the addition of trained enterpreters. They were coached in 'nineteenth-century commercial practice, modes of behaviour, patterns of deference, and even physical bearing'. However, despite painstaking research and the emphasis on accuracy, it soon become clear that the visitors to the store were uncomfortable with the deferential behaviour of the interpreters in role as shop assistants and impatient with the unfamiliar slower rate of service.

There was a further incident in 1989 involving the portrayal of death that had a profound influence on policy at the site, underlining the importance of careful consideration of the nature of interactions organised for visitors. Such experiences need to be carefully designed to ensure that visitors feel sufficiently comfortable to participate:

> An attempt to 'de-sanitise' our treatment of death failed because the
> situation which was created - a widow beside a coffin being consoled
> by a priest - caught visitors so unawares that they did not feel
> comfortable with the re-enactment. This made it impossible for the
> interpreters to communicate with them. (Evans, p.151)

When BG visited Sovereign Hill she joined a group of visitors being addressed by a soldier explaining the forms of punishment meted out for misdemeanours on the gold fields. On joining the group, she noticed that one of the women visitors seemed to be tied or manacled in some way to a flag pole on this part of the site. Visitors were in a group around the soldier, listening intently to what he was saying in first person characterisation. As she hadn't seen whether the woman volunteered or the action was carried out in jest, BG found this incident disturbing. She felt herself caught up in an interaction in which she was unsure of the nature of what was taking place between interpreter and visitors. The point we are making here is that however the management policy for 'peopling' a site is devised, in practice it may result differently from what is intended. Visitors may see partial performances of interactions or 'read into them' unwarranted assumptions.

Old Sturbridge Village (United States) had few problems when they introduced their funeral programme. It was deemed a great success with people forming lines to view the coffin. GB was told that the marketing department had said it couldn't be done as it would turn people away. It was important to the interpreters that the death and funeral were not presented in a gruesome way, but as a fact of life in the 1830s that could be interpreted interestingly and informatively. Interpretations that deal with the sadder or more shocking side of life must, clearly, be handled sensitively and the visitor prepared for what they are to see.

These issues cannot be avoided if a living history reconstruction is to represent life accurately. The issue of censorship arises here. Are all aspects of life acceptable to the visiting public? Can an interpretation recreate 'life as it was' if, for example, violence and brothels are absent? There are interesting issues of context here. The reconstruction of life is not life itself. The site is a public amenity, which presumably has to uphold standards of public decency, if it is to continue to receive funding, either from charitable or governmental sources or from the fee-paying public. It can therefore only offer a sanitised version of the past; its claims to 'authenticity' are therefore limited.

Not all interpreters are as concerned as this about offending visitors. In 1997 one of the Sunday papers in England ran a news story about military re-enactment groups distancing themselves from what was described as a 'new, "extremist" wing' of such re-enactment. This new group was described as performing 'live, no-hold-barred reconstruction of the blood and savagery of war for a family audience.' (*The Sunday Telegraph* 19 October 1997, p. 9) The group, Viking Middle England, performs at local festivals and events and even schools. Someone who had seen one of their displays was reported as commenting that 'it all had rather too intense an edge to it. I suspect that they enjoy shocking people.' Although the group's event co-ordinator claimed that adverse reactions among visitors were few and that 'if we started worrying about upsetting people or giving kids nightmares, we would have to pack up and take up tiddlywinks. We are historically accurate, we are not just a bunch of bloodthirsty loonies.' He also quoted an American group specialising in First World War re-enactments who distributed fake body parts across the battle field, adding that 'we would not go that far.....but people always want to go that extra yard. Let's face it, 99 per cent of people go to Grand Prix racing hoping there's going to be a crash.'

These examples illustrate that different groups of interpreter perceive their visitors or audiences, and their needs and sensitivities in different ways. This in turn can influence the form of living history that they use.

## 2. Visitors' attitudes and expectations

### a) Attitudes to history as a subject

On one internet site (http:www.gulf.net/~vbraun/FloStar/intro.html), a page entitled 'Meet the minds behind The Florida Star', a wife told of how her husband was a Civil War re-enactor who enjoyed taking pictures of the battle re-enactments. His wife thought that re-enacting also provided 'a wonderful outlet for his love of history.' On the other hand, she had 'always hated history' having got stuck 'with "teachers" whose only stipulations were memorizing dates.' Accompanying her husband to re-enactments and seeing his photographs - 'like daguerreotypes sprung to life' and always having 'loved checking out old pictures', she joined him behind the camera and in turn this led to the development of their web page, with its photographs and graphics as well as information about the Florida Star group.

Lowenthal (1985) thought re-enactments 'enliven history for millions who turn a blind or bored eye on ancient monuments, not to mention history books.' (Lowenthal , 1985, p.301). Kirsch (1996) believed many people attending re-enactments found the spectacle quite overwhelming because he suggested 'adults, teenagers and children alike found history in school a lifeless collection of dates, facts and boring textbooks.' Attending a re-enactment they are 'confronted with history more alive, vibrant, and three dimensional than a novel or movie ...'

These examples illustrate what seems to be a commonly held idea among living history exponents, that many people have been put off history because it has been presented to them as a boring academic subject with little relevance to them and holding nothing of interest. People may be bored by a particular presentation of History or its content, but re-enactments and living history museums can, it is claimed, bring 'dry as dust' history to life and *entertain* the visitor. Although, for the interpreter, there may always be the haunting spectre of invoking the visitor's boredom and subsequent inattention.

Although this is a common perception amongst re-enactors there is evidence to suggest that whilst visitors' main motivations for visiting living history museums may be social, they do espouse an interest in history. During his visit to Old Sturbridge Village GB was told of a survey of visitors showing that their main motivation for visiting was for social reasons but that this was explained as having a good day out with family and friends in pleasant surroundings and to explore *America's past*. Repeat visitors and first timers had similar motivations. It was not felt that visitors came for entertainment. At Williamsburg GB was told that most visitors came to be educated and were surprised at how entertaining it could be:

> Education does not have to be boring. Some visitors come for the
> aesthetics which can be a form of entertainment but they don't come
> with a theme park mentality. They expect education and are surprised
> that it's fun. To learn how a crosscut saw was used, to try and get the
> characters out of character and to be harangued by an auctioneer is fun.
>
> (Williamsburg Conversation 1)

The ways in which programmes are modified, also indicate what interpreters think about visitors' attitudes to history. We have already mentioned the funeral at Old Sturbridge Village. At this site there has been a shift away from the drier forms of interpretation such as debating to deal with more controversial social issues:

> In some ways this is popularisation in other ways I'm not sure. We are
> still focussing on subjects that to many people would be controversial.
> Death, illness and sexual relations are subjects that a lot of places
> don't want to touch on. They are a major focus for us. (Sturbridge
> conversation)

## b) Visitors' prior history knowledge

For many different reasons, the visitor may indeed have little or insufficient
historical knowledge. We have already mentioned Honour Horne-Jaruk's
paper. In this she reported a somewhat informal survey which she carried out
of visitors attending three re-enactment events. She was surprised by the
answers they made to some simple questions regarding what happened to
people with severe injuries or disabilities in the past. She found the answers
unexpected and even frightening:

> If you got a bad cut you rotted and died.
> If you couldn't work they fed you to the wolves.
> Deaf people had to be monks.
>
> (Horne-Jaruk, 1996)

She believed that the pervasive idea in the answers from visitors was that
'people in the past had few handicaps, because almost all illnesses were fatal,
and that people with disabilities were routinely and casually killed by their
families or communities.' The major part of her article dealt with how
people with physical handicaps can and should be incorporated into re-
enactments not only as an opportunity to educate the public but also as a
model for how those with disabilities today can find a role and
companionship in participating in re-enactments. Towards the end of her
article she concluded that today's re-enactments are educational, exciting
and appeal to people 'who never related to "book history".' For her, re-
enactors have the dual responsibility of representing the handicapped
people of the past accurately and enabling the handicapped of the present to
participate to the limit of their abilities.

Some visitors will have considerable historical knowledge and use it to
show off and try to outmanoeuvre the interpreter. The source of this
knowledge, however it is used, will be various and variously 'accurate'. At
Williamsburg GB was told that many people acquired their knowledge from
television, especially the cable history channel. Cinema played its part too.
Merchant Ivory's 'Jefferson in Paris' had recently been released in the
United States:

> which plays a lot with what Jefferson got up to as minister of state in
> Paris. People take it as gospel truth. Merchant Ivory must be true,
> the costumes look good so it must be true
>
> (Williamsburg Conversation 1)

At Williamsburg it was accepted that people come with different preoccupations and are enthusiastic about history. 'We have to go back and try to teach the realities of it. We have to be diplomatic.' (Williamsburg Conversation 1)

This type of relearning is familiar to museum educationalists. At Yorvik , the Viking museum in York (England) it is acknowledged that visitors come with powerful, mythological views about the blood thirsty Vikings which often have to be reconstructed.

Visitors' subject knowledge can influence their ability to take part in the interpretation. In first person interpretations, where the interpreter assumes a character from the past and only interprets from within that character's experience, certain areas of knowledge can only be discussed if the visitor knows what questions to ask. A visitor to Plimoth who knows something of the religious beliefs of the time can enter into conversation at a different level and maintain more control over that conversation than someone who only feels confident to ask 'what are you doing?' It is a basic criticism of first person interpretation that the information flow may be restricted in this way. We will return to this later. Many of the living history sites we visited attempt to prepare the visitor with historical knowledge through the orientation film and associated 'traditional' museum displays. One of the strongest examples of this is at Jamestown where the museum provides information on the Powatan Indians and their social structure, and historical background on the settlers and their reasons for leaving England. In this museum there is clearly an attempt to address visitors' attitudes to what they are going to see by instilling respect for the Powatan culture. For visitors not only bring knowledge but attitudes as well.

Visitors' attitudes can cause problems when an unfavourable image may be presented through the interpretation. Plimoth Plantation has to carefully consider how it portrays the pilgrim fathers who, for many, are icons of American culture and the realisation of the American dream. There is a lot of residual guilt because of the ways in which the pilgrims treated the Native Americans. Interpreters at Plimoth felt that it was important not to apologise for the pilgrims but to objectively present their way of life and beliefs. At Williamsburg a different problem was explained to GB:

> People try to make you condemn people and situations in the
> present:.... to validate gun control and bigotry in religion and racism.
> They then go home and say that people at Colonial Williamsburg
> support that....Visitors will think that they can get away with putting
> down Black people. Blacks [interpreters] have a terrible time
> maintaining integrity as people and portraying a degrading
> experience. [slavery]

It is therefore very important that the visitors understand how the characters work. This need to understand the nature of the interpretation on the part of the visitor is akin to an understanding of how History as a discipline operates. It depends in part on the previous experiences of museum visiting which people have had.

## 3. Visitors' approaches to museums and sites

*a) Visitors' previous museum experience*

It is sometimes suggested that visitors fail to visit museums and galleries because they find them intimidating and are doubtful as to how to behave, or at least understand what is deemed to be appropriate behaviour in such buildings. Certainly if the visitor has rarely been inside such institutions it is possible that open-air museums, historical buildings and re-enactments using the living history approach might be something of a surprise, quite the reverse of what was expected. GB carried out a survey of teacher education students' museum visiting patterns and we were initially somewhat surprised by their limited experience and their expectations of visiting, especially those who went with their own children. Such visits tended to be seen as implicitly and primarily educational and not necessarily recreational. Following discussion and further thought on the matter, it became obvious that most had their first experiences of museum visiting on organised school visits and journeys. For this generation of students in the United Kingdom the living history approach was comparatively unfamiliar compared to sites in the United States and Canada where the approach has a much longer and probably more successful history of co-existence with formal museums. (Robertshaw, 1997). If museums and historical sites are recalled as the destinations of school visits and if the living history approach as the method used in such institutions is comparatively unfamiliar, then the visitor may require guidance on what is expected of them. A complicated situation such as a worker's cottage or a schoolroom may need to be introduced to the visitor in such a way that they can understand how they are expected to behave. (Shafernich, 1993, p.46).

It is possibly for this reason that many sites where there are costumed guides or demonstrators and the living history approach is used, make a deliberate attempt at informing the visitor of what awaits them. In doing so, sites not only need to describe what is to be seen but also the type of encounters and possible emotions that may be experienced. At the Black Country Museum (England), there is a short video showing parts of the sites and the costumed characters, and especially the schoolroom and the type of discipline that is encountered there. Such films and videos are often referred to by the museum professionals as orientation material, as they aim to orientate the visitor and prepare them for their experience. An analysis of film/video content also can, of course, indicate what it is that interpreters think visitors need to know and probably are perceived as not knowing. Such material might be seen as a controlling mechanism, except for the fact that the placement of such films needs to be carefully monitored and researched for maximum effectiveness. When BG and her daughter visited the Black Country Museum, the video display was at the opposite end to the tourist shop, adjacent to the lavatories, positioned fairly high up on a wall with seating for at most half a dozen visitors, almost underneath the video screen. The video played continuously. It seemed to be visitors seeking out the lavatories who noticed the video, but few stopped for more than a few minutes to view the images being screened, let alone attend to the voice-over commentary. Few saw this orientation material in its entirety.

At Plimoth Plantation 'Where history repeats itself', it is difficult to bypass the orientation film as visitors are shown into the cinema first. This film explains that:

> Pilgrims to this day evoke powerful images of America's past. Images that often refer to myths and stereotypes instead of facts. Today Plimoth Plantation strives for the most accurate representation of pilgrim life possible. Everything in the village is based on painstaking research. The animals, gardens and houses, the food cooking on the hearth, the tools, clothing and furnishings, even the dialect, personality, the politics and the world view of each colonist have been carefully studied....
> As you leave the building also prepare to leave the twentieth century behind. You are about to travel to another world. Open your mind to the ways of life of two very different seventeenth century peoples. Be ready not only to look and listen but also to ask questions about many things unfamiliar to you. There is much to learn.
>
> (Plimoth Observation Notes)

Despite similar efforts at Sturbridge, as we have seen, people still do not always understand that the village is a composite drawn from all over New England and not built on the site of an actual town.

At Williamsburg GB was told that generally visitors trusted the interpretation:

> Most visitors do not know what goes into it. [i.e. substantiating the interpretation with sources] When we use the spontaneous combustion story we don't quote the source on the street but the visitors trust us. If we say it, it must be true. We are sticklers for detail with a public reputation.
>
> (Williamsburg Conversation 1)

Visitors also vary in their acceptance of the time shift. Interpreters at Plimoth said that some visitors seem really taken in and talk as if it is the seventeenth century. On the other hand, others seem confused. One anecdote tells of a pilgrim who was complaining about the lack of merchant supplies only to be told by an indignant visitor 'don't you know that they are taking money out there.' [i.e. on the gate] (Plimoth Conversation 3)

*b) Visitors' attention span*

The visitor's attention span is constrained not only by physical tiredness, thirst and hunger but also by the sheer amount of what is to be seen and the unexpectedness or unusual nature of much that is laid on for the visitor's 'experience'. At battle re-enactments, for reasons of safety, visitors are often corralled behind some form of fencing or boundary line. Even so, they can usually move about, seeking more advantageous positions 'behind the tape' as the battle enactment moves from one area to another of the site, or even to avoid the smoke and noise of the cannon and muskets in a Civil War Re-enactment such as BG experienced at the Battle of Marston Moor. This was a thrilling experience but it was a hot summer's day, and she sought the shade of trees surrounding the taped off battle area. More experienced visitors had brought deck chairs, rugs to sit on, and picnic hampers. A loud speaker commentary directed visitors' attention to what was happening on the various parts of the battle field, the words of which often became inaudible in the din and shouts of the charging pikemen or the mounted cavalry. The conflicting claims of sight and hearing were a distraction and an invitation to inattention. Indeed BG eventually found shade under a tree and took time off to 'close her eyes', ostensibly to restore her stamina for the rest of the day's spectacle.

The interpreters understanding of the visitors attention span can also influence the interpretation. At Old Sturbridge village GB was told that in the 1830's sermons lasted for two hours. There was then a break and then another two hours. Modern visitors could not be put through such an experience. The average 'performance' would be twenty minutes with interpreters focusing on one main message. (Sturbridge conversation 1)

*c) Visitors' curiosity, willingness and ability to ask questions*

Lowenthal (1985) wrote of visitors hesitating to enter Lincoln's log cabin while a period meal was being eaten, because it seemed so real. In this example, the visitors were intimidated and distanced from the interpretation by the completeness of the reconstruction and their every day sense of modern politeness. Lowenthal also pointed out that the Plimoth Plantation brochure claimed that the Pilgrims were always eager to converse and that 'the past is a world into which time travellers may pry without embarrassment or fear of rebuff.' (p. 296). Visitors can pick up objects - the possessions of the costumed characters - and examine them, and make remarks to their friends about their fitness of purpose. They can 'pry' in a way that would be considered unacceptable in 'real' life. If the costumed character then should appear or the visitor becomes aware of his or her presence in the room, the visitor may find it difficult to think of what to say or an appropriate question to ask.[1]

As we have seen, visitors' willingness and ability to ask questions is also restricted by their subject knowledge and their ability to understand the interpretation, especially if it is conducted in first person. The following observation was made by an interpreter at Mystic Seaport:

> Interpreters in displays should give information. Visitors cannot ask
> questions if they have no background information. When using first
> person you must give the background... A first person dispute
> between interpreters could raise questions in the visitors' minds.
>
> (Mystic Conversation 1)

Having considered these ways in which visitors might influence the living history interaction we will finish this section with an example that reminds us of how difficult it is to generalise about the visitor.

## TALKING ABOUT VISITORS

We have described certain features about those who constitute the different groups of visitors and shown that generally it is the interpreters and those who write about the living history approach who provide a 'voice' for the visitor, guessing at what the visitor needs and sometimes supplying reasons for such requirements. Such motivations have much in common with how the interpreter wants to envisage the visitor as the 'other' in the interaction that is fundamental to the living history approach.

In 1995 on a riverside site in Leeds, in the north of England, Tetley's Brewery Wharf complex opened. In a circular building, displays cover the story of brewing and the place of the inn in English history. There are working displays by craft people, such as the painter who demonstrates the making of inn signs. On the upper floors, visitors can 'time travel' by passing through a series of rooms (with costumed characters) which illustrate eating, drinking and hospitality through the ages.

Writing about this site, two writers described similar experiences in different ways depending on the type of visitor they had in mind. The first to consider is an article about the Tetley Brewery, which was composed by Kevin Berry and for which the readership was likely to be teachers. (*Times Educational Supplement* 'Going Places', 3 February, 1995, p.38) He described how full and flexible programmes had been planned for school visits and the time spent in each historical period was substantially lengthened for school visits. The public however had 'only five minutes in each room and are then whisked on':

> Visitors are first greeted by a jolly monk in the cellar of a 14th-century abbey. Then they go into the courtyard of an Elizabethan inn to encounter an actor rehearsing his lines, thence to a Jacobean tavern to meet some plotters and on to a Georgian room, a Victorian pub for a piano-led song, an Edwardian bar and a wartime pub in which they meet an air-raid warden. (Berry, 1995, p.38).

Let us consider the actions (verbs) which the writer used in this description to indicate what the visitor would expect to experience. These are that he or she would

- be 'greeted' (by the interpreter as 'jolly monk'. Is the visitor expected to reply?);
- 'encounter' (an Elizabeth actor);
- meet' (some plotters);
- be 'led' (in the sing-song) and finally
- meet' (the air-raid warden).

How does the writer's choice of the actions he attributes to visitors suggest the type of role expected of them? Are they to be passive or active participants in the form of living history approach adopted at this site?

Jane Malcom-Davies also wrote an article about Tetley's Brewery Wharf about the same time but for a different audience than Kevin Berry - the journal *Museum Visitor*. (Malcom-Davis, 1995, pp.23-29). As a researcher of the use of live interpretation at historic sites and a skilled exponent herself, she most certainly considered that its use at the Tetley Museum could have made the approach more constructive for 'visitors' enjoyment'. She advised as follows:

> What would be more appropriate than to sit down for a chat in the bar/pub/inn and enjoy the company of your guide as he or she paints the picture of a convivial gathering from the past? Drinking is a social activity, offering opportunities for news, jokes and scandal to be exchanged. But Tetley's visitors became passive receivers of monologues which tell little of the history of beer and find themselves the butt of poor jokes. Silence is the order of the day: if visitors keep quiet, the actors perform. (Malcolm-Davies, 1995, p,.29)

We would like to leave you to consider the way in which she uses the language resources available to her to represent the interpreters as 'guides' and how her focus is more the entertainment of the visitor (an important question of revenue for museums and historical houses) rather than familiar historical periods (for school visits being able to fulfil the requirements of national curriculum teaching)[2]

These two examples we have used, are secondary sources - we have not visited Tetley's Brewery Wharf for ourselves. Indeed, if we did we are sure any account would depend on the audience for whom we were writing, as well as the focus we adopted because of our different interests and disciplinary backgrounds. However we would suggest that written accounts of visits, where they do exist, should be considered in the same way as the text of tourist brochures or the orientation film for assumptions about visitors' needs and desires and museums' expectations of their likely behaviour. Such sources may reveal expectations about the role of the visitor. For instance, just how 'active' is the visitor assumed to be where an interactive approach like living history is used to recreate the past?

---

Footnotes

1   In report of Live Interpretation Conference in Springfield, Ohio by Jane Malcolm-Davies Heritage Interpretation, Summer 1990 No 45, Ken Yellis the director of public programs at Plimoth Plantation was stated to have said that 'one area we are looking at is the ways in which visitors can be encouraged to open conversations with the pilgrims they encounter.'

2   We have found the articles and conference contributions of Jane Malcolm-Davis particularly useful because she has a wide experience having researched the use of live interpreters at historic sites as well as being involved in the training of guides and character interpreters in historic properties and museums. She works in England but has visited sites and attended conferences in the United States, where there seems to be more systematic research being carried out on the larger and longer established heritage sites and living museums.

# Chapter seven

❧

# THE INTERPRETERS

This chapter is concerned with the interpreter, the third category in our analysis of the participating factors that go to make up a living history interaction. As in the previous two chapters, it has sometimes been difficult to decide under which section the data should be discussed. The overriding principle for deciding the content of this chapter is that it deals with the interpreters, how they are described and how they describe, how they see their role and how it is observed, and the techniques which they use to people their historical space.

This section is organised in the following way:

1. We identify the interpreters and consider the terminology which is used to describe them.
2. We approach the interpreter rather as a visitor might, noticing their appearance, listening to them speak and discovering the characters that they portray. This section will deal with issues of authenticity and the distinction between first and third person interpretation.
3. We look at some of the techniques which interpreters use to play their role and the way in which this might be varied according to their perceptions of their audience.

In this section we will also consider methods by which interpreters can be said to control the interaction.

## IDENTIFYING TYPES OF INTERPRETERS - DIFFERENCES IN NAMING

In historical representations and recreations visitors react to and interact with the people, the interpreters, who produce these presentations. These interpreters attempt to appear as they believe people involved in the specific past events or periods portrayed would have appeared. Usually the feature with the greatest salience for the visitor is that the interpreter is dressed in a markedly different 'costume'. Hence living history exponents are often referred to as **costumed guides** or **costumed characters**. Other terms used may be **re-creators** or **re-enactors** (with or without the hyphen), **actor/guides**, **actor/interpreters**, **demonstrators** (activities such as glass blowing, chain making or sweet making), or **activators**; the last term is used at the Australian heritage site depicting the early days of gold mining - Sovereign Hill. Terms can be used with or without a capital letter. However, there is no general agreement on the terms to be used.

A quick look at the publicity material or articles on several historical buildings and museums in the United Kingdom produced the following examples of terms used to refer to Interpreters; (the site or institution is identified first, then the name used for the person or staff involved in the use of the living history approach, and then any reference to the role or function achieved):

### The Tower of London

*Name:* encounters with **costumed characters**;
*Function/role:* 'bringing the past to life'

### The White Cliffs Experience, Dover

*Name:* encounters with a **Roman**, an **usherette** and an **A.R.P. warden**;
*Function/role:* 'unforgettable journey into the past' (*presumably these are costumed interpreters*)

### Bowhill House and Country Park, Selkirk, Scotland

*Name:* non-paid staff dress-up in **character**;
*Function/role:* subject in a painting that stepped out of picture to talk about themselves'

### Craigside, Rothbury, Northumberland (National Trust, late Victorian mansion)

*Name:* volunteers in costume as **'housekeeper'** and **'maids'** use role-play;
*Function/role:* 'shows history as the study of events and real people's lives - not just words in a text book. It's also fun!'

### Llancaiach Fawr, Nelson, Wales

*Name:* **costumed interpreters** take on roles of **servants** from the household to show visitors around with fascinating tales of every aspect of seventeenth century life;
*Function/role:* 'taking a step back in time to experience life as it would have been in the past.... interact with the costumed interpreters.'

### London Transport Museum

*Name:* **actors** as various characters;
*Function/role:* 'bring history to life'.

### Wigan Pier (Centre of Learning Excellence)

*Name:* **actors in Wigan Pier Company** perform Victorian schoolroom, theatre workshops and promenade plays;
*Function/role:* 'meet and greet the characters of the day'; 'what life was like in the year 1900.'

It somewhat surprised us that in some places using the living history approach, no reference was made to this fact in their advertising literature or that the reader had to interpret phrases such as 'a journey into the past' as an indication that they might 'encounter' (a favourite word) costumed people representing characters from the past. These could be individual characters but often were emblematic of the period or representative of a trade or skill. e.g. Mrs Abercromby, the 'housekeeper' ; 'a Roman', etc.

Most of the interpreters referred to in this chapter are adults. As we saw in the previous chapter on visitors, 'living history' interactions sometimes take place with the visitor in costume especially if these are school children. We have come across children taking part as interpreters at Kentwell and in the recreation of the battle of Marston Moor. Children usually take part in what have been called 'every day' re-enactments, in which families or women and children are likely to take part rather than in the military recreations. When BG visited the recreation of the Battle of Marston Moor by the The Sealed Knot, children in costume watched the battle re-enactments and also were to be observed in the recreation of the camp living quarters. Indeed one young lad fell asleep with his large mastiff in the grass near to where BG was observing. He lay undisturbed by the battle shouts and gun fire, while several younger children in costume played around a large oak tree with visiting children, mimicking what was being re-enacted on the battle field in this skirmish between visiting and re-enactment children.

## APPROACHING THE INTERPRETER

### What do interpreters wear?

As already mentioned, an important way in which Interpreters using the living history approach can be identified is the nature of their **costume and dress**. You may recall our example of the visiting couple who were enthusiastic proponents of the method and who wore their costumes (appropriate for the period) on one of their day visits to the historical site. On the bus taking them into the site, other visitors assumed that they must be site staff because they wore costume.

As this example demonstrates, visitors' first impressions of Interpreters are likely to be based on their perception of physical difference between themselves and 'others' in the setting. This is usually 'clued' by the costume worn by such others who are seen to 'inhabit' the place, or in the phrase used earlier, are part of 'peopling the historical space' of a building or site. There are few references in the literature to the effect on visitors of such perceptions. We might guess that those that are seen as 'peopling' the site are classed with the replica aspects of the setting and any approach by visitors may be cautious, uncertain about the conventions of approaching such individuals. Are they costumed guides, employees of the site and part of what the visitor has 'bought into' as part of their visit? What makes for the legitimisation of the role of such people? To what extent are Interpreters seen as strange or unfamiliar? Whether the interpreter initiates an interaction and how they are heard to speak may be an important point in the visitor's perception of the interpreter and to the practice of their attitudes to 'peopling' the site?

The main concern of interpreters in regard to their costume, their character and sometimes their speech might be the achievement of **accuracy and authenticity**. The credibility of the living history interaction depends on the visitor trusting the interpreter to be accurate in their reconstructions (at least that is the espoused view of an interpreter at

Williamsburg). Whether many visitors are bothered or could even spot inaccurate and inauthentic material is a mute point but if living history claims to be an historically educative medium its case rests or falls on its ability to recreate an experience that is as authentic as possible.

From the interpreter's point of view historic accuracy of costume and 'props' seems to assume enormous importance as a means of legitimating the living history exponent's portrayal, whether of a distancing, third person-speaking guide or demonstrator, or of the more unusual first person speaker creating a character or what is often termed amongst exponents, a 'persona'.

Certainly re-enactment groups often recommend that for costume details the exponent should study period pictures and artifacts and not rely on 'modelling their clothing after other re-enactors.' (Dingman, 1996) Museums and historical sites will probably have access to primary sources such as portraits and original costumes in their archives.

This desire for accuracy has commercial repercussions particularly in the United States where there are a number of firms manufacturing and providing the materials of the appropriate weave and texture used in the period when a costume was made and worn. War re-enactment as a growth industry has also given rise to providers of authentic armour and weapons. It has been estimated that there are 'more people involved in the armour industry in Britain now than there have been at any time since the Middle Ages.' ( Kenworthy,1995, pp. 8-9).

The need for historical accuracy and authentic finish in respect to armour is of course, also necessary for safety purposes and to avoid embarrassing accidents. One re-enactor who made his first breastplate out of the steel front of a washing machine, discovered that no matter how much he polished it, the brand name was still visible in sunlight! (Kenworthy, 1995). Certainly armour needs to be correct in every detail because of the:

- nearness of visitors during often realistic combat demonstrations;
- armour possibly being used almost on a daily basis at some sites;
- combatants having to be able to move in the same way as the original users. (Kenworthy, 1995)

Interpreters' attitudes to historic accuracy of costume are likely to be influenced by the purposes for which the living history approach and re-enactment techniques are used. In museums and historical sites, where interpreter guides are employed, paid and trained, part of the institutional management system is likely to be the control of standards of dress as part of the preservation of the institution's status and reputation. In a similar fashion, re-enactment groups proud of their reputation for truthful and realistic enactments of past events and living conditions will strive to exert similar forms of control but often with more difficulty. Contributions to discussion groups on the Internet provide evidence of criticism of the 'hobbyist' element; those people joining re-enactment groups, who do not take the activity seriously enough or put their own physical comfort first. As one contributor insisted, his group does require that people must make an effort to dress as the period dictates, and that this didn't just mean removing baseball caps or unsuitable footwear. He believed that when members had been in the group for some time they wouldn't just continue to make clothes or buy material simply on the grounds of 'merely liking it.' He viewed the latter as 'deliberately not playing the game and being quite inconsiderate to those who did.' (i.e. strive for historic accuracy). The wearing of 'sneakers', 'trainers' or similar footwear seemed to produce similar outrage and condemnation by those who valued historical authenticity highly. There was often much discussion of how to control or discipline non-conformers and whether a Society should try to enforce a dress code on its members.

## What do interpreters do?

Visitors soon realise that interpreters are not only dressed differently but are more than likely to be involved in activities that are different to those of the visitor. Granted he or she may stroll along the same path as the visitor but they may also stand on a box extolling the benefits of some quack 'snake oil' or demonstrate to a few visitors outside their shop, in the role of a nineteenth century dentist, how a tooth was extracted - usually with 'a liberal drink of whiskey if he were a man' or 'a sweetie afterwards if he were a wee child'. (Swan Hill Pioneer Settlement, Victoria, Australia: BG's notes of visit)

Activities that interpreters are involved in are likely to include demonstrating, telling, narrating, explaining, discussing and arguing. They may sing and dance, and tell jokes, and look after and attend to animals, and plant and sew (corn and cloth), and make many things, from candles to wooden tops and whips. They can demonstrate how to light a fire, wash for gold, how to use a mangle and a flat iron, and serve tea from a trolley or ale in a deer horn. And they can march, advance on foot, mount a pike charge, gallop into battle, and drive a Second World War tank as well as an ambulance. Many are the actions and activities in which one can become involved as an interpreter or re-enactor.

Perhaps the strangest is burning down buildings (Pedley, 1996, p.3). The Companies of the Torrington Cavaliers (Torrington is a town in Devon, England) commemorated the 350th anniversary of Torrington's Civil War battle by building the church of St Michael's and All Angels and then razing it to the ground. The original church had been blown to pieces in the battle of Torrington in 1646 and 200 Royalist prisoners died, trapped inside the building when stored gunpowder exploded. This was by no means the first fire razing re-enactment carried out by this group. They had previously torched a 100-foot Viking ship in 1974 and other buildings had included a western style fort.

The near perfect, full sized replica church was made almost entirely of waste wood, the grey granite blocks of painted chipboard, the roof tiles constructed of the bottoms of discarded cheese boxes from a nearby creamery, the Perspex stained glass windows created by a signwriter, and the replica organ pipes had once held carpet rolls. The building held pews and a pulpit and an altar decorated with handmade replica candlesticks. So vast was the project that planning permission had to be sought. It was all burnt to the ground, an example of the physical Setting being completely destroyed. The complicated attitudes of re-enactors towards authenticity and motivation for their actions are illustrated in the words of one of the founder members of the Cavaliers:

> People say 'it's a shame you're burning it'. But they know deep down that it's only a bon-fire. It's just the fact that we've made it so well. You take pleasure in something that look's (sic) perfect. I just wanted people to look .... and gasp. (Pedley, 1996)

This example leads us to consider the accuracy of the content of an interpretation which depends on the subject and context of the interaction.

At Jamestown, modern day visitors can be guided by Master John Pore, Secretary of State to Virginia 1619-21. Substantial records exist about this man and his work. The occasion re-enacted is when he was returning to Jamestown as a King's Commissioner to make a report on the colony. He dressed, spoke and conducted himself as a King's Commissioner might have done but he was acting as a guide to visitors, a role which he would not have undertaken in 1620. Here we have an example of a real person reconstructed from historical records but undertaking a job that would not have been part of his original life. Would a fictitious character using Pore's information or a modern guide have been more effective and less of a distortion of the past? Pore's language was often difficult to understand and GB, admittedly suffering from jet lag, experienced unmitigated boredom. Other visitors were, however, enthralled. One man turned to the lady with him and remarked. 'He had you really believing you lived 400 years ago didn't he.'

The problem of behaving 'authentically' is simplified if the characters are not based on people who actually existed.

Old Sturbridge village is a composite site, the historical events portrayed there did not actually happen at that place. The crafts and processes that are demonstrated and explained, however, can be verified through written or archeological sources. The craftsman's accomplishments, however, can be distorted by the expectations of the visitor. A metal worker confessed that he could solder a perfect seam but visitors would not believe that the artifacts were made in the village by him unless they were imperfect!

Events can be recreated with specific accuracy however, where records survive, for example in the Lyceum debates at Sturbridge. The funeral on the other hand was reconstructed from several sources:

> Should we tell a real or composite story? Does it make history less in a composite or does it strengthen it because we can tell more of a story? One problem and strength is not having a specific year or town. So we can only show composites. Information often has big holes. We struggle. How do you tell the whole story without having it?
>
> (Sturbridge Conversation 1)

This leads us to one of the main criticisms of the living history approach. It cannot acknowledge its sources and the gaps in the historically 'provable' account that is being portrayed whilst the interpretation is going on. So it is in danger of misleading the public and presenting as a complete version of the past, a falsification of what actually happened:

> Interpreters react to this problem in different ways. At Williamsburg, when we use the spontaneous combustion story we don't quote the source in the street but visitors trust us. If we say it, it must be true. We are sticklers for detail with a public reputation. Some museums don't have it, they manipulate and play.
>
> ( Williamsburg Conversation 1)

Third person interpretation does not carry this problem, as the way in which we know that something was done in a certain way or happened at a certain time, can be discussed. The authority of this information can be conveyed by quoting sources and pointing out areas of supposition or through such phrases as 'the curator believes that' (Jamestown Conversation 1). This relieves the interpreter of the responsibility for veracity and leaves open the possibility that the curator may be mistaken!

> At Williamsburg a point is stretched when it comes to the time scale of specific events.We will play with time scale for instance in the Gunpowder Incident when the Governor was trying to stave off revolution and so took the gunpowder out of the magazine. In our time, this takes days so that people can follow the story. It took three weeks in real time. We have not made up or transposed events. We can never know what is true. In twenty years people will laugh at our interpretations.
>
> (Williamsburg Conversation 1)

Having considered the accuracy of the appearance of the interpreter and the authenticity of their actions, we now consider how they speak.

## How do interpreters speak and talk?

The interaction between visitor and interpreter may take place in several forms. It can be on a one-to-one, face-to-face basis, or it can be a group of visitors watching and listening to a single interpreter, or more rarely, several interpreters talking to each other. In the last interaction there are fewer opportunities for individual visitors to carry on a sustained conversation with an interpreter because other visitors may become restless. Some may feel that the 'experience' is being monopolised by one person or the individual may feel constrained by the situation wondering whether they have a 'right' to prioritise their particular interests or curiosity, particularly if the group of visitors is a large one. In these circumstances, visitors' participation may be limited to a single question.

### Responding to visitors' questions

Interpreters sometimes reply to visitors' questions with some such evaluation as 'that's an interesting question' or 'I'm not surprised you should ask that.' Such a response enables the interpreter to justify their evaluation by launching into an explanation based on their more extensive knowledge of the site and its history. This continuation of the interpreter's 'right of reply' may be used by the interpreter to change the topic of the discourse or determine the length and nature of the verbal exchange in the interaction. The interpreter may exert **mechanisms of control** in the situation by how they linguistically choose to respond to the visitor.

Our impression from our visits and taped material, was that interpreters were generally willing to accept questions from visitors. However, the size of the group and whether it resembled an 'audience', seemed to influence the extent and nature of the verbal exchange that resulted. Examining transcriptions of several conversations suggested to us that it was likely that the interpreter's experience and training enabled them to adopt subtle ways of retaining 'the right to speak' in such verbal exchanges. Certainly visitors, being less practised in their role in the living history interaction, are likely to be unfamiliar with the 'moves' in such conversations and usually content to leave the linguistic initiative to the interpreter.

*Do interpreters use first or third person?*

Once the visitor hears the interpreter speak, they will know if the interpretation is to be in first or third person. **First person** is often considered to be the more demanding style of presentation, where the interpreter takes on the 'persona' and role of a real historical character - someone whose life and character can be researched, or a 'typical' or composite character based on accounts of several people living at the time. The usual form of first person interpretation involves the interpreter using the present tense to talk about the past and never expressing any views or knowledge of events occurring after the time in which their character lived. First person interpreters are often able to 'employ a combination of techniques including storytelling, demonstration, question and answer, and discussion; encourage verbal interaction from the audience; and avoid breaking character.' (Roth, 1998, p.183) They will strive to share their knowledge of the period with the visitor in such a way that the visitor may be able to believe in the period being recreated, and to do this, authenticity is of great importance. The first person interpreter will be concerned to know about specifics such as concerns of daily life, family, occupation, education, religion, food and drink, and pastimes, and the history of the site up to the period being recreated. The interpreter will be conscious of speech patterns as well as accuracies of dress and manner.

**Third person** or 'costumed interpretation' has many of the characteristics of first person interpretation in that the interpreter will be informative, talk with visitors and often demonstrate period skills or encourage the visitor to try for themselves ways of carrying out every day tasks; e.g. starting a fire with flint and steel. They will not however attempt to role-play a character. In contrast to first person interpretation, visitors and interpreters will be able to make comparisons between past and present.

*Interpreting living history for the visitor*

We should mention here that a British group, Historical Re-enactment Workshop (HRW), have for some time been experimenting with an alternative form of third person interpretation called 'red T-shirting' as in some of their projects interpreters appear as twentieth century guides and commentors who are identified by wearing distinctive red T-shirts. Robertshaw (1997, p.6) has argued:

> The visitor is thereby offered the opportunity to question not just the activities as they develop, but also the research and assumptions upon which it is based. This is an example of an approach that could benefit any museum or site, if it was prepared to accept that we cannot 'know the truth' about the past and that what is offered in galleries or open air sites is an interpretation, based upon available evidence and open to speculation and discussion.

This would seem to be an important development since it enables interpreters to provide 'references' or acknowledge the sources for their information.

Stacy Roth in her book *Past Into Present* (1998) cites the HRW red T-shirt version (p.14) as well as the use of 'contextualists' on some Colonial Williamsburg programmes. These 'contextualists':

> 'introduce upcoming scenes, explain the significance of key issues, and hold a wrap-up session at the end. At Old Sturbridge Village, similar content bracketing is conducted by a selected role-player who steps temporarily out of character for the task.' (p.15)

Roth conceives such versions of the living history approach as examples of a 'mixed interpretive medium' and believes that there are 'many creative possibilities for mixed interpretation.'

*An important decision*

We have come to realise that the most fundamental question for interpreters and institutions is whether to adopt first or third person interpretation or to employ a mixture in various settings around the site. The decision seems to be taken against two basic criteria: the extent of historical information available to create historically verifiable persons and a choice over which method in which setting is most effective in communicating information to a particular audience. At both Jamestown and Old Sturbridge Village GB was told that the lack of specific historical information was one reason for using third person interpretation.

Although policy decisions are clearly made, interpreter preference also seems to play a large part in deciding the style of interpretation adopted. At Plimoth, perhaps the most highly developed example of first person interpretation, the initiative to adopt this form originally came from the interpreters themselves. (Plimoth Conversation 1)

At Sturbridge:

there is no institutional statement. Interpreters have the freedom to decide to use first or third. Interpreters have their preferences. [This can cause] problems on the stations, of deciding roles beforehand. We have struggles over this.

(Sturbridge Conversation 2)

Specific programmes are often designated as using first person. At Mystic, which uses a mix of third and first both in costume and out, first person tends to be reserved for specific events and a distinction is made between 'theatre type events' and role play:

The first is used for theatre type events for example the lantern shows at Christmas using 120 actors in six scenes. They interact with the guides who are in costume and in role. The scenes are scripted. When we have role-play we develop composites, characters who are like themselves [the interpreters] and reflect their own interests like the female physician. It is different working with actors and ordinary museum staff. When I made a video with an interpreter who was not an actor I had to direct the cameras as if it was a live sporting event.

(Mystic Conversation 1)

At Sturbridge, specific programmes were rehearsed rather than scripted. At the Town Meeting they used to read from scripts but then threw the papers out and developed scenarios with a variety of positions for outlined topics.

Other interpreters work in different ways with different groups. Again GB was discussing this issue with an interpreter at Sturbridge who preferred to role-play with school groups rather than with ordinary visitors, many of whom did not understand the method. He said that visitors felt that it was a waste of time as they wanted specific information which may not be conveyed. With adults around he preferred to role play with someone else playing off each other for two minutes or so and then 'get down to brass tacks'. (Sturbridge Conversation 2)

Here it seems that the choice of which type of interpretation to use varies depending on the particular part of an interpretation: a prelude to set the scene or the conveying of information. This particular interpreter was happy to slip from first person into third.

I am used to going in and out of first...and do more than when I started. It is sometimes easier to get the message across. Maybe the bottom line is that we're not trained to get the message across by using first person and I know that I have the safety valve of third.

(Sturbridge Conversation 2)

GB found that once absorbed in an interpretation it was sometimes difficult to detect this switch. An interpreter could be in first person but 'if you had been coming to my school (or shop) in 1835 you would have..... or 'oh you're referring to (in answer to a question)... Well let me tell you this.'

The problems of communicating in first person were explained by an interpreter at Sturbridge:

> I admire first person interpretation but don't know how to get the
> message across. Sometimes you just can't unless the visitor asks the
> right question. I know from personal experience as a visitor there have
> been times when I can't find a way to ask the question.
>
> (Sturbridge Conversation 2)

Our description of first and third person interpretation may have given the
impression of a marked dichotomy between these approaches whereas in
practice one finds more variety depending not only on interpreters' personal
choice but also the setting and institution in which the past is portrayed. As
described above, some sites make use of a halfway solution to the restraints
of a particular interpretative style. They have some twentieth century guides
or commentators on the site, identified by their clothing. Visitors can
approach these employees to ask questions not only about activities
performed by the living history interpreters but also about the research and
assumptions on which the interpretations are based.

### Speaking authentically?

As in other areas mentioned above interpreters are also concerned with
accuracy and authenticity in their speech.

Bambi Dingman (Dingman, 1996) quoted a re-enactor, Tony, who worried
about his 'French' accent, which he perceived as an important and necessary
feature of his first person interpretation and creation of a particular character
from the past. He was aware that accents could be 'dangerous' since if the
re-enactor is 'doing a bad job, people will stop listening to what you're saying
and will only concentrate on how ineffectively you are saying it.' Tony's view
assumed that all his listeners would be familiar with hearing French and
therefore knowing how a 'real' French accent should sound.

At Plimoth considerable efforts have been made to reconstruct the dialect
of the areas of England from which the Pilgrims had originated. Apart from
the academic difficulties in undertaking such a task, this is dependent also
on the skills of the interpreter. The general effect of visiting Plimoth is that
the Pilgrims speak in archaic tones with different grammatical structures that
may be difficult for many to understand. Coupled with the first person
nature of the presentation (which means that the pilgrims are only conscious
of concepts and objects that were understood in 1635) there can be
difficulties in responding to visitors' questions.

At Old Sturbridge Village they have not pursued such an approach to
language. 'We use an 1828 dictionary and make assumptions that the
language is similar. Weeding out anachronisms in first person is an issue
however.' (Sturbridge Conversation 1)

At Williamsburg, GB was privileged to witness a training session in which
a conversation about spontaneous combustion was generated from a
contemporary account. The approach to language was more impressionistic
than at Plimoth. Whilst obvious anachronisms were avoided, authenticity
was limited to an attempt to sound like Jane Austen. Clear communication
with visitors seemed to be the main concern. (Williamsburg Observation 4)

The problem of speaking authentically is not restricted to linguistic features but interpreters are also faced with the problem of ensuring that their characters express the opinions their 'originals' might be supposed to have held. This is made more complicated when attempting to answer questions relating to present-day issues. As we have already mentioned, at Williamsburg it was pointed out that there is:

> no problem in damning eighteenth century Popish Irish rogues but talking about Pope John Paul II (the pope at the time of visiting) is different. People try to make you condemn people and situations in the present and justify their own positions; to validate gun control, bigotry in religion and racism. They then go home and say that the people at Colonial Williamsburg support that. So people must understand the nature of how characters work. You have to be careful (for instance) that characters do not go as far as to say overtly that slavery is a good thing.
>
> (Williamsburg Conversation 1)

The appearance of the interpreter, his or her deeds and words, are all part of the role they create and perform in the historical presentation.

## THE INTERPRETER'S ROLE

### Establishing the role

There are many ways in which an interpreter can establish his or her role depending on the extent to which they are expected to immerse themselves in the persona of a particular character or be themselves in a period costume. Much depends on the context and how the situation of the portrayal is 'policed' and controlled by external factors or by their personal concern for accuracy of presentation. Undoubtedly for some living history exponents, there may be considerable appeal in losing yourself in creating someone from another time.

Even with historical records, the personality of a recreated person may still end up being different to that of the original. This problem was explained to GB at Williamsburg where the characters are based on people for whom some records exist:

> We have their names, where they were born, and who they married but there is little written information so we have to extrapolate from their class etc. There is a big thing in America. Do you make up the characters creating the personalities you want or do you use people who used to live in which case you may be assigning them a personality which they never had.You follow the documents. Some have lots e.g. Robert Harvey Nicholas, a man grounded in principles, Treasurer of the Colony.
>
> (Williamsburg Conversation1)

Another example is Mistress Anabelle Powell:

> We don't know her values and opinions, we know a little about her
> personality which is surmised from her class and how the interpreter's
> character comes to it. You have to use the interpreter's personality
> because there is not enough time to train them in true character work
> so that they really learn to develop someone who is totally different
> from themselves.
>
> (Williamsburg Conversation 1)

Characters therefore arise as an interaction between historical evidence and
the interpreter's personality. The characters are chosen to people
Williamsburg so as to be able to interpret a cross section of the community
and give visitors a general view. This function is usefully fulfilled by the
midwife as someone who would know a lot about other people, get all over
the place to see gentry and low life, and be respected because of her training.

At Plimoth, the characters are based on well documented pilgrims:

> carefully documented characters are filled out by lived experience.
> The problem is the shift of mind set - the seventeenth century
> cosmology of God and the stars. It is hard for many interpreters as
> they have no religious background. Pilgrims believed that their lives
> were predestined.
>
> (Plimoth Conversation 1)

It was acknowledged to GB that this lived experience within a different
mind set has an effect on the interpreters. The interviewee confessed that it
had effected his attitude to disturbances in his life.

This method of interpretation can be successful though. Another
interpreter at Plimoth, who portrayed an Alchemist, told of how he was
visited by a professor from Leiden who studied alternative sciences. They
talked enthusiastically about alchemy. The professor said that it was so good
to meet a natural philosopher out there in the backwoods. This was for the
Alchemist the highest accolade. (Plimoth Conversation 3)

In establishing a role, the interpreter may have to choose between assuming
the character of a known, historical person or a composite character resembling
real people of a particular period. The former choice means the adoption of a
role in which the character is based on known and documented life events,
attitudes and values of a real person. This is likely to demand considerable
study of the historical personage and is close to acting a scripted part.

The alternative, the composite character, is the type of role in which the
aim is to create an authentic 'sort of person' who might have lived in a
particular time and place. To assume this type of character and role, the
interpreter might need to study and empathise with social and physical
features of an unfamiliar way of life. Some interpreters claim that
experiencing the practical difficulties of such 'role-play' can be more
challenging and personally satisfying than just acting a real life character
however much interesting research the latter may have entailed.

Both forms of interpretation and role are likely to involve an element of **immersion in the character** demanding more than mere role-play. It is possible that the reward for such study, dedication and empathy with people of the past is to gain a different identity from which to view the present. Living history exponents in their created identities have a temporal and physical existence, although the visitor's perception of their portrayals can never be more than a sampling of the behaviour they create. The interpreter may strive to bring to life a character but must maintain a healthy balance between 'being' or 'creating' the character and their own personality. For it is through the latter that contact must be made and maintained with the visitor.

**Communicating the role to the visitor**

Most interpreters are not content to simply 'dress up' and adopt a role for their own enjoyment but also want to 'communicate the attitudes and perspectives' of the period they are portraying. This issue of communication with the visitor is at the very heart of living history. It influences the method of interpretation chosen and as we shall see later, decisions about the kind of people who should be employed as interpreters. Indeed the purpose of this book is to explore the context, function and impact of this communication. In the following section we will look at methods of communicating with visitors and, as a part of this, the issue of control. As our work has developed we have come to see this issue of control as dominating any living history interaction, not just in terms of the interpreter managing the movement and safety of visitors, but also in attempting to control the visitor's experiences and consequent knowledge.

The intention of living history interpretations was summed up by an interpreter from Williamsburg:

> We try to create a situation where a visitor has to react, has to think. It is not good enough to spoon feed them and expect them to appreciate and accept it. We find that they have to come to grips with it and we challenge them with it.
>
> (Williamsburg Conversation 1)

The intention then, is to provide a stimulating situation in which the visitor has to become involved and work to create meaning. A number of interpreters have said during our research that a principle way of involving visitors is through making connections with their modern life and concerns:

> Adults retain and appreciate information if it relates to their own experiences. In some cases you never know it happens. For example, if they are shown a bill of exchange and then two months after they write a cheque and it reminds them.
>
> (Williamsburg Conversation 1).

It is therefore necessary for interpreters to find parallels between the period they are interpreting and modern life. This can be seen clearly at Williamsburg:

> The class structure was challenged in the third quarter of the
> eighteenth century with the rise of the middle class. There was
> increased consumerism and religious awakening. Everything was in a
> state of flux. This is confusing for us but it's challenging to show
> people this colonial period and show them how modern American
> society was born. It wasn't just the middle class that were challenging
> the gentry but rational thinking and science - Newton and Locke.
> What and how we think started then. You have the birth of
> modernism in this period.
>
> (Williamsburg Conversation 1)

The parallels with modernity are clear. Both societies are in a state of flux and
just as there was a shift from mysticism to rationalism in the eighteenth
century, one might detect a shift from rationalism to mysticism now. (See
Williamsburg Curriculum statement cited in Chapter 9, pp184-188).
Interpreters at Williamsburg do not make these parallels, obviously, but take
advantage of contemporary concerns to illustrate eighteenth century parallels:

> Characters do not overtly do this. When an American was caned in
> Singapore this was on visitors' minds. There had been a lot of press so
> characters used the issue, not overtly but by talking about the nature
> of punishment in the eighteenth century knowing that it was going to
> elicit this contemporary response about what is acceptable.
>
> (Williamsburg Conversation 1)

The same ideas are apparent at Sturbridge:

> The Town meetings in New England are unique and the main issues
> are the same as now, education, roads, finance, poverty. Of course it
> was different then as now you can't let animals run loose in the
> community. We try to draw on connections.
>
> (Sturbridge Conversation 1)

Examples of using this technique are often more apparent in third person
interpretation.

At Old Sturbridge Village bookmaking was being demonstrated and the
interpreter was using glue with poison in it to kill the bugs 'like today's
wallpaper.' The school teacher skillfully used the familiarity of visitors with
a school situation to make comparisons with a schoolroom in the 1830s
without breaking role. By teasing an adult who sat in the front row she made
the point that these seats would have been occupied by four-year-olds
learning the ABC.

That the parallels have been driven home often becomes clear from the
visitors reactions. On the 'Family programme tour of the capitol: Putting a
bill through the legislature' (Williamsburg) visitors are told that Washington
introduced a Bill about controlling animals. This was lost. He was advised by
Edmund Pendleton to redraft it and 'come down hard on the environmental
stuff.' There was lots of laughter from the visitors.

A criticism often leveled at first person living history re-enactments is that they fail to illustrate and explain change. The use of similarities to make contact with the past could exacerbate this situation if changes in values were not also clearly illustrated. Certain interpreters and visitors may be critical of the accurate historical portrayal of social attitudes. For instance, the activities demonstrated and issues discussed by interpreters will usually reflect the gender differences of the period. At Fort Clinch in the United States, a genuine historic setting where Civil War living history interpretations take place, men demonstrate the use of rifle and cannon, marching manoeuvers, guard and fatigue duty while the 'ladies' assist in the kitchen and 'mend, wash, iron and repairing soldier uniforms. They also make candles, work in the hospital, read to and write letters for the soldiers. Children, who are authentically dressed, stay near their mothers.' (http:www.addy.corn/ftclinch/history.htm ) If a mother was adopting a first person interpretation, it would probably be difficult for an exchange between her and a visitor to occur on the theme of the marked division between the sexes in respect to their duties at the Fort. However, if third person speech was adopted then contrasts could be made and discussed between these practices and those of the present, and to what extent social division in activities is culturally or physically determined.

In the Magistrates court at Williamsburg, GB was involved as a 'magistrate' for three cases which were designed to show how the values of the time effected the administration of justice. Visitors could then compare these values to those in their own society. There were three cases, that of the:

(a) slave seamstress which illustrated the rights of women and of slaves.
(b) catholic man who did not attend church which showed attitudes towards religious freedoms.
(c) woman who sang bawdy songs against the king which showed attitudes to the monarch and a man's duty to curb the behaviour of his wife.

In first person interpretation change may be understood by the visitor through reflecting on the differences between the attitudes portrayed in past times and those current today. In third person interpretation they may be explained. The issue of indicating change is also helped by anachronism. We have noted the continuous interest among living history exponents in authenticity, but as visitors we have also noted and been interested in the function of anachronisms - those mistakes made by placing something in the wrong period of time, which we occasionally observed. More often than not these were 'modern' things appearing in the created past. The notice informing visitors that the Aborigines at Old Sydney Town had 'gone shopping' or the ambulance parked in the trees by the lake waiting at the battle of Marston Moor were anachronistic but reasserted the present in the recreation of the past. Re-enactors may deplore the wearing of trainers or track shoes with full Civil War uniform, but such 'mistakes' assure both visitor and interpreter of the reality of their existence in the present.

Having considered these basic principles of communicating and contrasting values, we now turn our attention to specific methods used by interpreters to involve their audiences in the interpretation.

## COMMUNICATION AS CONTROL

The devices which interpreters use to communicate with visitors also control their experience. To illustrate this we will follow through the stages of an interpretation from gaining attention to maintaining interest and then to the timing of the finish. Throughout this account, we will distinguish between methods used in third and first person interpretation. We will then look at different approaches used when interpreting to different audiences - most particularly to children.

The third person interpreter can demonstrate and explain unrestricted in the references made to the present or the past. They still, however, have to gain and sustain the attention of visitors. One of the techniques observed was to encourage the visitors to explain what the interpreter was doing. This is signalled by the phrases 'what am I doing now' and 'why do you think I am doing that?' (book maker at Sturbridge).

Visitors can be recruited to help in demonstrations as at York Town Victory Centre where visitors were used to demonstrate the firing of a cannon, and at Old Sidney Town where they were subjected, humorously, to the parade ground drill of the militia. Although this technique may be more common in third person interpretation it was also observed at Plimoth where visitors were helping a Pilgrim carry firewood to heat the oven. An extension of this device is to put visitors 'in role' which is discussed later.

First person interpreters can gain attention by greeting the visitor, perhaps even commenting on their appearance. At Sturbridge an interpreter in the general store selling molasses commented on GB's tie. ('I am the only one wearing one. I wonder if they have been primed about my visit.' Observation notes). Having gained attention she did not risk the loss of her advantage by launching into a potentially unproductive conversation, but swung round to talk about men's and women's work and how the children were in school when they were not in the fields. GB was left wondering why she wanted him to have that information.

A similar approach was observed at Plimoth. The Pilgrim called across the greeting 'good day to you.' The visitors asked him what he was planting and he used the simple request as an excuse to give information about farming techniques, the use of Indian corn, some biographical and family detail, and to explain the need for everyone to co-operate. (Plimoth Observation notes).

At Jamestown the soldier interpreting the settlement immediately accosted visitors with the question; 'Why have you come here?' This also had the effect of throwing them into role as he kept questioning them until they had told him that they had come to Jamestown to make money. He then encouraged the visitors to consider ways of making money demolishing all suggestions except that of growing tobacco. (Observation notes)

It is obviously important to put visitors at their ease. In the school room at Sturbridge everyone was welcomed. A baby then cried and the school mistress said, 'Welcome to you too.' A woman arrived late and was greeted with 'you may come in.' (Observation notes)

Having grasped visitors' attention, interpreters must work hard to keep it. The shoemaker at Sturbridge, working in third person, gave an informative demonstration and talked about how shoe sizes had derived from the time of Edward II. He broadened this into a mini lecture about New England trade and industry in the 1830s and some of the group left. At the end, no one asked any questions. He had either dominated the situation too much and given information that people did not want or he had told them everything that they wanted to know. (Observation notes)

Third person interpreters can hold attention by giving the visitor things to think about and to notice. A good example of this is the costumed, third person guided tour of the Governors house at Williamsburg. Firstly we were asked to look out for symbols of power and then to explain how the style of the two floors was contrasted (Walnut panelling in the official rooms to the pea green upstairs.) (Observation notes)

Another way of keeping the interpretation going is to question the visitor as the soldier did at Jamestown. This technique is probably more naturally used in first person interpretation. At Williamsburg Dr Baker asked if he could be of service to visitors. He then used various things that the visitors said on which to hang his information. He inquired where visitors had come from so that he could then tell them of his own crossing from Ireland. Interpretations can also be personalised. Dr Baker asked GB for his card. This was standard University issue with no individual details. The good doctor seized on the opportunity to talk about his own qualifications and express his contempt that GB's card displayed none. (Observation notes)

The School Mistress at Sturbridge also used questioning to pace her interpretation. In answering the visitors questions she treated the adults as children:

> <u>Visitor 1</u>    I have a question
> <u>Sch Mis</u>    Rise please young man (laughter)
> <u>Visitor 1</u>    Who do you live with ...at the present time?
> <u>Sch Mis</u>    I have boarded around with families. I believe I'm going
> to your house next week. Be ready for me,

So the answer is made personal to the questioner.

> <u>Visitor 2</u>    What about discipline?
> <u>Sch Mis</u>    Come up here (in a threatening voice.)
> (Sturbridge observation notes)

All of these examples have an element of interpreter control about them. This can be seen more explicitly when issues of timing are considered. Staying with the same setting, the dismissal was neatly linked to a question about recess:

> 'I'm glad you brought that up because I was just about to dismiss you
> for recess.
> Class dismissed.'
> (Sturbridge observation notes)

GB discussed the issue of timing with another interpreter of the school house at Sturbridge:

> People feel trapped and feel that they have to sit. The interpretation
> has to be delivered to a constantly changing audience and limited to
> three to four minutes so as not keep people waiting.
>
> Interpretations for school parties can happen in 5-8 minutes. I always
> ask if there is anything else they want to talk about and always avoid
> 'Do you have any questions?' because I have been embarrassed
> myself in other museums. I skip punishment because the children
> always ask about that and its useful to close. I give a quick bit on
> punishment and then excuse them.
>
> (Sturbridge Conversation 2)

Visitors can also be controlled by being put in role. We have already seen this
used as a way of gaining visitors' attention but it can be used as a way of
managing the whole experience. A good and enjoyable example of this was
at the Boston Tea Party in Boston Harbour.[1] Here the visitors were seated on
board ship each sporting a blue feather. They were then harangued about
the injustices of colonial rule, encouraged to cheer and boo until whipped up
into a frenzy, when they then moved to the side of the ship and cheered as
children threw tea bales overboard. Amidst this, interpreters playing the
roles of the key protagonists, delivered speeches giving the visitors the
background issues and the outline of the story. (Boston Observation)

This method is also used, perhaps more seriously, at Sturbridge and
Williamsburg.

At Sturbridge, visitors can take part in the town meeting and in a
programme called 'Your Day in Court.' Here the Justice of the Peace
discusses his role and then hands out scenarios to visitors who volunteer.
They have a lot of freedom with the scenarios.

> When 'Your Day in Court' is not set up well its disaster: Visitors need
> help in understanding what their role is.
>
> (Sturbridge conversation 2)

A similar technique is used at Williamsburg for the court room
interpretation, already referred to, and the family tour of the Capitol. In the
courtroom, the scenarios for the cases are handed out to the visitors who
improvise their responses. On the occasion when GB was a magistrate, the
interpretation nearly went wrong because a visitor was uncertain about what
he should do. This technique may involve those taking part in a way that
improves the communication of the past to them but it can work against the
educative experience of other visitors, should it go wrong.

The Capitol tour was specifically geared towards children and explaining
the ways in which the legislature operated. The process was demonstrated
by re-enacting, with the help of visitors in role, the first bill that Washington
presented. In this case, the words to be used were printed on prompt cards.

In the previous examples, the content of the interpretation and the
resulting visitors questions are controlled by what the visitor is told, has seen
or has done, all of which are dictated by the interpreter. Additionally the

setting itself can dictate the interpretation. At Sturbridge this was explained to GB:

> The store is interesting as it dictates the interpretation itself, even with children. You can control the situation by where you stand.
>
> If you stand by the textiles and fancy goods children will usually come over to where you are. They often ask if they can buy something. I don't say flatly, 'No', but it can take too long to develop a response through role play - 'Do you have an account or do you have gold or silver Spanish or English coin?'
>
> Children may get out their money. And I may identify that as a learning situation. Children love being rich and have found out that people made fifty cents or a dollar a day. I pay no attention to the denomination.
>
> 'It's not National Bank so you must have made it yourself, put it back in your pocket before someone sees it. You can see the copper on side of a quarter so it must be forged!'
>
> Many times the store starts the conversation: What is that? How much does it cost? We don't know many of the prices so we give the range.
>
> (Sturbridge Conversation 2)

We were struck at times with the similarities between classroom teaching and the interpreter/visitor interaction. Information is likely to be difficult to communicate if class or visitors are restless. However, if the latter were bored, unable to hear, or understand the verbal exchange, they can move away - even while the interpreter is in mid sentence. In the real schoolroom, the teacher has a 'captured' audience whose escape is more likely to be by day-dreaming or 'getting up to mischief', than the 'blatantly rebellious' action of leaving the room.

**VARYING THE INTERPRETATION ACCORDING TO THE TYPE OF VISITOR**

This brings us to the way in which interpreters recognise the need to vary their interpretations according to their audience, especially in the case of children. The following account gives a flavour of the language and strategies used in the Family tour of the Capitol at Williamsburg.

The tour starts outside the Capitol and we are asked to notice features that made it look like an important building. One visitor offered the Coat of Arms and the interpreter took the opportunity to inform us that they are the arms of Queen Anne. Another visitor pointed out the shiny bricks. The interpreter responded that these things combine with the size of the building to make an impressive statement. For eighty years this was where the laws of the colony were made. Talk for a minute or so was about Virginians being proud of being Englishmen and doing things the way they did 'back home'. The interpreter continued:

well, one of the things they did the way it was back home in England
was organise the government. They had a bicameral legislature.
Bicameral - that's a big word, know what it means? Two houses!
There was a lower house, a lower chamber where the men - the
representatives there were elected by the people, two from each
county. They were called burgesses. And then there was an upper
chamber called the Virginia Council. This was a very small group
appointed by the king. Now the Virginia council was just like the
House of Lords - in the English parliament - and the House of
Burgesses, the elected body, was like the House of Commons. A lot of
famous people sat in the House of Burgesses, any of you know any?

(Williamsburg Observation )

The interpreter deliberately captured our attention with simple
observational questions and then gave a relatively simple explanation of the
legislative process. Unfortunately she made the comparison with the
contemporary British system and not with the American. How many
American children would have understood this?

Further into the tour we had an example of the way in which interpreters
had to be sensitive to the insecurities of a young audience. The trial of an
indentured servant was to be re-enacted using visitors to take the roles of the
sheriff, the felon and his master:

A child was chosen to play the sheriff. An indentured servant was the
felon. GB was told afterwards that the interpreter tried to avoid
choosing a child for this role as children can get upset if they are
found guilty in the trial and are told that they are to be taken off to be
hanged. The outcome of the trial is up to the visitors. Mr.Hornsby, his
master was then chosen. Someone recommended the boy's father.
The interpreter was uncomfortable with this. 'I don't like the sound
of that' she laughed. She then tried to choose a girl who really did not
want to take part, so she checked that the boy did not mind his father
being his master.

(Williamsburg Observation)

The problems of communicating to young people were clearly appreciated
by these interpreters but others at Williamsburg:

say that if children don't get it, its not their problem. In the last two
years it has become their problem, or better - their opportunity. We
have some training on how children learn. If interpreters try to teach
abstracts to an eight-year-old it's a waste of time.

We now work on how to teach families - parents learn as much as
children when the interpretation is geared to children - not
condescendingly - but instead of a walk through the capitol we show
them how the legislature worked.

(Williamsburg Conversation 1)

Interpreters, like teachers, are aware that the children will not learn from the interpretation if they are not paying attention. Interpreters need, therefore, to manage children. One interpreter at Sturbridge was adamant, however, that he never put children down unless they misbehaved or were silly:

> If I'm working in the store and one child dominates with silly stuff - maybe trying to be twentieth century. We deal with the issue. I pretend that I don't know what they are talking about. If they keep on I might say 'why do we waste every body's time, we're imagining we're in 1835 so let's talk in those terms.'
>
> With a child you make sure that they think they ask OK questions. You use more interrogatory answers with children, to try to get them to think things through. Children are used to thinking: we're not [adults that is] in the real learning mode.
>
> I never let children think they have given a stupid or wrong answer: it's interesting but not quite right.
>
> (Sturbridge Conversation 2)

With adults, his attitude was different:

> With adults if they ask a dumb question and try to get you to validate a stupid idea I try to bring them round but not awfully gently. I don't say - 'of course people were shorter in 1830s' but according to military records the average height was half an inch shorter than today. Do you know the average height of a man in America today?
>
> (Sturbridge Conversation 2)

This survey of the interpreters part in the 'living history' interaction has, we hope, shown the complexity of reliving the past and communicating it to a visitor. We cannot leave this chapter, however without considering the training of interpreters, their backgrounds and motivations for undertaking such a complex task.

## INTERPRETERS' TRAINING, BACKGROUND AND MOTIVATION

### The Training of interpreters

The amount of training which interpreters receive varies enormously. To illustrate the variety of methods we will give a few examples of training methods which arose in visits and during conversations. Common features seem to be induction, the development of knowledge, interpretational skills, self study, mentoring and in-service training on specific issues.

Different types of training are clearly needed for different types of interpretation. Craft interpreters need to learn the craft and understand its cultural and historical background. At Jamestown an interpreter had watched and read. She had learned the crafts and become well practised. Doing the craft had made the explanation easier and through doing it every day she had developed a sympathy with the Powatan way of life. (Jamestown Conversation 1)

The limitations of time in training interpreters in role play techniques have already been mentioned but at Williamsburg such techniques are paid some attention:

> Training is not just to sound better but to look at techniques to draw the visitor in - get them to understand different attitudes.
>
> Every one has an overview of the period. We train people in local and regional history and how it reflects or opposes national history. Interpreters receive two weeks' presentation and communication skills on how to organise information and how to speak properly. For three years layers of sophistication are added. Interpreters have to look credible, become more comfortable in history so they can win increased respect from the visitor.
>
> Then characters have specific training; e.g. in language - how to get around twentieth century-isms; interactive skills - how to draw visitors in and how to cut off and how to act toward another person.
>
> For most of it we throw them out and see how they do with mentoring, to catch them if they fall down and provide feedback. Even neophytes provide acceptable experiences.
>
> Surveys say that visitors are impressed by the level of knowledge. Our interpreters are people who are willing to read in their own time.
>
> (Williamsburg Conversation 1)

At Sturbridge interpreters receive:

> four days of institutional introduction. Then they go out for a month with a supervisor: somebody to work with and see how it goes. Then back for detailed Economic, Religious and Government history. There is too much to be bombarded with as there is so much information. We also arrange call back time when we discuss issues that interpreters encounter, and historical information is reviewed. We run specific courses in the summer, for instance, on nineteenth century medicine.
>
> (Sturbridge Conversation 1)

Training can also be supported by the production of high quality handbooks. Singman (1996) writing for re-enactors, believes that the 'quality of re-creations is very much dependent on the information on which we base them' and cited three general categories of information which he thought should be disseminated; historical information, supplier information, network information, suggesting that the media for this would be journals and monographs to include bibliographies, reprints and translations, and handbooks. The last of these he described as consisting of 'digested' information, covering all essential objects and activities at a level of authenticity appropriate to re-enactment. It is worth while here to quote in full how he conceived the purpose of a Handbook in relation to re-enactment groups or societies, as it deals not only with establishing the authority of the claim for authenticity but the practical experimentation of recreating past practice by which the veracity of historical knowledge may be established:

> To ensure the quality of our living history, it is desirable for a Handbook to stick as close as possible to the primary sources without becoming unusable; e.g. instead of offering a pattern for a generic doublet, it should offer a pattern for reproducing a specific doublet; instead of telling us about social classes, it should quote what contemporaries had to say about them, etc. A Handbook should also include information on the purpose of suppliers, and a listing of contacts. The principal purpose of a Handbook is to provide basic information on a broad range of topics. At the same time, it can also be an important document for those engaged in primary research, since it can establish the state of our basic knowledge on any given topic, giving researchers a beginning point (and something with which to take issue, in many cases.) Over time, research would doubtless identify points at which the original information was incorrect.
> (Singman, 1996)

The cost of training, researching to establish authenticity, costumes, and wages will determine the number of people who can be employed as living history interpreters on the site. Sites may not stay open all year, and employment that can be offered may be part-time or occasional. These are all reasons for historic buildings and heritage sites drawing upon either the skills and support of 'Friends' to act as costumed volunteers[2] or on the experience and enthusiasm of re-enactment groups who may be paid or unpaid. The larger institutions may use various means of ensuring the 'peopling' of the site, either by undertaking the training and supervision of their paid, professional staff or inviting and collaborating with approved living history and re-enactment groups.

For instance, the Living History Foundation , a tax exempt, non-profit corporation promotes the use of the living history approach as a method of interpreting historic sites and events along the east coast of the United States. The Foundation provides living history exponents with research-based information and experiences, which are simulated if necessary, to enable them 'to create a believable impression of reality, and to communicate accurately and effectively the facts of history, as well as the attitudes and perspectives of other times.'
(Web page http://members.aol.com/lhcourier/page5.html) .

### The background of interpreters

A wide variety of people make up the interpreting profession, motivated by a number of reasons. GB explored these issues at Williamsburg , Sturbridge and Mystic Seaport Museum:

> At Williamsburg our third person interpreters are made up of ten to fifteen percent of teachers and about fifty percent have History as a primary focus in college. We are looking for a universal enthusiasm

about history. Twenty years ago we hired interpreters for their
background in history more than maturity. Now we look for people
who are good with people, have good judgement, and are mature. We
can teach history but can't teach good judgement.

Our turnover is only ten to fifteen per cent. This is one of the few
places in America where you can make a career and reasonably good
living by talking about history.

For our characters we prefer good interpreters who know the history
with the personality to create a Character rather than good actors. You
rarely find a good actor in Living History. Actors are easier to push
around and do the same thing for twenty hours a day but that doesn't
work well. About a third to half have acting experience; others
enthuse for social history; a few have both.

(Williamsburg: Conversation 1)

Similar concerns were expressed at Sturbridge where they also prefer good
people skills to historical knowledge:

We can teach the history and skills. It is easy to deal with gaps in
history but personalities are hard. This shows up on visitors comment
cards. We employ people from a wide range of backgrounds;
housewives, truck drivers, factory workers and some historians with
MAs and Doctors.

(Sturbridge Conversation 1)

Similarly at Mystic Seaport:

Interpreters come from various backgrounds. They have an interest in
maritime history and are trained to have broad knowledge and then
become more specific. Some take maritime studies courses.

(Mystic Conversation 1)

## The motivation of interpreters

Obviously interpreters are motivated by a love of history and the enjoyment
of communicating that to others and doing the job convincingly. We have
already heard from the alchemist at Plimoth who was praised for being a
'natural philosopher' by an expert in that field. He went on to enthuse about
learning and the need to instil that zeal in children.

Anderson and other writers in the 1980s believed that nostalgia played an
important part in the appeal of the living history approach, both to visitors
and to those who chose to be costumed interpreters. Talking to living history
exponents, Anderson found that three reasons were usually given for
wanting to get away from the present and take part in 'simulated but realistic
ventures into the past.' They were:

a need to escape from the tyranny of abstract time; a nostalgic
preference for the past - usually a particular epoch; and a curiosity
about the nitty-gritty nature of everyday life in a specific period.
(Anderson, 1984, p.183)

Other interpreters were reported as having more specific social motivations. At Williamsburg again:

> This needs close supervision. One interpreter has made it through a bad alcohol and drugs problem. He is proud that he has seen his way through. He uses his interpretation to young children to stay off drugs etc.
>
> (Williamsburg Conversation 1)

One is tempted to see this as admirable given current social concerns but:

> It's not in keeping with the free Black character he plays. His subjectivity gets in the way of the aims of the foundation. It's not our job to teach the young to stay off drugs. If it were in character, OK, but interpreters should not use a Hyde Park soap box.
>
> (Williamsburg Conversation 1)

We have already seen that the job can be particularly uncomfortable for Black interpreters given some visitors attitudes to them and the degrading role that they may have to play:

> Many Black interpreters want to set the record straight, to correct the stereotype. They want to tell the story properly and not have it forgotten. Some are crusaders in that regard and most want people to understand how it used to be and remember it that way.
>
> (Williamsburg Conversation 1)

In this chapter we have moved from the physical appearance of the interpreter, usually the initial impression received by visitors, to what can be attributed to the interpreter's character on the basis of how they act and perform (including the significance of their costume and their actions) and what they communicate by means of the content and form of their talk.

In the next chapter BG takes a closer look at this communication process between interpreters and visitors. A functional model of language is used to clarify the language resources inherent in such interactions and how they can determine the choices available to interpreters and visitors.

---

Footnotes

1  All the visitors represented the rebellious crowd and were presented with a blue feather to be worn on their head. This minimal costuming was intended to remind them that the protesters had been disguised as Native Americans.

2  We described in the previous chapter the importance in the development of Sovereign Hill (Victoria, Australia) of the creation of a volunteer organisation, the Friends of Sovereign Hill (FOSH). When BG visited Sovereign Hill she joined with other visitors to request songs of the period from a small group of musicians dressed in period costume and using first person to encourage visitors to join in their music making. This entertainment was particularly popular as there was a torrential rain storm outside and visitors crowded into the small room to shelter. It was only two days later that BG was to see one of the musicians again performing but this time in modern dress during the evening celebration dinner at an international reading conference. This 'Friend' in his 'day job' was the headmaster of a large school in Victoria.

# PART THREE

---

# REFLECTIONS ON LIVING HISTORY

*Chapter eight*

❧

# A CLOSER LOOK AT
# THE LANGUAGE OF INTERACTION

## WHAT THIS CHAPTER AIMS TO DO

U sing a functional model of language and a linguistic form of analysis I want to outline how we can identify the purposeful and meaningful nature of living history interactions by a study of the language choices made by interpreters and visitors in their conversations.

The transcriptions we have, were collected when we observed on sites, acting in the role of observer/visitors and were able to use a tape recorder. We do not have data for the experience of students visiting sites where a programme is organised by museum education staff or where the approach is used by interpreters who visit schools. To our knowledge, although descriptions of school visits usually identify the living history approach when it is being used by interpreters, comment is often made about the character's costume, activities and representation of the past, rather than his or her talk. We have found no examples of the linguistic analysis of the transcribed speech of interpreter and visitor interactions, based on a functional model of language.

Firstly, I have been interested to see whether such a language model can be used to examine, even in a limited way, what might be some of the ways in which language is used in the living history approach to produce communication between interpreters and visitors. and secondly, the extent to which such conversations are likely to convey historical knowledge in any way similar to that of the organised and structured, written texts used in school history.

## WHAT IS MEANT BY A FUNCTIONAL MODEL OF LANGUAGE?

Contributions from the areas of semiotics, systemic functional linguistics, discourse analysis, and critical literacy would all be relevant to the theme of this chapter but I have decided to draw mainly on only one of these four areas of language study, that of systemic functional linguistics (SFL) as developed by M.A.K. Halliday and others (e.g. Halliday 1978, 1985,1994 and Halliday and Hassan, 1985). Systemic functional linguistics (SFL) is the school of linguistics that describes language in use and recognises that language changes in different situations and contexts.

The literacy approach which draws heavily on SFL (e.g. Christie 1990, 1997; Derewienka 1990, 1996; Martin, 1989) suggests that using a functional model of language helps school learners to understand the different effects that can be created by using different forms of language. In a verbal interaction, our choice of language depends on such factors as what we want to achieve in the exchange, to whom we are talking, what the conversation is about, and where it takes place. The systemic approach theorises the links between language and social life, so that verbal interaction can be approached as 'a way of doing social life'. (Eggins and Slade, 1997). Such exchanges can be analysed as 'involving different linguistic patterns which both enact and construct dimensions of social identity and interpersonal relations.' A powerful aspect of the systemic approach is that language can be viewed as making not just one meaning at a time, but several simultaneously and, therefore is more complex than just focusing upon a single factor such as the turn-taking organisation of verbal exchanges (Sacks et al. 1974 quoted in Eggins and Slade, p.323). Also, a functional model of language focuses on language at the level of whole text, and 'text' is taken to mean any connected stretch of language, spoken or written. 'What is important is that a text is a harmonious collection of meanings appropriate to its context.' (Butt et al., p.11)

## Two research projects using a functional model of language relevant to this study

### School history and written texts

A major literacy research project *Write It Right* conducted in Australian classrooms between 1991 and 1996 by what was known as the Disadvantaged Schools Program, studied the demands made by school subjects on students' literacy competencies within and across the curriculum. The project's reference book for teachers, *Exploring Literacy in School History* published in 1996 described, using a functional view of language, certain key reading and writing demands of history as taught in schools and provided teachers with a ' language to talk about language'. The reference book traced 'the relationship between history students' expanding linguistic repertoire and their movement from constructing the past as story (with a focus on particular, concrete events unfolding through time) to constructing it as argument (with a focus on abstract theses organized in text time).' (Coffin, 1997, p.196). It was argued that school students are in effect learning how to think like historians as they construct historical knowledge within the secondary school context. The research focused on the range of written texts encountered by students when reading history and required of them in their writing of the subject.

In all, a thousand texts were collected and analysed and the findings were related to the history curriculum taught in Australian junior secondary schools. Drawing upon techniques available from SFL, some of the collected texts were examined revealing various things 'about how different forms of historical consciousness are constructed through text.' (Coffin, p.201). Such constructions were seen to follow a developmental progression. It seemed likely that many teachers might be unaware of the literacy demands of the written texts being used in school history, particularly for the student experiencing reading difficulties.

## Conversation and living history talk

Suzanne Eggins and Diana Slade from the University of News South Wales, Sydney published their book *Analysing Casual Conversation* in 1997. It drew upon a range of functional and semiotic approaches to language to provide a theoretical framework and analytical techniques. They used these to describe and explain how language enables people to initiate and sustain casual talk. As they state near the beginning of their book 'we treat conversation as an exchange of meanings, as text, and recognize its privileged role in the construction of social identities and interpersonal relations.' They suggested that despite its centrality in people's daily life, casual conversation had not received as much attention from linguistic research as written texts or what they referred to as 'formal spoken interaction'. They offer in their book a very comprehensive set of techniques for analyzing patterns in casual conversation at a variety of linguistic levels.

I found their chapter on the various ways in which spoken interactive discourse has been analyzed from different perspectives very useful for understanding living history talk. This was especially so in relation to the way in which texts position participants and give rise to different discursive practices that would seem to have relevance for studying the verbal interaction between interpreters and visitors.

### THE CONCEPT OF CONTEXT

As explained earlier, a functional model of language places emphasis upon context proposing that language can only be understood in relation to the context in which it is used. Thus, it is the different cultural and social purposes for using language and the different contexts that produce different types of text. It is the construction of such texts that in turn influence or impact upon the context. As Halliday expressed it, 'the text creates the context as much as the context creates the text.' (Halliday, 1985, p37)

In fact, a text always occurs in two contexts, one within the other as it were. Functional linguists think of the outer context as the **context of culture** and the inner as the **context of situation**. The combination of cultural and situational contexts results in differences but also similarities between usage and resulting texts. (Butt et al., 1997, p.11)

I should like to look at each of these contexts in turn and then use them to consider how the past is conveyed through the institution of schooling in the form of the curriculum subject, History, and the relevance of the living history approach for achieving this social purpose.

### Context of culture

The word culture is often used in slightly different ways but here it is used to include the attitudes, values and experiences of any group of people having shared expectations of ways of behaving and getting things done. These accepted ways of behaving have probably evolved over time but they are mediated through language and different types of texts, created by means of speaking, reading or writing to become appropriate forms of communication:

> In any culture, different kinds of texts are used to get different things done in various social settings (e.g. shopping for fruit, chatting with friends, recording personal experiences, explaining why a particular historical event occurred, organizing a protest rally). Each of these **social purposes** results in a distinct type of spoken or written text known as a **text type or genre**.
>
> (*Exploring Literacy in School History*, p.12)

It is in this way that text types develop for many and various reasons. They inform, entertain, instruct, explain, argue, purchase things, and so on. They evolve and change as the original purpose for which they were instigated, changes within the culture.

*Different text types or genres*

Such text types can be recognized by the distinctive form and linguistic features of the spoken or written text. The text usually has a beginning, middle and end structure through which the social function of the genre is realised. A genre has been described as 'a staged, goal oriented, purposeful activity in which speakers engage as members of our culture'. (Martin, 1984, p.25) and as it unfolds, each stage has a part to play in the organisation of the information and experience being constructed.

*Written genres of school subjects*

Considerable work has been carried out on the analysis of written genres based on the staged and purposeful model described by Martin. He and Rothery in the 1980s analyzed in considerable detail the key written genres that they had found being used in Australian schools. (Martin and Rothery, 1986 quoted in Eggins and Slade, p.57). These distinctive text types included reports, narratives, explanations, procedures and argumentative genres such as exposition and discussion. Eggins and Slade reported that this research 'had a wide impact on education in Australia, and has formed the theoretical underpinning of what is now referred to as the genre-based approach to the teaching of writing in schools.'

The work by Martin and Rothery led in turn to the *Write It Right* project mentioned above and the publication in 1996 of a reference book for teachers *Exploring Literacy in School History*, the purpose of which was 'to identify and characterise in objective terms some of the key communication tools and **text types** that junior secondary history demands.' Its main focus was on the written word - on what students in the early stages of secondary schooling in the Australian education system would need 'to read and write in order to access and construct historical knowledge.' The book's writers identified text types that they had found to be typical of the learning area of History and examined how they were different from those other learning or 'subject' areas of the school curriculum.

## Narrative and different subject areas

Early in the book, the writers raised the question of why different learning areas seemed to value different written text types. Using two *narratives*, one from the English and one from the History subject areas, they suggested that the answer lies largely in the different *social purposes* that different types of narratives fulfill in the Australian culture. They distinguished between the two forms of narrative in the following way. They suggested that the overall purpose of the narrative as used in the English subject area would be 'to entertain and construct solidarity between writer and reader' and belonged to a group of text types generally known as **story**. The writers suggested that usually such texts were used 'to entertain and draw a personal response from the reader to the experience shared between reader and writer.' The overall social purpose of the History narrative, usually identified as a Historical Recount, was considered by Martin and Rothery as being 'to inform by building up a historical understanding of events.'

Historical Recounts were seen as belonging to a family of text types called the Chronicle text types. These text types by retelling past events could build up a systematic record of the past. Other types (reporting, explaining and arguing History) are progressively less concerned with people's personal response to experience and are directed more towards the public sphere, where events and public affairs can be debated and appraised in a more impersonal way. (*Exploring Literacy in School History*, p.4) The writers concluded that within the context of school History, many teachers seemed to see the Chronicle text types as having more potential for learning about History and demonstrating that type of learning than Story text types.[1] However, they conceded that 'contemporary theories of teaching and learning history, as well as the concept of empathetic understanding, have led other teachers to focus on story texts as a suitable medium for accessing and demonstrating historical knowledge.' (p.5)

There would seem to be a strong parallel between this latter group, the champions of story texts for retaining students' interest - particularly that of young children - by means of character and plot in the unfolding of historical events, and the living history exponents who enact events through real or fictionalised characters and make use of the first person approach.

To return to *Exploring Literacy in School History*, the writers provide two examples of the instructions given to students asked to construct a story and to imagine themselves as a particular type of historical character in a given period or involved in an historical event. The writers considered that setting students a task such as this, could raise several issues. They thought that the 'kind of text it seems to be requesting has entertainment as its social purpose and the kind of interpersonal meaning which would be brought into focus is personal and to do with people's inner feelings.' The writers go on to ask whether this is the kind of interpersonal meaning that Historians, History teachers and History Examiners generally require of students and are likely to value and reward. If it is not, and that really what is generally valued and therefore required of students is an objective and evaluative response, then the purpose of this type of task may not be clear to learners and create confusion.

That is, if the role of the historian and (as an apprentice historian) the student is to inform through showing an understanding of historical events, then requesting texts where the *social purpose* is largely to entertain, is likely to result in student responses that could elicit the following types of teacher comment:

- This would be better as an English essay then a history piece.
- Too much feeling and not enough information.
- You have used too much emotive language and focused too much on your own personal opinions.
- Too much opinion and not enough fact.

(*Exploring Literacy in School History*, p.5).

The above argument could equally be applied to the use of the living history approach as an appropriate method for learning school History, since for many living history exponents, especially those paid employees in theme parks, the verbal text produced in interpreter/visitor interactions would have as 'its social purpose and the kind of interpersonal meaning', a purpose and meaning to do with people's inner feelings . As often stated by exponents, such feelings would bring the 'past to life' for visitors and 'entertain'.

*School History conceived as moving from the personal to generality and abstraction*

In the Australian study, a number of distinct written text types or genres were identified as being important for learning the skills and knowledge of the subject area of History as taught within junior secondary schools. An overview of these text types is provided in *Exploring Literacy in School History* - Table 3.1, (p.13) which indicates a progression through four groupings of the text types, moving from the personal to less personal, grouped according to four broad themes:

- chronicling the past
- reporting the past
- explaining the past
- arguing the past

For each text type - there are eleven in all - the social purpose and stages for how the text is likely to be organized and how they build on each other, are explained. (Footnote[2] for more details of the text types and their social purpose). The writers note that 'there is not a fixed number of text types which conform to a set of prescribed rules' and that sometimes 'it can be difficult to identify a text as belonging to one or other text type.'

It is claimed by the writers of *Exploring Literacy in School History* that learners need to understand how written History texts are constructed and adapted for different situations. This can be done by identifying and writing the different text types and in the process becoming aware of the most typical structures and linguistic features of each type of text. Understanding the social purposes and characteristics of such 'typical' texts of History as school subject, provides the student with a resource for critically analyzing what they read. The authors of *Exploring Literacy in School History* make use of a functional model of language to describe the linguistic features of such text types and show how the context of situation affects the language choices made by the writer. The focus is on the written word but through this approach students are learning to use communication tools and to share a language for talking about language. These tools help the learner to recognise the techniques used by writers of History and so to analyze texts' effects. It is worth quoting the synopsis of Chapter 4 of *Exploring Literacy in School History* since it outlines some of the language resources it is intended that junior secondary students should explicitly understand. It describes those:

> language resources which enable writers and speakers to colour a text
> by appraising people's behaviour and emotional responses, and by
> giving value to historical phenomena. An understanding of how these
> resources work to position a reader will enable students to critically
> interrogate both primary and secondary sources. In addition, an
> understanding of these resources will enable students to build new
> interpretations of the past. (*Exploring Literacy in School History* : page
> VIII)

There is considerably more in the book about the concept of text types and the reading and writing demands, which the main text types used in learning school History, make on the learner.

In living history, if the interaction between interpreter and student in the role of visitor is considered as a 'text type' we do not know how such 'experiences' could be integrated into learning school History and to what extent teachers use a developmental model of progression in teaching the subject. Certainly preparation for visits and 'de-briefing' sessions afterwards would seem to be very important if visits to sites are to have a pedagogical purpose rather than merely an 'entertainment' purpose. In respect to children and young people visiting sites with parents or other adults, discussing the living history experience might seem to be more opportunistic.

### Cultural differences

I have been concentrating on describing the role and function of text types within the concept of the context of culture. Within this 'wider picture' of context, like other social phenomena, genres can change over time, though Christie has suggested that possibly written genres do so more slowly than spoken ones. (Christie, 1997, p.11) Institutions such as the school may contribute to the more conservative function of written genres since they emphasise the value of writing as a means of record keeping, or present evidence of pupils' ability to re-present learnt knowledge as required in examination systems.

Genres or text types are related to the values and expectations of the *culture*, so genres in other languages might be quite different to those observed and noted in English. Even between different English speaking countries there can be culturally determined differences. For instance, evidence for this may be found in text types that are designed to entertain and amuse. Pictorial humour may cross cultural barriers more easily than spoken or written jokes, as may be seen by the vast and increasing popularity throughout this century of the animated antics of cartoon characters. The Internet appears to be developing a cross country purpose which aims at global communication with 90% of usage being achieved through competence in the English language.

Within the **context of culture** we can conceive of the institutionalised ways in which the past can be represented and in which historical knowledge is selected and organised by means of text types or genres. Museums and historical sites, tourism, and schooling are involved in this social process of institutionalising the past into a knowledge commodity that can be valued and preserved for future generations. Of course, that valuation is likely to change with the passage of time, particularly in respect to the significance of individual events and the access of particular groups to achieve their own 'voice' to present their version of the past.

At this point it is useful to introduce Halliday's idea of metafunctions of language and the notion that three types of meaning can be identified. (Halliday, 1994) He described these as :

(1) *ideational meanings* : meanings about the world and representation of reality (e.g. topics, themes and subject matter talked or written about)

(2) *interpersonal meanings* : meanings about roles and relationships between people (e.g. perceived status of interactants, degree of intimacy )

(3) *textual meanings* : meanings about the message and channels of communication (e.g. spoken or written, use of expressions/idiom, types of cohesion)

The first of these, **ideational meanings**, can include the meanings we make about the world in which we live. People in different parts of the world, now and in the past, live and have lived their lives, in different societies and cultures in which language enables them to conceive and name different aspects in making sense of their world. (So as we remember and think about our past and at the same time as we develop a notion of *the past* these will be socially and culturally influenced in their conception.) In discussing the content and issues raised in *Exploring Literacy in School History* I have been writing about how a particular group of people, called *Historians*, in the context of the Australian culture, conceive of the past. This is in a different and specific way to an 'everyday' meaning, identifying concepts and forms of knowledge that can be stored and passed on to future generations by means of the recording function of written language. Such genres exist and change in relation to a society's needs and purposes over time. The existence of a group who determine an area of knowledge as History and themselves as Historians, in order to distinguish what is important within the society's past by selection and recording, is an important cultural feature.

In other parts of the world, the past may be differently conceived. The existence of the museum as a storage place for collections of artifacts of past times stored in glass cases may seem alien in the context of Aboriginal culture. In the traditional Aboriginal society it was the responsibility of tribal or clan elders to be the guardians of the creation myths and stories and determine who should have access to them and thereby understand the ideational meanings in which the past and landscape are integrated. This conception of a past time found expression in both verbal language and artistic expression but now with access to schooling, Aboriginal children may learn how to read and write History text types, appropriate for a 'western' understanding of the past. But in doing so will be expected to assimilate the social values inherent in obtaining competence in such linguistic genres.

I think the Australian work on History texts used in some of the secondary schools in that country, based as it is on a functional model of language, can help us to understand how text types, verbal or written, might be 'doing a job in a social context' within the context of culture. *Exploring Literacy in School History* provides information about how students in a specific school system are apprenticed into how to think and write like 'Historians'; that is, Historians in English-speaking, 'western' culture and its societies - at the present time. A degree of formality and legitimacy can be given to the process of forming the past through the social and cultural institutions of schools, museums and 'heritage' sites. Certain text types and genres are valued as means by which this cultural valuation of the past can be identified and passed on to the future. How the individual experiences these cultural influences is very much related to that other aspect of context, the **context of situation**, to which I now turn.

## Context of situation

Language is used in a context of situation as well as one of culture, so that while our social purposes in speaking and in writing determine text types and their structures, the language used will be influenced by the specific setting and our perceptions of what we sense and make meaning of in what we 'experience'. Halliday and Hasan (e.g. 1985, pp5-9 ) have suggested a framework for describing context and three dimensions likely to effect our language choices in making different kinds of meaning. In the context of situation three dimensions can be identified, which can be used to *analyse* the role that language plays in that situation. These are

Field:  the particular social activity or topic focus; that is, what is the text about?

Tenor:  the relationship between the participants;  that is, who is taking part and what position are they adopting?

Mode:  the channel of communication; that is, how is the text structured? (spoken or written for example)

Field, tenor and mode are seen as determining the choices that the speaker or writer can make from the language systems of discourse, vocabulary and grammar available to them and collectively Field, Tenor and Mode are known as <u>Register</u>.

There have been studies of classroom talk, using video and audio recordings that can enable the process of communication between teacher and students to be recorded and studied. Using transcripts, the linguistic choices of teacher and students can be analysed and studied.

To understand how language 'works' in the interaction between interpreter and visitor in the adoption of the living history approach we would need to know more about the context in which the language is used. Why a particular type of text or different types are used during the course of the interaction? Who is involved, the relationship between the interactants, and what their talk is about? What role does language seem to play in different types of situation?

Using a functional model of language, could one describe the type of language that might be seen as typical of the different types of situations in which the approach is use? If such a systematic and patterned discourse could be identified, would it indicate similarities to a pedagogic form of discourse? In the context of schooling, certain pedagogic discourses can be identified (Christie, 1997, p.135) in which different registers refer to sets of language choices, which seem to arise from teaching-learning goals. It might be assumed that any similarity in discourses would be related to shared social purposes within the particular culture.

However, at this stage, the first practical step is to try to see whether an analysis based on a functional model of language and using the three facets or dimensions of field, tenor and mode, can be used to describe a verbal interaction between interpreters and visitors in a context of situation.

### Context of situation and a living history interaction

The transcript of this interaction is quite brief but can be used to illustrate the terms field, tenor and mode determining the concept of text register. However before presenting the transcript I have included some written text available to visitors about this living history museum located in Dudley, which is in the Midlands region of England:

> The Black Country Museum is an open air site where historic
> buildings and features have been brought together to vividly recreate
> a past way of life. Friendly guides in traditional costume will give you
> a warm welcome and help you to make the most of your day at the
> Museum.(Site plan and visitor information pamphlet.)

The context of situation for the interaction between a woman guide as interpreter and a woman visitor described below is the interior of what is known as 'The Tilting Cottage'. This reconstructed building is described in the caption to a picture in the guide book *The Black Country Museum* (1994, p.10) as being 'one of the collection of buildings from throughout the Black Country that has been dismantled and relocated at the museum.'

### Transcript of the interaction

Woman guide in costume seated at a table, says 'goodbye' to mother and small child at the same time as visitor enters the tilting cottage. 'Bye bye darling, goodbye.' (Waves to child as the two move into the next room) 'Linda. Good bye Linda.'

| | |
|---|---|
| Visitor (speaking to guide) | What was this place? Was it a shop? |
| Costumed Guide | No, no it's the tilting house. ..subsiding a bit. |
| Visitor | Why does it tilt? |
| Costumed Guide | It was on a mine shaft many years ago... so we've sort of taken it down .. measured it first ... and built it back on the same tilt as we found it ..and of course made it safe ... |
| Visitor | Yes |
| Costumed Guide | It's around 1913 with decorations and furnishings, all other buildings would be 150 years old.... |
| Visitor | um? |
| Costumed Woman | This was how it was in 1913 .......[indistinct] ... white collar workers were better paid so it was a nice house, quite comfortable you can see. |

The costumed Interpreter stops speaking to the visitor since other visitors have entered from outside. The woman visitor moves into the next room.

## ANALYSIS OF THE TEXT REGISTER OF THE INTERACTION USING FIELD, TENOR AND MODE

### Field

This refers to what is happening in a text - who or what is involved; that is the Participants (usually written with a capital letter) and can include the people, things, places and ideas of the content. Participants are realised by nouns and noun phrases, and one of three functional components of a clause. The other two are Processes and Circumstances; Processes are realised by verb phrases such as 'have taken', 'measured' and 'built', whereas Circumstances (how, when, where and why a Process takes place) are realised at the phrase and word level by adverbs and adverbial or prepositional phrases such as 'on a mine shaft' (Circumstance of Place) and 'around 1913' (Circumstance of Time) in the text above.

In any given text there are things that we associate with particular activities or topics and we are likely to be able to identify the field of the text from such items. For instance, if the text includes activities such as 'swimming', 'surfing' and 'balancing' and names such as 'boogie board', 'wet suit' and 'Bondi' we might recognise the text's topic as probably being concerned with a popular Australian sporting activity. In a similar way, the words or vocabulary in the above text such as 'house', 'mine shaft', 'buildings', 'decorations and furnishings', and 'white collar workers' will indicate that this is a conversation about the sort of homes that certain people occupied in the past. Circumstances of time as in 'many years ago', 'around 1913', and '150 years ago' will also indicate to us that this text deals with historical information and meanings.

The visitor in asking 'what was this place', chose to use the past tense. In so doing, she was seeking information about the past - she was asking for historical information. She queried whether its function had been as - a 'shop'. Why? Certainly there were some scales on the table where the interpreter was seated, but also a teapot. The room the visitor had entered was furnished somewhat simply, providing the appearance of a 'living' or small 'sitting room', but possibly this visitor had already seen other 'shops' on the site. What was her concept of a 'shop' at this stage of her visit? Current experience would enable the visitor to have a concept of 'a shop' on the basis of the 'everyday' activity of 'shopping', but the situation of visiting a recreated site may lead to revision of the everyday concept, and possibly the development of a construct of greater complexity and finer differentiation. This could be based on historical knowledge as well as current, experiential values.

The costumed guide replied 'no, no' to the visitor's question 'Was it a shop?' She specified that it was 'the tilting house' (she didn't refer to it as a 'cottage'), pausing to elaborate on the attribution 'tilting' to explain the word's meaning as 'subsiding a bit'. The dictionary meaning of 'subsiding' is 'sinking bit by bit into the ground' and indicates a Process, being realised by the verb 'subside'. In a functional model of language, typically Processes are realised in the grammar in the form of a verbal group. Processes are a resource for representing events or happenings such as activities - e.g. swimming, fighting, or shopping - that can be categorised as involving:

*action* (given the term **Material Processes**);
*saying* (**Verbal**);
*feeling and thinking* (**Mental**);
*being and having* (**Relational**)

The visitor immediately asked for an explanation of why this Process, an action happening - 'tilting' or 'subsiding' or 'sinking' - was currently happening since she worded her question 'why does it tilt?' in the present tense.

The interpreter's utterance was a much longer response than her previous answer because the visitor had provided a different type of question - a 'why' question, which involved the interpreter in a more detailed answer covering several themes;

where the original house had been built;

its movement to the present site in the living history museum;

its re-erection to present the same tilt as in its original location and most importantly, its safe construction.

The interpreter continued to expand her reply beyond the original concern of the visitor's question, providing a date as to the time or historic period of which it was representative and also a class or type of occupation 'white collar-workers' based on the house's type of occupants. She attributed a value - 'it was a nice house', based on it being 'quite comfortable', which she invited the visitor to confirm for herself by looking around the room. The visitor did not reply. The interpreter stopped talking at this point and the conversation came to an end. Other visitors had entered.

The interpreter in her reply had moved from answering the visitor's immediate query to providing more general information of a historical nature realised through references to time and dates. What is especially interesting is her use of the nominal group 'white-collar workers' which in SFL terms can be conceived as **generalised human Participants**, an important feature in historical text since it enables groups to be talked or written about as entities that act on other entities or are acted upon and thereby become elements in the construction of causal relationships. Generalised Participants can be categorisied as either human or non-human. For instance, examples of other **generalised** *human* **Participants** would be the 'the Vikings', 'Tudor monarchs' and 'Socialists' whereas generalised *non-human* Participants would be 'the first reason', 'the invasion' and 'European states'. (*Exploring Literacy in School History*, p.111).

*Text type*

It could be argued that the interpreter was expanding her answer and moving towards a more abstract view of the world and what might be described as a **factorial explanation**. This is a text type that explains the reasons or factors that contribute to a particular event or outcome. Explaining how a number of reasons or factors contributed to past events or happenings, is common in historical investigations and often expected in students' responses to examination questions or essay assignments undertaken in learning school history. (*Exploring Literacy in School History*, p.110) Factorial explanations have a different social purpose to **historical accounts** of events. The writers of *Exploring Literacy in School History* have explained the latter as being concerned with explaining the past in terms of a single sequence of causally related events, whereas factorial explanations are concerned with multiple-layered causes that can be appraised or rated in terms of their importance.

A *scientific* factorial explanation could equally have been offered by the interpreter as the cause of the house tilting. It would probably have involved the choice of the technical term 'subsidence' but this interpreter chose instead to assume that her listener understood the dangers and to assure the visitor that although the tilt had realistically been recreated, the building was safe as well as apparently 'authentic'. Indeed this was so, because there wasn't a real mine under the building!

By moving towards a factorial explanation, the interpreter had a means by which the individualistic experience of the living history situation, in this case that of the recreated tilting house, could be used to progress her listener's knowledge towards greater historical understanding. She did not however proceed beyond an implied relationship between occupation, level of paid employment, and housing conditions. If the conversation had continued, what would the visitor have asked next? Alternatively would the visitor have had sufficient historical knowledge, interest and confidence not to have asked another question but instead to have made a statement? Would the conversation have then assumed the features of an exchange of views between interactants of equal status? This is speculation but at least analysing this piece of text in relation to its field suggests how it might be interpreted as being 'historical' in content. However, since language can convey more than one meaning we can now turn to the second dimension of the context of situation - the tenor of the text.

**Tenor**

This depends on the roles of the participants and their relationship. For example, how well the interactants know each other, their ages and gender, their relative status, and how they feel towards each other. (Derewianka, 1990). In our text the costumed guide knows the child's name and repeats it as she says goodbye to the woman and child. She uses informal language saying 'bye, bye Darling' to the child as well as 'goodbye'. The intimate nature of this farewell procedure is in marked contrast to her conversation with the visitor, for which there is an absence of greetings and no formal closure or farewell.

Halliday (1985) emphasised that what he called the speech function could be identified in the type of utterances used in an interaction, usually on the basis of providing information or seeking or offering a form of action or service. For such speech functions there are usually a range of possible responses, some more acceptable and cooperative than others.[3] For instance, if we ask a question we usually expect an answer. Silence or the reply 'I don't know' would be likely to be viewed as a non-compliant response, and could quite probably bring the interaction to a stop. Utterances anticipate a response and although the speech function of an utterance, or each interactant's move in a conversation, may not completely determine the response, it tends to set up a range of possible responses.

The visitor's first question indicated that she sought *information* from the guide, implying that she believed the costumed guide could respond in an informative and knowledgeable way. That the guide was 'in costume' possibly indicated a different type of role to the usual form of dress for guides - everyday clothes or uniform. Even if the visitor was unfamiliar with the living history approach, she might have inferred that a 'living' response might be 'demanded' of the guide since the woman was clothed in the costume of the period of the room's setting. By modern, Western standards the room would be likely to be seen as simply a room in a somewhat humble dwelling that with its occupant, is representative of a past time and different social and cultural values.

*Implications of first or third person as a linguistic choice*

I have used the 'tilting house' transcript to illustrate some of the linguistic resources available to interactants in what might be identified as the use of a living history approach. The costumed woman interpreter used **third person**, and made no attempt to assume the persona of a fictional or real life character by using **first person**. When we 'read' a text, as a written text or a spoken interaction, we are entering a relationship with both the text (its content) and with the person (their motivations, perceived status, linguistic choices etc.) producing it. So the choice of first person or third, a linguistic choice, if consistently followed has content or field implications in the sense of what can be talked about in the interaction but also in relation to tenor.

For instance, first person exponents usually refer to the past in the present tense (a grammatical choice) and therefore their contribution to any conversation is limited by lack of knowledge of what has taken place for what, for the historical character, is still 'in the future'. Those adopting third person do not have to deal with this limitation and therefore can comment and evaluate from the position of looking back on the past from a greater length of time. This distinction on the basis of linguistic choice, has immediate repercussion in respect to the nature of historical knowledge and meaning which the interpreter can convey to their listener and the nature of the discussion between them that can follow.

It may be a somewhat simplistic generalisation, but third person interpretation seems to be a context of situation in which the living history exponent can talk like a Historian, reflecting, evaluating and arguing, whereas the first person exponent is more the historical 'primary source', inevitably drawing more upon the text types of autobiographical recount and descriptive report. Argument is less likely because the first person speaker and present day listener are not 'equal' in terms of historical context of situation, even if participants in the same physical context. This is not to say that they may not be able to exchange views but first person presentation if consistently followed, means that the two participants come from different time periods and different worlds; i.e. Halliday's ideational strand of meaning, those meanings about the world and representation of reality. Indeed, the first person interpreter's social purpose may be to entertain and maintain contact with their listener by emphasis upon feelings and the humanity the two conversants have in common. In the language exchange constructed, the text type produced by the interpreter could be closer to the anecdote and story type narrative, than the text types of chronicling or reporting History.

If the visitor runs out of questions with a first person interpreter or becomes impatient with the control exerted on the conversation by the interpreter's linguistic choice, then the conversation may cease to be a dialogue and interactive, as the talk becomes a monologue. Indeed where there are several or many visitors, it may be too difficult to sustain a dialogue, although some interpreters are skillful at combining the two forms by using the strategy of picking out individuals in the group or crowd with whom to exchange remarks

Eggins and Slade (1997) noted that even in casual conversation, a speaker might indulge in both forms but monologue often enabled the speaker to recount an anecdote or develop a line of argument. Also, questioners in a group are in effect often 'nominating' themselves for a dialogic exchange. What we never observed was a *visitor* making the linguistic choice of entering into a first person conversation with an interpreter. The linguistic choices implied by impersonating a character of the interpreter's period would seem quite a challenge for any visitor, unless they were equally proficient living history exponents.

### Conversation as exchange

The brief 'tilting house' interaction was in the form of a dialogue and to obtain a semantic understanding of such an interaction, Halliday's concept of what is in effect a symbolic exchange among the participants provides us with two notions;

(1)  the role taken by an interactant in the exchange;
(2)  the nature of what is being exchanged.

Halliday has conceived exchanges as involving goods and services versus information, which are realised through the traditional speech function categories of the statement, question, offer and command. Statements and questions are seen as involving exchanges of information and are called propositions, while offers and commands are exchanges of goods and services and are referred to as proposals. (Martin et al 1997, p.58). If we take the first pair, question and statement, for which we have examples in the 'the tilting house' transcript, not only will the extent of the information conveyed by the resulting propositions depend on the type of question asked but also by the attention of the questioner in their role of listener, or the extent to which they are distracted by other events occurring. In the exchange between interpreter and visitor in the tilting house, the interaction is terminated by the fortuitous entry of other visitors. The interpreter in an exchange may not be able to say as much as they intended. The listener may of course choose to encourage the interpreter in the role of speaker, as the visitor does in two places in the interpreter's propositions, by responding with 'yes' when the interpreter refers to making the recreated building safe. The visitor's second interjection was transcribed as 'um' after the interpreter had made a distinction between the 'dates' and age of the tilting house and other buildings on the site.

To return to thinking about the field of this discourse, did this distinction imply that the tilting house was the only recreated building on the site and that all the other buildings were in their original locations on the site? It is interesting that this proposition about the recreated buildings on the site, follows the reference to safety, since as we have mentioned previously, safety and authenticity often seem to be major concerns for museums and sites using the living history approach, since complete authenticity would endanger the visitor. When given the opportunity to respond to a question, the interpreter may be tempted not only to answer in detail the query, that is, to act as 'expert' and 'educate' the visitor, but to offer assurances about concerns which perhaps are more apparent to the site provider than the visitor.

This brings us to consider how a participant has to balance his/her own purpose against that of the other participant in any dialogue. In order to achieve what we want we need to give the other person enough of what they want to keep the conversation from flagging or breaking down completely. A form of negotiating is often needed. My children eventually rumbled my strategy of saying 'we'll have to wait and see' as my response to a direct request or demand. For me, it often provided time to consider what was involved or even to avoid immediate agreement or refusal. They learnt to have persuasive arguments at the ready, so negotiation could be entered into as part of any request!

*Controlling the situation*

Cultural and situational contexts determine who can speak, whether or not they will be listened to, and to what extent the speaker's contribution will be valued. Research has been carried out on identifying those linguistic features that identify a power difference between conversation participants. (Poynton 1985 as in Schirato & Yell, p.85) It is held that power tends to exist in the asymmetry of interactions and the meaning choices available to who is more or less powerful in the situation. Those who are powerful and can exert control in a speech interaction, do so by such strategies as interrupting, talking more in the turn-taking of dialogue, or what is usually thought of as 'monopolising' the conversation. In so doing, they are converting their 'turn' in the conversation into a monologue. This enables the speaker to nominate the topic to be discussed or introduce a different topic and hence the content or field of the text changes. Schirato and Yell consider that Fairclough (1989, p.46) summed up the exercise of such power in his statement that 'power in discourse is to do with powerful participants controlling and constraining the contribution of non-powerful participants'. What has been described as 'watching what you say' has usually been found to be more the action of 'non-powerful participants'. Several times we observed that visitors who spoke to first person interpreters seemed anxious about whether they would be understood by the interpreter. E.g. Elizabethan house: costumed man speaking to teenage girl with her mother 'why be this young woman a wearing of trousers?' to which the young girl turned to her mother saying 'Mum, is he talking about me jeans?'

I have raised the issue of the exercise of power in interactions because we have previously mentioned the living history exponent's discourse as sharing similarities with teaching or pedagogic speech patterns in that the register adopted in both situations seems to have two functions; management of the listener's attention and interest, before information or instructions can be conveyed.[4]

## Mode

This is the third of the three systems of choice or dimensions of situation available to language users and is the channel of communication: the two most basic channels for communicating being speaking and writing although communication can be by means of non-verbal, visual and auditory channels. For instance, the message of a cartoon is often largely communicated by graphic means rather than the language. In spoken communication, speaker and listener are often near to each other as in a face-to-face situation. They share what might be called the same 'here and now' situations in which gestures, facial expressions and perceptions of what is happening can suggest that shared meanings and therefore communication is being established. Transcripts of spoken conversations contain hesitancies or pauses (usually indicated by ....) , backtracking and interruptions or overlaps as one speaker speaks before the other has finished what they were saying, or even finishes their utterance for them! The conversation may contain references to the shared situation or immediate physical environment as in 'do you want me to do these for supper?' or as in the visitor's query 'what place is this?'

*Relationship between spoken and written language*

In communications over time or distance however, usually written language is required. The writer has time to construct the text and because they are physically distanced from the reader, all the meaning has to be in the text. This can lead to dense or compact writing as more information is packed into the text, for the writer cannot assume a shared context or even shared knowledge. Although the spoken and written modes of language are often contrasted, the relationship between them may be more usefully viewed as a continuum from 'most spoken' to 'most written' (Hammond et al., 1992, p.5). It is increasingly difficult to draw a clear dividing line between spoken and written language. For instance, plays or scripted conversation between living history exponents may have been written to sound like spontaneous speech but are based on written records for accurate presentation of period language. Some written texts on the other hand contain features commonly associated with spoken language.(e.g. on the Internet, use of e-mail or the 'conversation' of chat rooms). In history textbooks, the Mode of the discourse may often change because the writer moves from secondary to primary sources, such as from a dense, abstract explanation to a quote from a politician's reported speech and 'actual words'.

The major similarity between the two modes of communication, however, is that both speakers and writers draw on the same language systems of discourse, vocabulary and grammar.

Speakers and writers are likely to make different language choices according to the situations in which they find themselves. Differences between spoken and written language can be shown in the language patterns of each mode of communication which has evolved because of the different functions that spoken and written texts fulfill in society, but technological developments make for changes in such forms of communication. People with access to computers send written e-mails across distances which have the linguistic features of talk. 'Smileys' are used to convey emotions but you have to know their meaning e.g. <g> or <G> means 'grin'; I'm joking, don't take me seriously. Forms of communication are changing all the time.

*Some conclusions about living history talk based on the analysis*

Using the living history approach, exponents speaking to visitors on a one-to-one basis, are likely to produce talk that resembles conversation, the transcripts of which have language features typical of spoken language. Such texts are dialogic in nature, in that they are jointly constructed by two or more participants. As can be seen in the 'tilting house' transcript, even when one participant just nods or murmurs 'mm', such feedback contributes to the discourse construction. However, as we have already seen from the above discussion, an important distinction made by living history exponents is whether they choose to use first or third person speech. Third person talk may be expected to have some of the features of written texts and seem more like the text of history textbooks than the reality of speech in the give and take of conversation. Unless of course, the interpreter is very concerned about accuracy of presentation and is speaking scripted text or alternatively their talk has become structured and patterned on the basis of 'what seems to work with visitors' and repeated presentations. The size of the group and the need for control may lead the interpreter to distrust the spontaneity of casual conversation and prefer to depend on memorised written text.

## TYPES OF SITUATIONS AND MAIN FORMS OF INTERACTION IN LIVING HISTORY

From our analysis in Chapter five, we were able to distinguish three different types of context of situation; that of

1. a museum, historical or heritage site in which costumed interpreters are paid or volunteer employees, and visitors are adults and children who may or may not pay entrance fees and situations may be in a variety of settings such as interior or exterior areas of different types of historic buildings.
2. a museum, historical or heritage site in which children and their teachers are visitors and interact with costumed, employee-interpreters, usually on the basis of some form of payment made to the museum or site, and situations may be the various settings but also a specially dedicated facility such as a classroom or activities area.
3. a school or educational institution in which the interpreters are visitors and interactions are with the children or young people and their teachers, and where the situation is likely to be a classroom, hall or outside area such as a playing field.

Re-enactment groups are sometimes employed as interpreters by museums and sites or they may visit schools and public places to present performances. Less frequently they prefer to perform for their own enjoyment and education - not for a paying 'public'. Then the interaction is solely between the re-enactors for their own purposes

We have only a small number of transcribed interactions and these are all from the first type of situation. We do not therefore know to what extent the living history exponent's choice of language might be effected by what could be called a 'pedagogical' context in that the situation is in a classroom within the site or the school. The register of the interpreter's speech might be quite different to that used in the more 'tourist' situations of the museum or historical site.

Previously we have talked of visitors and interpreters mainly in the plural and earlier in this chapter my example was of a one-to-one interaction. It needs to be borne in mind that the situation can change in relation to the composition of the interactive group possible in any of the three contexts outlined above. For instance, the educational sessions planned for children and their teachers are more likely to follow a set programme. Material provided for schools that suggests the type of preparation for the visit may include details of the experience, whether or how the school group should be costumed, and the facilities provided by the museum or site. The determination of the group size or the number of interpreters involved is less likely in the spontaneous situations of visitors and interpreters encountering each other on the various site locations.

Within the context of situation, there is the one-to-one interaction between interpreter and visitor, but the former can also interact with several visitors or a whole group. Interpreters may talk to each other. Visiting Kentwell, an Elizabethan manor house in Suffolk (England), when I came to the stone flagged dairy two costumed women were standing in the sunlight from a high window, chatting in low voices, as one teased out wool thread on a spindle. I liked the image of the two figures, their heads bent together, and moved back into the shadows, trying to see how I could capture the image in the view-finder of my camera. At least two different visitors stopped and glanced through the doorway. They did not choose to enter. Somehow the two costumed figures were part of their setting. I took my photo and also moved away, leaving them undisturbed by questioning, deep in the privacy of their talk.

The situation created by the number of interactants is also an important factor in whether an interaction even occurs, the nature of communication experienced, and how long it lasts. To summarise, the main forms of interaction are:

- One-to-one
- One visitor to several costumed interpreters
- One costumed interpreter to several or many visitors
- Several costumed interpreters to several or many visitors

### Using the interaction analysis in different types of situation

What follows is an example of the verbal interaction between an interpreter talking to three female visitors in a shop setting of a recreated industrial town. The analysis attempts to show how using the dimensions of field and tenor, some understanding may be gained of the language register used by this particular interpreter in his use of third person. Two further examples of interpreters' styles of communication with groups are given in the Appendix. All three have in common the same mode, being transcripts of verbal exchanges between an interpreter and a group of visitors.

The intention in producing the example below is to provide an illustration of the actual talk of an interpreter and discuss how his choice of language can shape the experience of the physical setting for visitors. This example and the two in the Appendix start with a brief description of the context of the talk between interpreter and visitors, followed by using field and tenor to analyse and discuss the text that resulted.

## The Pawnbroker's shop, Black Country Living Museum (UK)

Male costumed character 'stationed' in the pawn broker's shop behind the shop's counter. He had answered a female visitor's question about the shop's content. He continued to talk, using third person, about the pawnbroker's knowledge of his customers and what he charged them. The shop was tiny and the three female visitors occupied most of the available space. The interpreter's talk developed into a monologue. The three visitors listened to his account. However one theme followed another and the visitors shifted uneasily in the cramped space. The interpreter returned to the topic of the shop's stock and how it had come from a real pawnbrokers. One visitor whispered something to her companion, and the interpreter, possibly sensing a loss of attention in his audience, continued

| | |
|---|---|
| Interpreter | ...and this is as it would have looked in the 1930s, genuine gas lighting, pop license to pawn father's best suit |
| Visitor | oo-eh! |
| Interpreter | there's a suit (pointing at one on a rail behind him) he wears for Chapel on a Sunday. During the rest of the week he wears his dirty old working clothes, so he doesn't want his best suit. So by Tuesday when mum runs out of money for shopping, he's got no more to give her cause he went in the ale house at the weekend....still expects his food for tea of a Wednesday...Thursday.. and Friday breakfast. So in comes his best suit. Soon as she gets his wages off him on Friday, she gets as much as she can, runs round, does the shopping, collects his suit, puts it back in the wardrobe....He gets up of a Sunday with a bad head, picks his suit and puts it on...goes to chapel ...and he doesn't even know its been out! |
| Visitor (*emphatically*) | YES (giggles from the other two visitors) |
| Interpreter | As long as he's been fed during the week, he's not too bothered. |

**Text type:** The purpose of the text type called a Recount is to tell what happened. To achieve this purpose, the text moves through a set of stages, such as an orientation that lets the listener (or the reader) know who is involved, where, when and so on as well as the retelling of a series of events in chronological sequence. (Derewianka, 1990, p.18). Although, as we know, texts differ not only in terms of their purpose and structure, but also according to the particular situation in which they are used. So that although this extract could be identified as the text type known as an Historical Recount, since it is the account of a common practice that exploited the way that money could be borrowed on clothes and then the items redeemed at a later date, also, it is probably a practised rendition of a well structured **narrative** with two central characters - 'father' and 'mum'. It might be thought of then as just an anecdote, told with a degree of dramatic enthusiasm, to hold his audience's attention.

However, the interpreter sets the scene with an introduction which provides a *historical* period - the '1930's. He then refers to two items associate with the period - 'genuine gas lighting' and the 'pop license' that hangs on the wall, the latter enabling the speaker to introduce the theme of the anecdote, the pawning of 'father's best suit'. He doesn't explain that 'pop' is a slang word for 'pawning'. It is a word of the period though.

Whether one sees this extract as a Historical Recount or a form of Narrative or an account might be considered in the light of the influence of disciplinary background as mentioned in *Exploring Literacy in School History*

**Field:** The subject-matter of the text is an example of a practice popular during the period being recreated - the wife borrowing money by taking her husband's best suit to the pawn broker. The field is established by means of the noun and noun phrases and the actions or processes by the verbs chosen by the speaker. Naming gives significance to 'genuine gas lighting' and the 'pop license' as features identifying the building and the shop's purpose at a particular time period - the '1930's. However, the listener had to infer that 'genuine gas lighting' was a change (from candle light) and an indication of modernisation. Furthermore he or she would have to read the license to understand that it was evidence of the trade of the pawnbroker and that authorisation was required in that period.[5]

Naming the characters a 'father' (when the spoken text is transcribed should we write the word with a capital or small case letter?) distances this personality from the episode in comparison with the less formal naming by the word 'mum'. 'So in comes his best suit' is a comic line, achieved by personification of the suit through the use of the action verb 'comes'. It isn't brought in by 'mother', which would give a different picture. Naming the days of the week provides a cyclical progression, starting with 'Chapel on a Sunday' and closure with 'of a Sunday'. Mum also 'runs round' with a sequence of actions to be completed to get the best suit back in the wardrobe in time - 'does the shopping, collects his suit, puts it back in the wardrobe...' The interpreter tells the whole of the episode in the present tense, which adds to the continuity of the actions and immediacy of the events.

However, it can be noted that the interpreter's completed rendition encompasses gender roles, religious observance, family finances, and an almost mythic presentation of working class life and habits through generalisation of practice from an incident. The assumption is communicated that it is illustrative of a common practice at the time. There is dramatic quality and human appeal in the contrasted behaviour of mum and her unsuspecting husband. Surely this is an anecdote which has been improved with repeated telling and one of the interpreter's aims was to 'entertain' his visitors, retaining their attention, as well as conveying historical information to them.

The interpreter and his visitors shared the physical setting of the pawnbroker's shop but to 'bring it to life' the interpreter adopted the monologue form to talk of the past and recreated the 'pawning' practice by narration. Interestingly he changed into the present continuous tense, very similar to the way in which a commentary would be constructed, so that his audience can 'see' it happening. That was successful with at least one visitor seems to be indicated by the strength and volume of her interjection at the climax of his account, when she acclaimed loudly 'YES'.

**Tenor:** As Schirato and Yell have pointed out:

> Meaning making is a form not just of social action but of interaction. .....Communication acts are not just simple exchanges of information, but are about the allocation, negotiation, acceptance or rejection of a variety of social roles. Tenor refers to the interactive dimension of communication.
>
> (Schirato & Yell, 1996, p.56)

First, in our example, we can note that the communication is a *temporary* relationship in which there is some uncertainty for the interactants as to its duration. Second, the tenor involves the interpreter taking on the role of informant of past practices and thereby assuming a status of authority. The visitors adopt a supportive listening role - they do not argue, contradict or ask for references to validate the historical information the interpreter is giving them. They adopt a less active role in the interaction, which however indicates that they are familiar with a readily recognised relationship, that of guide/interpreter and visitors in a museum and site situation. However, relationships such as mother-daughter, patient-doctor, or teacher-pupil may be more familiar and since they are embedded in the culture through social roles and literature and media depiction; i.e.influence of the context of culture.

In the transcript dots have been used to indicate the pauses and hesitancies, which are characteristic of spoken language as participants engage in construction of joint meaning. However, the part of the transcript I have selected is that where the interpreter produced a monologue. The minimal interruptions from the three visitors, his 'audience', indicate that, at that point in time, it was a monologue not a verbal exchange of equals. Lack of backtracking and self correction tend to indicate that this was a practised performance, the interpreter knowing what he wanted to convey, the form he constructed exhibiting elements of narrative through providing setting, characters, and climax.. Although the interpreter's narration took on some of the features of written text, his rendering conveyed something of the informality of spoken language by his use of phrases such as 'runs out of money' or 'he's got no more to give her cause ..'.

**Summing up:** This analysis would seem to suggest that an experienced interpreter using third person, can use language to go beyond the immediacy of the context of situation. The interpreter need not 'talk like a history book' but try through experimenting and making choices from their language resources, enable the listener to 'see' people and actions that took place in the past. If asked for references for his or her 'view' of the past, the interpreter might find that they had to change his or her choice of language to fulfill this purpose. Then the subsequent text might be closer to that of the conventional written texts of history as a subject of detailed study.

Our purpose in this book has been not just to describe but by analysis to indicate how the living history approach with its emphasis on verbal rather than written communication may work in practice. We acknowledge that there are many useful papers and books offering advice on what *ought* to work.

## CONCLUSION

Early in this chapter I wrote that two publications using a functional model of language had used a form of analysis based on systemic functional linguistics which might be applicable to examining in more detail the nature of the language choices available to interpreters and visitors in the use of the living history approach. *Exploring Literacy in School History* demonstrated how written history texts used in school might work as models for students learning history as a school subject and the other focused on casual conversation and the purposefulness of speakers in such interactions. Since living history is concerned with the presentation of the 'past' and primarily through interactive talk, the ideas and methods emerging from these two recent publications might be relevant to taking a closer look at how this type of approach might work in practice

At the beginning of the chapter I posed two questions. The first was whether a functional language model could be used to examine the talk of interpreters and visitors and secondly whether such talk resembled the written texts used to teach school History.

I used work from SF linguistics and the three dimensions of register to show that living history talk is purposeful but that there is considerable complexity in such talk particularly in relation to the interpreter's role in conversations with visitors. Entertaining visitors and retaining their attention may be as important as conveying historical information. Several meanings may be communicated simultaneously by the interpreter's speech which can only be effective if the visitor and interpreter share similar experiences and sufficient knowledge to make meaning. Of course, a prior factor is that the visitor attends to the interpreter in the first place! Using the three dimensions - field, tenor and mode, illustrated the complexity of making meaning, and as Butt and his colleagues have commented 'it may seem astonishing that the situational differences between texts may be accounted for by just three aspects of the context.'(Butt et al., p.12)

As for the importance of knowing how language functions and considering the living history approach from that angle, Butt and his colleagues (1995, p.156) have argued that 'the more we are able to articulate what is going on (linguistically) in a given situation, the more likely we are to notice when someone is using language to play power games with us, and the greater our chances of using language to suit our own ends.' This is not to say that I think interpreters are attracted by the opportunity to control interactions and 'play power games' but rather that greater linguistic and critical awareness, on the part of both interpreters and (adult) visitors may make for more interesting encounters! Interpreters may become more aware of the interplay of the two strands of the living history approach. 'Living' means active interaction and the subsequent 'human' emotions that may surface. At the same time knowledge of the past is created that has some of the excitement, rigour and argument of 'History'. Visitors may become more aware of the process that is taking place in living history interactions and ask different and varied questions or in first person interpretation enter the 'play' and extend their imagination.

Professional linguists, particularly in Australia, are currently using grammatical or functional forms of analysis to explore many aspects of human discourse. Even on the very limited 'closer look' of this chapter, the living history approach is clearly an area of research with much to contribute to this developing area of scholarship. Interesting avenues of enquiry are:

- the language used when museum staff act in an 'educational' role with school students, in and out of school;
- the language used between interpreters and visitors as an indicator of the power dynamics within the relationship;
- the impact of living history on children's ability to write in a traditional 'historical' register.

Turning now to the second question concerning the similarities between living history verbal texts and the written texts used in school History, in my judgement there is a misunderstanding. Spoken and written texts are different in their use of language. They do different things.

Frances Christie (1997), another Australian researcher using SF Linguistic techniques to examine the generic structures of school texts, has suggested that written language and speech differ grammatically and that the grammatical differences result from the different purposes the two modes serve:

> Whereas speech is learned in face-to-face interaction and continues to
> be used that way throughout life, writing evolved to deal with
> experience at some remove, and it is for that purpose that it continues
> to be used. Thus, the grammatical features of writing reflect the fact
> that it creates information for the audience that is removed in terms of
> space and time (Christie, 1997, p.70).

Since speaking and writing fulfill different functions, and the living history approach is primarily verbal, it might be expected that the linguistic features of the approach would be different to those of the mainly written text forms encountered in school . The Australian research has suggested that such text forms make considerable demands on students' literacy. If this is so, the living history approach may have little to contribute to the learning of History in school at least in terms of mastering the genre. Although it may contribute enormously to awakening children's interests in the subject of history and in developing their understandings of it.

Writing, especially in History, has as its purpose a 'distancing' effect, as Christie acknowledges:

> The term 'most written' refers to language texts where distance from action is greatest and where distance between participants is maximal. Examples of 'most written texts' include abstract reflections on causes and effects of distant events such as history or economics, theoretical arguments and where an author writes for an unknown future audience. (Hammond et al., 1992,p.5)

Is this distancing also present in the verbal interactions of living history? There are instances in these interactions when conceptualising a clear dividing line between spoken and written language may not be easy because some texts are neither *exclusively* spoken nor written. For instance, the living history exponents' choice of first or third person speech leads to identifiable differences. In third person, the interpreter can discuss ' abstract reflections on causes' and mount theoretical and highly abstract arguments more often typically associated with written language. Using first person the interpreter can present verbal language more often associated with spontaneous speech, revealing emotional reactions and attitudes.

The major similarity between spoken and written language, the texts of living history exponents' speech and the texts types of written History, is that 'both speakers and writers will draw upon the same language systems of language discourse, vocabulary and grammar.' (Hammond et al., 1992, p.5), therefore an understanding of the relationship between this aspect of language usage may be of help to teachers. I stress that this is not just having a descriptive model of language, which can be used to identify and name parts of speech accurately, but rather a process orientated and functional model which illuminates how language 'works' in different contexts.

At this early stage of examining living history speech forms and written History text types, the following implications for **teachers** are emerging:

- consider carefully what the living history approach might contribute to students' historical knowledge and understanding;
- prepare students before visits to sites where the approach is used and 'debrief' them afterwards. Consider whether the approach might be more relevant to a particular stage of schooling, such as being more appropriate for use with younger rather than older students or whether the discussion and debate surrounding the visit can make such an approach suitable to all;
- encourage children to reflect on their own understanding and critical awareness of the linguistic features of texts which carry historical meaning.

## Footnote

1   This discussion of which narrative form is valued by different school subject areas led me to recall my son's experience in his first year in secondary school. Following a History lesson on the Battle of Hastings, he had been asked to write about this historical event for homework. He had only recently discovered the detective story text type and the writing he handed in was modeled on this genre, with Harold's death being treated as the climax of the event. His effort was returned with the teacher's comment: *An exciting story Steve but history is not about stories.*
I think this teacher was trying to indicate that stories belong to the English subject area and writing in History is different. However, her comment did not make clear what was the type of understanding and its form that students were required to demonstrate in writing History-in-school.

2   Within the junior secondary school history, the writers of *Exploring Literacy in School History* were able to identify a number of distinct text types that were important for learning the skills and knowledge of this subject as conceived through the *NSW History 7-10 Syllabus;The Statement on Studies of Society and Environment for Australian Schools*; History text books currently in use in schools; students' assessment tasks, and teachers' programmes and notes.
Each text type was analysed for its social purpose and the stages by which this social purpose was achieved, so producing a functional description of each text type. There was a progression in that an overview of the identified text types (p.13) appeared to enable students to 'broaden their focus from sequencing particular events within their own lives and areas to explaining and analysing more generalised events and categories of time, causes and consequences.' (p.9). The writers conceded that the development of learning specified in such an overview could to some extent be achieved through listening and speaking activities, but that it was reading and writing that played a critical role. They thought it important that teachers should 'understand how different historical skills and forms of historical knowledge are related to, and made possible by, students gaining control of different kinds of text types and language resources. (p.10)
This developmental way of characterising history is a feature of the SFL approach to curriculum research and school studies carried out in Australia during the past two decades. For instance, the disciplines of science and history make use of reasoning differentially, which is reflected in the linguistic features and grammatical patterning which characterise the texts of such areas of knowledge as conceived in the particular culture. Martin, writing of the grammatical patterns of the report text type as used in the two disciplines, described scientific reports as defining, classifying and exemplifying in order to construct new technical taxonomies whereas history reports classified and described in order to generalise across classes of participants. As he concluded (Halliday and Martin, 1993, p.233):

> The scientific reports in a sense construct new knowledge while the history reports generalize and rearrange the old. Science *invents*, history *interprets* - this at least is how the grammar of their discourse works when the genre focuses on how things are.

Since this Australian SFL research is based on the school texts, pedagogical methods, and conceptions of disciplines in the context of that country's educational and social systems, these findings and interpretations may not be transferable to other contexts and countries. For instance, in the United Kingdom there has been at least a decade of continuing argument about the place and content of the subject of History in the school curriculum let alone whether the sequence of teaching should proceed from the learner's subjective experience to more abstract and generalised thinking.
The reproduction here of part of the overview devised by the writers of *Exploring Literacy in School History* (p.13) suggests just such a sequence of development. They named a sequence of History forms - chronicling, reporting, explaining and arguing - each of which gave rise to several identifiable text types differing in their social purpose and stages that needed to be understood:

Chronicling history
| | |
|---|---|
| Autobiographical Recount | to retell the events of your life |
| Biographical Recount | to retell the events of a person's life |
| Historical Recount | to retell events in the past |

Reporting history
| | |
|---|---|
| Descriptive Report | to give information about the way things are or were |
| Taxonomic Report | to organise knowledge taxonomically |
| Historic Account | to account for why events happened in a particular sequence |

Explaining history
    Factorial Explanation       to explain the reasons or factors that contribute to a particular outcome
    Consequential Explanation  to explain the effects or consequences of a situation

Arguing history
    Analytical Exposition      to put forward a point of view or argument
    Analytical Discussion     to argue the case for two or more points of view about an issue
    Challenge               to argue against a view

[Extracted from Table 3.1 <u>Overview of key written text types in school history Years 7 to 10</u>:, *Exploring Literacy in School History*, p.13; it is the elements in the Stages of each text type which have been omitted from the above outline]

3    The form of basic speech functions is usually considered to be:

    the statement which provides information;
    the question which demands information;
    the offer which provides an action or service;
    the command which demands action or service. (Schirato and Yell 1996, p.82)

4    Registers of curriculum genres: Christie has written of a curriculum genre observed in schools in which two distinct registers can be identified as operating in which the management element is related to 'activities' required of the students and content is in regard to knowledge and skills. The first called a regulative register refers to sets of language choices, which are mainly involved in the establishment of goals for teaching and learning activities and their achievement. The second identified as an instructional register, refers to language choices in which 'the knowledge and associated skills being taught are realized' and 'the two registers operate in such a way that the former fundamentally determines the introduction, pacing and ordering of the other.' (Christie, p.136 in Christie and Mission, 1997)

5    Chronicling of events as *change with the passing of time* is probably one of the historian's chief concerns but in relation to the representation of historical events, the experienced historian writer also makes use of Circumstances of Cause, often introduced in text by linking words such as 'as a result of' or 'because of'.

At the end of Ch5 of *Exploring Literacy in School History* the authors refer to how nominalising of time into an entity (such as an era, an age, or a period of time rather than a numerical date) enables time to act or to be acted upon, to become a causative element or it can be brought into relationship with other Participants and given a value or an Attribute: E.g. 'By 1942 a *disastrous period* of the war had set in, bringing about wide spread fear of the ultimate outcome'. Time periods and events can be used by the writer to become agents in the construction of causal relationships, and this 'agentive role of time' may be ideologically significant, requiring critical awareness in the reader. As the authors concluded:

'understanding the resources used by historians to construct and label waves of time enables students to critically analyse the ideological perspectives inherent in history.' (*Exploring Literacy in School History* 1996, p.92)

The costumed man in the pawnbroker's shop (page 159) provides an example of chronicling of time by recounting the events in the passing of the week before father's suit can be redeemed and also in his account of the pawn broker's trade, he refers to the '1930s'. He can do this as he is speaking in third person. It is difficult, although not impossible, for the first person interpreter to use periods of time that can be used to construct causal relationships. This is just one way in which I suspect that the linguistic structure of living history interpreters' conversing may be constrained, in comparison to the written text forms developed by historians to convey the abstract thought and reasoning of their discipline and to explain and discuss historical content.

Where living history exponents use *scripted* speech between historical characters in an interaction performed before visitors, it could be argued that this text type comes very close to the *literary genre of the play*, the main difference being that it is performed in a historical setting or situation rather than a theatre.

*Chapter nine*

⚜

# A CLOSER LOOK AT
# LIVING HISTORY AND IDENTITY

In this chapter, I (GB) want to pursue the idea that our conception of the past contributes to our perception of ourselves and the ways in which we perceive others. In short, our learning and experience of the past affects our identity. It is important from the outset to stress, as does Daniel Mato, that this does not imply that identities are 'legacies passively received but representations socially produced, and - in this sense - matters of social dispute.' (1998, p.598). I argue that the constructed history or interpretation of past events is just one of the many ways in which this disputation is carried out. In this sense, it is in our construction of, and arguments about, our pasts that we identify ourselves. It is the purpose of this chapter to see if 'living history' can help us in this process of extending our understanding of the identities of ourselves and others.

For over twenty years I have been interested in the study of the past, History, as coming to an understanding and an accommodation with the present. In teaching History in primary schools and university, I have become convinced of the importance of History as a way to develop self understanding and to consider matters of moral and political importance. Taught in an appropriate way History provides a safe environment for considering how real people behaved in certain circumstances. We can come then to an understanding of the consequences of their actions and by reflection consider the ramifications of our own decisions. Of course, this must be done with sensitivity to the historical evidence and its limitations and with a developing understanding of the cultural mores of times past. As the curriculum in both schools and universities becomes increasingly utilitarian and skills - based, History provides us with one of the few opportunities to develop an understanding of ourselves and others.

These ideas have already been raised in Chapter two. However, now I want to examine the claim made earlier that History education is about the exploration of identity wherever it takes place and at whatever age the learner may be. This educational process of identity exploration is concerned to develop a greater understanding of oneself and of others in terms of individual and group identities and to explore relationships between them.

I undertake this exploration in seven stages:

- I recall the definition of History education developed in Chapter two;
- I consider notions of identity and the contribution made by the past to the construction of identities;
- I examine the role of memory, both individual and collective, and the concept of lieux de memoire;
- I explore the contribution to these ideas of identity made by museums and the role of living history as a method of identity exploration;
- I illustrate ways in which different aspects of visitors' identities can be examined through the experience of living history;
- I consider the part played by living history in the identity exploration of the interpreter;
- I attempt to assess the validity of the contribution of living history to identity exploration and its usefulness to this aspect of History education.

## HISTORY EDUCATION

In Chapter two we developed the idea that History education can be seen as establishing and exploring a critical relationship with the past. This can take place through museum education, heritage education or, perhaps more traditionally, in the school. This relationship can be explored in different ways and with different degrees of complexity by different groups of people. The professional Historian and museum curator are concerned with explaining historical issues to fellow professionals and the 'public'; History teachers are developing their pupils' thinking skills and establishing methods of critical inquiry; members of the general public may be interested in reading the products of the Historian and visiting the exhibitions organised and interpreted by the curator. These groups are bound together by their attempts to make sense of the experience of living in an historic environment surrounded by images of the past and attempts to order and explain their relationship to these images.

The process of History education was explained as converting gut or lay 'mini theories' (Claxton, as cited in Husbands 1996, pp.80-81) into an area of knowledge recognisable as the discipline of History. This conversion was seen as an uncertain process given that everyday historical consciousness (Heller 1982, p.55), or beliefs that may have no grounding in 'provable' historical 'truths', may prevail in determining people's actions and therefore their relationship with the past. Our view of History education was that it should attempt to establish a critical view of this relationship, enabling people to understand that various versions of the past are established as 'history' depending on the perspectives and purposes of those creating them.

Taking the idea of a relationship one stage further we speculated that living history is a particularly powerful way of establishing and exploring that relationship because it attempts to personalise historical experiences and can be interactive. At the end of this chapter I will return to this speculation. In the previous chapter BG has shown that there are linguistic limitations to the interaction and has described some of the communicative problems involved in first person interpretation and the reluctance or inability of some museum visitors to ask questions. I will also consider whether a relationship with the past established through such an interaction can be said to be critical.

In order to consider the contribution which this particular relationship and living history as a method might make to our understandings of ourselves and others, I now consider some notions of identity and the contribution that the past might make to identity construction.

## WHAT IS IDENTITY?

Here I want to combine two notions of identity. The first is from ethnographic research and the second from feminist moral theory. I think that taken together they give us a working definition particularly useful in considering the influence of the past on present identities. MacDonald (1993), writing from the point of view of an ethnographer sees identity as the ways and circumstances in which people define themselves and are defined by others. Identities are socially created in specific historical contexts. (This parallels Mato's assertion cited above). I would argue that one's identity is not, therefore, given but created, neither is it static because in different circumstances and at different times it may change. Individuals therefore have *multiple identities* in the ways in which they project themselves in different situations and the ways in which they are identified as fulfilling different roles by others. These roles have attributes with which individuals choose to identify and which are ascribed to them by others. I am not seen in the same way in the lecture hall as I am in the back garden with my six year old nephew (neither would it be appropriate to romp with my students or lecture my nephew although sometimes it's difficult not to!). It is tempting to consider that there is a difference here between role and identity, the role being something which the deeper core identity adopts or casts off. On the other hand, what you see may be what you get. This personal level of identity might be summed up by the following question. 'How do I as a human being project myself in certain situations and how am I seen by others?'

Here we are concerned with personal, individual identity but people also identify and are in turn identified with groups. For example, gender, sexual orientation, class, ethnicity, regionality or nationality might be considered important in defining who a person is. Our identities are not, therefore formed in isolation but through a social process alongside and in contrast to those around us. We belong to a group of similar individuals defined against other groups who are different. Mato usefully reminds us that 'every and each collective identity construction highlights assumed similarities while obscuring presumed differences that at times may become more or less significant.' (1998, p.598). As with individual identities, collective or group identities are not static and may be redefined in different circumstances. A crucial aspect of this form of identification within and between groups is the notion of power. This is particularly important when the groupings are of class, gender or ethnicity.

Additionally identity at an individual or group level might be defined by the choices or moral judgments made by oneself or by a group to which one belongs. These judgments might also be made by others in order to identify an individual or group as 'good' or 'bad'. This leads to a notion of moral identity. Am I, and is this particular group to which I belong, acting in a moral way or not?[1]

I am particularly interested in the three aspects of identity which emerge here; the individual, the group which may be political and/or social, and the moral. It is these three ways of identifying which I use when considering the potential of living history as a means of identity exploration.

Most of us, however, whilst recognising these facets of identity see ourselves as a cohesive whole. Here I think a second definition using the idea of narrative helps. Benhabib defines identity as being:

> how I, as a finite, concrete embodied individual, shape and fashion
> the circumstances of my birth and family, linguistic, cultural and
> gender identity into a coherent narrative that stands as my life's story.
> (Benhabib, 1987, p.166)

Here, I think, narrative is used in a less technical sense than the way in which it is defined by systemic functional linguistics or used by Gergen (1996, as referred to in footnote 1). This idea of narrative is as an unfolding story structured by choices made in its telling. This idea of narrative is particularly attractive, although its coherence may at times be questionable, as it enables us to consider the constructed narratives of the personal histories of individuals and also of groups and nations as expressions of identity. In this way, the construction of history parallels the construction of stories about people's lives. The idea also allows for the possibility for others to tell different stories and therefore to construct different identities as historians assemble different histories. It is to these histories that I now wish to turn.

## MEMORY, HISTORY AND IDENTITY

Personal, group and national identities are founded on 'memories' often aided by artifacts or images that substantiate the information recalled. Individuals may surround themselves with photographs, souvenirs and certificates that remind them of significant turning points in their lives. In a similar way groups and nations collect symbols and commemorate events through memorials and museums. In the sections that follow, these images will be approached in two ways. Firstly I consider how they can be invested with symbolic significance and stand for aspects of a group or, particularly, a Nation's identity as, what Pierre Nora has called, lieux de memoire ('sites' or 'realms' of memory). Secondly I consider these images in a more intimate way in the sense that they can provide material for individual and group identity exploration in terms of searching for one's roots and clarifying features of one's contemporary identity by making comparisons with similar features in the past.

## National identity and les lieux de memoire

In a fascinating multi volume study of the history and identity of France, Pierre Nora (1996) has identified 'lieux de memoire': those icons from the past which people choose to invest with certain significances. In a subtle discourse on the relationship between history and memory he argues that in modern societies, conscious of a discontinuity with the past, we are compelled by ever present change to organise the past into history. In effect, history has destroyed memory:

> Lieux de memoire arise out of a sense that there is no such thing as spontaneous memory, hence that we must create archives, mark anniversaries, organize celebrations, pronounce eulogies, and authenticate documents because such things no longer happen as a matter of course. When certain minorities create protected enclaves as preserves of memory to be jealously safeguarded, they reveal what is true of all *lieux de memoire*: that without commemorative vigilance, history would soon sweep them away. These bastions buttress our identity, but if what they defended were not threatened, there would be no need for them. If the remembrances they protect were truly living presences in our lives, they would be useless. Conversely, if history did not seize upon memories in order to distort and transform them, to mould them or turn them to stone, they would not turn into *lieux de memoire* , which emerge in two stages: moments of history are plucked out of the flow of history, then returned to it - no longer quite alive but not entirely dead, like shells left on the shore when the sea of living memory has receded. (Nora,, 1996, p.7)

These lieux de memoire are especially potent signs of our identity. It is not the events themselves that have the significance but rather the meaning for identity invested in them. In terms of the argument I offer here they can be seen to have political significance in that they often remind us of our group identities and moral significance in that they remind us of our responsibilities. Through the process of memory, or at least recognition and identification, these historical associations effect our identity.

In Vaclav Havel's writings against totalitarianism, these ideas come together. For him the notion of historical identity conveyed through memory gives life true purpose and liberty. He writes that individual identity consists in individual history and that one's own perceptions of one's own history rely to a degree on memory. 'As we know man [sic] is the history of man'.[2] Life without memory (history) is one which makes a man a machine, or the instrument of production that the system desires, 'a private life without an historical horizon is sheer fiction, window dressing, finally, actually a lie.' (Havel, 1989 cited in Pynsent 1994, p31). He also talks of responsibility as the prime mover of identity, one's sense of responsibility making the individual an individual. This responsibility has to be learned through living trials and dilemmas. Without responsibility we are overcome by a feeling of absurdity and hopelessness.

Taken together these views illuminate the process of political and moral identity formation by recreating the past through our memory to give life purpose. In terms of National identity the process is similar, working in this instance through a collective past and collective memory. David Lowenthal (1985) demonstrates the power of the past, the history, of a people to assert an identity. He cites the case of the town hall in Warsaw that the Nazis destroyed to crush the Polish spirit, which was restored to its former glory as soon as possible after the war (Lowenthal 1985, p.44). As the conservation chief explained: 'It was our duty to resuscitate it. We did not want a new city, we wanted the Warsaw of our day and that of the future to continue the ancient tradition.' (Lorentz in Lowenthal Op.cit.)

So far the role of the historical environment in ensuring and asserting individual and group identities is expressed positively and intentionally; almost as a requirement for healthy living. People may, however, refuse to see their identity in terms of their history or tradition. On the contrary, they can reject the past in order to create themselves anew. According to Marx: 'The tradition of all past generations weighs like an alp upon the brain of the living.' (Marx, 1852). For occupied countries the rejection of the coloniser and colonial history or the destruction of reminders of the conqueror's presence are powerful assertions of a new identity. And so, with the overthrow of a totalitarian regime, its icons also tumble. Thus, negatively, the influence of history on conscious identity is acknowledged.

It is interesting to consider the notion of 'truth' in relation to these 'lieux de memoire'. If we accept that history is an interpreted version of past events then sites of historical significance are going to stimulate the interpretations that are imposed upon them. In this sense, identities are based on a version of the past rather than any conception of absolute truth about the past. The same may be said about an individual's view of their own life. To return to Benhabib's metaphor of the narrative, the individual selects and is informed by their own version of the events that they choose to make a significant contribution to their life's story.

The interpretations of lieux de memoire can also change. This is powerfully illustrated in the following example. The concentration camp at Buchenwald near Weimar in Germany has particularly complex associations for the identity of modern Germans. Its proximity to Weimar is significant. Goethe and Schiller lived and worked there as did Bach, Liszt and Nietsche. As lieux de memoire for the cultural identity of Germany the town is highly significant. These associations were used firstly by the Weimar Republic, then the Nazis, then the communists of the former German Democratic Republic and in 1999, it was the cultural capital of Europe. (One might almost say as a symbolic celebration of the victory of capitalism - if that isn't stretching a point too far). On the hill overlooking the city there is a stain on this cultural enterprise. The concentration camp of Buchenwald. Firstly used by the Nazis and then the Soviets. Towering over the camp and clearly visible from the town, the GDR constructed a National memorial. In its conception of itself the GDR was identified as an anti fascist state (some now see this as having a certain irony given its methods of ideological control - others may see it as a positive form of state denazification). This memorial ritualistically mourns the victims of the Nazi regime and reinforces communist ideas of comradeship. This symbolic ritual was experienced by countless East German school children and other citizens of Eastern block countries with, I am sure, a mixture of genuine feeling, national pride and cynicism. Today the symbols may be interpreted by some with a certain irony as cynical instruments in the hypocritical brainwashing of a country: rather than marking a break with a fascist past it is seen as a bridge establishing continuity. To me, however, the power of the monument remains, arousing complex feelings of loss, horror and regret.

There is a further point to be considered. Does the site of a lieu de memoire have to be genuine or can it be reconstructed? In America, Plimoth Plantation, Williamsburg and Old Sturbridge Village can all be read as symbols of important aspects of American identity: they are powerful lieux de memoire. As we have seen, all of these sites are reconstructed to varying degrees.

Plimoth is a modern reconstruction of the first pilgrims' settlement but on a site a short way from the original. The story that it tells is also a reconstruction told by interpreters adopting the characters of the first inhabitants. When Americans visit this site, they may be in search of an aspect of their common past. Some may be exploring their European or religious roots (i.e. individual and group political and social identity), and others exploring their links with the Native Americans of the area and making judgments about the way in which they interacted with the European invaders (i.e. moral identity). What reconstructed identity do they come away with?

At Williamsburg, the site is genuine but the buildings have been rebuilt and the colonial past and its early attempts at democratic government are again played out by costumed interpreters or even visitors with prompt cards as we saw in Chapter seven. At Sturbridge the idyll of rural new England is reconstructed from mostly genuine buildings (excluding the Grist Mill - see Chapter five) collected from all over New England and assembled into a village, which never existed, peopled by fictional characters reconstructed from types. These places undoubtedly contribute to Americans' understandings of their pasts and are likely to influence their conception of modern American identity, in that the sites reinforce powerful aspects of the American dream (I will return to this later) and its associated 'myths'.

It is interesting here to consider the role of myth in the relationship between lieux de memoire and identity.

As Robert Hewison wrote:

> You will appreciate that if I describe something as a myth, that does
> not necessarily mean that it is untrue. Simply, that it's true in a special
> sense, in that it has truth for a great many people, and this general
> belief gives it a contemporary validity. It may contain elements that
> are unhistorical, or ahistorical, but it adds up to a cultural truth. It may

> indeed contain a great deal of historically accurate and factually
> testable material but this is transformed into a touchstone of national,
> local, even individual identity. (Hewison, 1989)

These myths may be harmless but they may contain prejudices and misunderstandings about 'others' that fuel a distrust of 'others' and lead to violence and intolerance towards those who are different from ourselves.

It is interesting to consider the role which myth plays in exploring moral identity. Any adoption of identity is an expression of values. When one consciously identifies with a group one is aware of, and generally in agreement with, the values that that group expresses. When concerned with moral identity the very judgment of goodness and truthfulness are describing factors. Myths of racial supremacy will attract individuals to racist political organisations. The ascription of these beliefs as myth is in itself an expression of my own values and an identification of myself as morally opposed to such views. To illustrate this consider the current debate about the European union that exposes such issues of identity. What version of recent European history do I ascribe to, what stereotypes of other partners do I give credence to, ultimately do I identify myself more strongly with the pro Europeans or those who want a Britain with weaker connection to the European Community? How much of this identity question is informed by an understanding of history and how much by myth, and what is the real difference in many cases in a world where history cannot be said to deal with absolute truths but a variety of truths!

This type of identity exploration is based therefore, on varying degrees of falsehood, either deliberate lies, ignorance or mistaken assumptions and conclusions. Is it any more false, however, or just false in a different way to the notion of national identity generated by Weimar-Buchenwald or the memories associated with a War memorial in a small English village? All history is an interpretation of the past and so to this degree all identity may be 'mistaken', but chosen, identity.

I have pursued these thoughts to illustrate the complexity of identity formation and exploration from powerful, indeed loaded, sites of historical significance. There is a serious responsibility identified here for those who interpret these sites in making explicit the extent of interpretation and reconstruction. We may be misleading visitors to identify themselves in inaccurate ways with the past and therefore influence their conception of themselves and others. This may be relatively harmless but in interpreting slavery as at Williamsburg, or commemorating the Holocaust as at Buchenwald, we may be reinforcing stereotypes which are socially and personally harmful.

## Individual identity and personal histories

Having considered history and identity on a grand scale, I want now to spend some time at the other end of the spectrum and consider personal histories and personal identity and the influence which the past is acknowledged to have on the self concept of people living in the present. I undertook a small scale investigation with seventy two First year teacher education students studying an introductory History education module in 1998. Students were asked to construct a public history of themselves and their families in order to understand some of the selective decisions historians might make. They were then asked to answer the following question: 'In what ways do you think investigating your family history helps you to understand your own identity?'

Not surprisingly all students felt that their understanding of their own identity was enhanced by investigating their family history: an obvious response to both the question and the task. What is interesting is the way in which students express their individual and family identities and the relationship between the two:

> My past defines who I am.
>
> This enables me to grasp a clearer understanding of myself and the way I live.
>
> This task prompted me to think about my identity and look back at what are essentially different parts of my make up. The family tree seemed to me to be like some kind of historical recipe to make me... I found it fascinating to think that all of my family history was occurring simultaneously in many different countries and the further back you look the more people come into play. It is amazing to think of the trials of life, the joy and the despair of all those people who contribute to my make up. I mean when ancestors in Ireland were starving due to the potato blight, some were in Austria, brewing beer while others were overseeing religious ceremonies in India.

A number of students reflected on the way in which they had an improved understanding of 'just where I fit within the wider family unit' as group or 'institution', and developing a sense of belonging whilst remaining unique:

> I would say that the process of researching your family history allows you to understand your position within your family, which in turn allows you to understand your identity. However it is important to remember that it is down to your judgment in the end. You shape your identity and although you are influenced by people or situations they cannot change your identity, this is something you develop yourself.

Two students also acknowledged that one might not like what one found out, particularly if the behaviour of one's ancestors was criminal.
Coming to terms with personal identity can be helped by investigating family history. What is discovered about a person's past may be disliked and rejected, but this still forms part of that person's identity because a conscious decision has been made to delete it.

A number of students mentioned specific historical events that defined their family's identity. Religious persecution was cited to explain the diverse nature of one family and the student's thirst for travel. Similarly, the Turkish invasion of Cyprus in 1974 explained the international links of another.

Many students mention their grandparents experiences of the Second World War and, in particular, financial hardships.

The influence of place was also important, not only in terms of specific ethnic origins ('I discovered I have roots from India, Tibet and Nepal to Scotland and Ireland.') but also in terms of regional identity especially the North South divide in England. A number of students listed the places in which they had lived and talked about regional accents as defining characteristics.

One student even spoke of his own lieu de memoire:

> Two years ago I travelled to India to see if I could find the family of my paternal grandfather over there; they live in Bombay. Even though it was my first time in the country I felt a sense of belonging. I sat on a swing in a small park where my grandfather used to play as a child, and I visited his old haunts. It was excellent. It was in effect, like going back in time, experiencing a living history.

Class, Culture, Religion and Values were mentioned frequently as identity characteristics which were illuminated by an exploration of family history:

> We can almost track down where our beliefs have sprung from. For example, looking at the history of my own family, it is made of both the middle and lower classes. Both sides of the family came together bringing two different classes of political beliefs with them. It is these merges of cultures that build a generation's 'identity' and certainly an individual's 'identity'.

The emphasis which students placed on inherited values as expressions of their identity is noticeable. Sometimes these were expressed in terms of religious faith but often in terms of providing an admirable role model:

> They may or may not, as individuals, have had any great impact on the world in general, but they were good, honest hardworking people.

> Much more of my nature and views coincides with family's than I had ever imagined and that in fact, many of the views I carry, are views that my predecessors have fought for. My Grandfather came down from Jarrow to London in the 1930's at the same time as the Jarrow marchers. He found work in London and settled in Edmonton. Although he came to London at the time of the famous march, he was not part of this event. However, he was so involved with the political events of the time that he would recall events as if he had been there. As a child I would listen to him recalling the historical events and now realise that his political views have been incorporated into my own value system as an adult.

These extracts illustrate the dimension of identity that has previously been characterised as Moral. The students responses clearly show their awareness of the influence of history on their identities in an individual, social, political and moral sense. They also indicate allegiances to groups such as the family, ethnicity, region and nation. The influence of place is a marked characteristic. I will end this discussion, however, with a quotation from a student which reminds us that not all identifications are of equal strength. In reflecting on the possibility of developing a European identity this student said:

> I have a strong personal identity which is quite detached from any
> need to belong to a National or International Group. I have a greater
> sense of belonging in my immediate environment, both at home,
> during leisure pursuits and now at University.

## MUSEUMS AND IDENTITY

The students' work and the memorials and venerated historic sites that surround us attest to the power of the past to help define who we are in the present. As has been suggested above, one of the key contributors to this process of remembering and constructing identity is the museum. In an article entitled 'Memory and Oblivion' David Lowenthal examined the problematic role which museums have in deciding what to preserve as 'keepers of the social memory' and what to forget. He talks of how 'collective memory sustained races and religions, neighbourhoods and nation states' and of how it was more important that heritage was seen as laudable than accurate. (1993, p.172). At the latter end of the twentieth century, museums can no longer solely sustain a laudable view of the past. When one in three Americans is reported as doubting that the Holocaust could have happened (Kakutani, 1993 cited in Lowenthal 1993, p.177) the presentation of our shameful memories takes on a certain urgency.

The problem for museums is not only to decide what to remember and what to forget but to acknowledge what it is suitable to represent. Lowenthal reports that some people feel that remembering events or aspects of our culture in a museum somehow condones it. Lowenthal cites the example of a museum to hunting which anti hunt protesters saw as 'part of our heritage which ought to be eradicated altogether... to museumise hunting implied approving of it. Inclusion in a museum signals moral endorsement no matter what display labels may say.' (Lowenthal, 1993, p.178). More recently the National Maritime Museum in Greenwich has been criticised for the unpatriotic and 'biased' nature of its new gallery, 'The Wolfson Gallery of Trade and Empire in the Eighteenth and Nineteenth Centuries'. Here the museum is attempting to explore some of the myths associated with British sea power and colonial exploitation and its legacies. The problem here, for some vociferous objectors, was not moral endorsement but the lack of it!

The process of institutional remembering and forgetting validates and excludes various identities. National state funded Museums are generally acknowledged as powerful and authoritative communicators of the National identity. Donald Horne sees traditional museums as trophy halls of imperial power (1992, p.173) as most collections in Western Europe grew from the spoils of nineteenth century imperial conquest.

The memorial and the museum will tend to present an official view of, for instance, the nation's story and as such these institutions are powerful symbols of a national identity. War memorials commemorating various conflicts throughout European history may be examples of this. Alternative versions may be mounted against them, using memories that have been previously 'overlooked' or 'forgotten', but they will tend to lack official support and essential finance until they in their turn, become official interpretations.

Examples of this can be seen in the presentations of history in the German Historical Museum in Berlin. Before the fall of the communist regime, this museum offered a Marxist interpretation of Germany's past. In recent years the museum has emphasised the common history of Germany before 1945 and has progressively underplayed the history of the German Democratic Republic. The final room of the museum, which had split to show parallel histories of east and west organised thematically, has more recently been reorganised into a confusing collection of images and artifacts arranged alphabetically. The museum has also been used to discredit the previous communist government of the GDR in an exhibition which portrayed the use of ritual in bolstering the regime. There was no suggestion that western governments had also used rituals in similar, if less obvious ways, and no acknowledgement that this exhibition itself performed a ritualistic function of discreditation.

In '*Museums and the Making of Ourselves*', Flora Kaplan recognises that 'Museums have long served to house a national heritage, thereby creating a national identity that often fulfilled national ambitions.' (Kaplan, 1994, p.9). These collections are now in public hands as a national legacy and it follows 'that legacy is then made available in museums for the enrichment, education and collective identity of the citizenry.' However unlike palaces, churches, temples and noble residences, there is no hereditary or ordained monopoly of access, possession and display of symbols of power. On the contrary, museums accommodate diverse contents and ideas and tolerate and even encourage access from a large differentiated population. (Kaplan, 1994, pp.2-3). She cites the example of the Nigerian initiative to set up Museums of Unity in each state that aimed to unite the various ethnic groups in the state, create mutual respect and present a coherent view of local, state and national entities.

The process of democratisation, which may have led to a continuing reinterpretation of a museum collection as more people seek to explore their identities and have them acknowledged, is not confined to state museums. In recent years there has been a massive growth in museums of many types where individuals and groups can develop an understanding of who they are. Local museums have, for a long time, presented local collections but these are now being made more relevant to the people who live in the locality they serve. Museums dealing with the histories of certain industries and various cultural activities, sports and past-times can fulfil a similar function for individuals exploring various aspects of their lives.

Museums presenting the cultures and histories of various social, ethnic, religious and political groups enable those groups to take charge of the interpretation of their own way of life as an explanation, consolidation and celebration of their identity within a pluralist society. For example, there are the museums of Gay history in Amsterdam and Berlin, the Koori exhibition in Victoria Museum in Melbourne, Australia, the various Jewish museums in major European capitals (Vienna, Berlin, London, Prague) and the museum of Labour history in London.

Even though museums are now accessible to more people, and more histories and identities are portrayed, the collections are still controlled by a minority in society who tend to represent the dominant group. 'To control a museum means precisely to control the representation of a community and some of its highest, most authoritative truths.' (Duncan, 1991, p.102). If museums are to 'become a centre where groups [are] working on their identity, their affiliation, their legitimacy' (Jeudy, 1986, p.44) then members of different groups need to be given more access to curatorial decisions about the displays which have the potential to reflect and explore the formation of their identities. Such initiatives are underway, for example, in the displays of the National Museum of the American Indian, New York where Native Americans have been involved in the selection and interpretation of their own artifacts. (See Chapter three)

It is tempting but simplistic to view the transmission of identity from museum to visitor, from ruling class to citizen as an uncontested process especially where national identities are concerned. Admittedly museums tell us what they want us to know and historians, consciously or not, write from a perspective influenced by their discipline and social background. But visitors are not empty vessels. Nick Merriman reminds us that people use the past in many varied and creative ways to suit their own needs and feelings about their position in the world (Merriman, 1991, p.131). Visitors may absent themselves if they feel that there is nothing in the museum for them or will interpret the message of the curator's presentation in line with their own preconceived ideas and understandings. There is no certainty that displays will be interpreted as expected. Merriman goes on to argue that museums should see themselves as services to the public so that the public can construct their own truths using the resources of the museum (p.138).

The process of identity formation and exploration in the museum is therefore an uncertain affair. The influence which museums, memorials and historic sites have on us will be modified by our own understandings of the past. These may be true in a traditional historical sense or as with some lieux de memoire they may be mythical.

Museums have a relationship to identity in that they present history and myth. They may enable us to recognise and gain a greater understanding of ourselves and our place in the world; they may help us to realise how our judgments and ideas have developed; they may develop an understanding of the development of processes within our society that fundamentally govern who we are as citizens; or they may ignore us altogether. Whatever the case, there is a relationship between us and these presentations of the past. I have arrived back at the idea of a relationship and given what I have argued above,

I see a vital need for that relationship to be critical; to question the basis of any historical interpretation and be prepared to seek out an alternative view. Without an understanding of how our relationship with the past works we are more vulnerable to prejudice, myth, and accepting an identification of ourselves and others which is ill informed and may be inaccurate.

In Chapter three we considered ways in which museums communicate with their visitors: ways, in fact, in which the critical relationship with the past may be developed. In the next section I want to consider ways in which 'living history' at museums and historical sites might contribute to identity exploration. I will then consider whether the consequent relationship with the past that is developed can be said to be critical. I examine this process from the point of view of the visitor and then that of the interpreter.

## LIVING HISTORY AND IDENTITY EXPLORATION

Earlier in this chapter I expressed the view that living history might be a particularly powerful form of developing a relationship with the past and therefore a useful method of identity exploration. Living history personalises history and can involve the visitor in interactive communication so that questions and perspectives that the visitor wants to address can be explored. The potential value of this form of museum presentation increases in the light of what has been said about involving visitors more in museums and providing them with opportunities to explore their own concerns and develop their own truths.

In this section I examine *four forms of identity* indicated earlier:

1. individual identity and the opportunities for the individual to gain an understanding of what it is to be a human being fulfilling certain social functions in western society (Schooling and shopping);
2. three aspects of group political identity; that of the citizen (in the United States), that of a member of the working class, (in the United Kingdom) and finally that of a pioneer, or at least the descendent of one, in an ex-colony (Australia);
3. issues of gender and race identity;
4. aspects of moral identity in terms of justice and the treatment of individuals.

Where appropriate I will also consider contributions made to the two forms of identity exploration I outlined earlier in the chapter: the operation of lieux de memoire and more frequently, the clarification of features of one's contemporary identity by making comparisons with similar features in the past.

### Individual identity

How can living history contribute to my own understanding of myself as I go about my everyday life? I will attempt to answer this question by looking at two situations common to most people living in the cultural context of western society which might illuminate the individual's identity when carrying out these functions. They are schooling and shopping.

*Schooling*

Many living history sites in America, England and Australia provide interpretations of schooling. This should enable the individual to develop a better understanding of schooling in the past and make comparisons with the present. The extent to which this helps individuals understand their role in modern society and hence illuminate an aspect of their identity, will depend on how much they can identify with what is being portrayed. This involves the consideration of similarities to and differences from the present and varies according to the various groupings to which the visitor belongs. The child who attends school will notice the similarities and differences in the layout of the school room, the materials available, the techniques used by the teacher to teach and to control, and the style of learning expected of the children. In some situations, for example the Ragged School Museum in London, children re-enact a school session in token costume using materials which poor Victorian children would have used. The teacher interprets in first person in an attempt to recreate the atmosphere of a Victorian classroom and the visiting children are in the role of Victorian children.

In Old Sturbridge Village, the schoolmistress that I saw was in role for part of the time but skillfully slipped into third person to answer some of the visitors' questions. She did not, however, teach visitors in the role of pupils but told us about schooling in nineteenth century New England. The experience was therefore quite different from that of the Ragged School and probably more suitable to her audience which was made up of children and adults, some of whom would have been parents and may have been teachers themselves. The different constituencies of visitors probably responded to the interpretation in different ways. As a teacher from another country I was interested in the training (or lack of it) and conditions of service of the schoolmistress, Miss Katy. The following examples are taken from her interpretation. In response to a visitor's question she told us that:

> Teaching is considered a part-time, unskilled teenager's job, often a first job. Men get twelve to twenty-four dollars a month plus room and board... this as a reward is less than they can make as field hands and so in the summer time the men will not apply for teaching jobs, they can make more money shovelling manure than they can teaching. Women teach in the summer, get six to eight dollars a month plus room and board.... and the more things change the more they stay the same...All you have to do to become a teacher is to be literate, have a good character reference, and that's it... It also helps to know someone in the school board. (Man's voice 'um um') But you don't have to have any special training. Howard Mann, that crack reformer up there in Boston is advocating that teachers go to school to be trained. In fact he set up in (indistinct) Massachusetts what he calls a normal school and you go to that for a couple of years and learn all these wonderful teaching techniques. What's so normal about learning to teach I'd like to know... I think it's a waste of taxpayers' money but that's what he wants to be able to do.
>
> (Sturbridge observation notes)

From this, I can draw parallels with my own concerns about teachers' salaries, equal opportunities and the value which society places on education. These concerns impinge on my professional role and therefore on my identity. To an American teacher it might place them in a certain tradition and help explain specific aspects of their job today.

The style of education is probably more interesting and meaningful to a wider audience:

> And then after you learn to read and write, after I teach you that, the rest is up to you class. You are responsible for your own education. (Male voice: oh!) How are you going to do that? It's easy. Just get yourself a book and memorise it. Page by page. You memorise a page, come up to one of these front seats... I know you are already to recite your lessons, are you not? (silence) Of course you are, I can tell, you have such a smile (subdued laughter) on your face knowing that you are brimming with knowledge... well, do your lesson and if then you do it to my satisfaction which means basically I look at the page and what you're saying looks like it is on the page (some laughter) then I will let you go and study the next page as a reward.
>
> (Sturbridge observation notes)

I quote this interpretation at length because it is clearly accessible to anyone who has been to school in the English speaking tradition and it is easy to make comparisons between the situation described here and one's own experience. This comparison can illuminate an understanding of oneself as a learner and reinforce or oppose one's attitudes and values with regard to education. As such, it can function as a stimulus to identity exploration.

The example also raises issues that it is useful to consider early on in this section. If apparent visitor attention, response and willingness to ask questions are a measure of success, then this interpreter was clearly popular with her audience. Her communication skills were effective and she projected a definite character who amused and conveyed information. The problem is that the information must be taken on trust. There can be no reference to sources. Additionally one of the ways in which she holds our attention is to be humorously opinionated. How widespread were these views in the 1830's and how typical was the situation she described? Visitors were invited to ask questions and these were answered with unattributed facts except for the mention of the ideas of Horace Mann but even this was glossed with her view. If opportunities exist in this situation for visitors to explore their identities by comparing their own experiences with the described situation and by considering the value issues which arise, do they do this conscious of these criticisms or are they unaware of the process in which they may be unwittingly involved?

### Shopping

All of the post eighteenth century sites visited described in this book offer examples of trading, usually through the shop. In modern society the choice

of where you buy your food or clothes may be an expression of your identity.
You are projecting an image through what you wear and what you eat. This
is often, in Britain at least, associated with social class, wealth, gender and
age group. In the sites mentioned here there is less evidence of this. In
Williamsburg there is a wig maker and a jewellery designer amongst other
purveyors of luxury goods, as one would expect from a centre of colonial
government, but in the shops at Beamish, Ironbridge, the Black Country
Museum in England, Sovereign Hill in Australia, and Old Sturbridge Village
in USA everyday foodstuffs, (often a thriving sweet shop), clothes shops and
hardware are interpreted. Two major issues arise here for the visitor. The
first relates to the goods on sale and how they differ from those available in
the present and the second relates to the prices and the means of exchange.

In this extract from an account of an interview with an interpreter at
Sturbridge we can see that he is concerned with making connections
between the children's own experiences of money and that used in
nineteenth century New England:

> Children may get out their money. And I may identify that as a
> learning situation. Children love being rich and have found out that
> people made fifty cents or a dollar a day. I pay no attention to the
> denomination.
>
> 'It's not National Bank so you must have made it yourself, put it back
> in your pocket before someone sees it. You can see the copper on side
> of a quarter so it must be forged!'
>
> (Sturbridge Conversation 2)

In this example, children are given the opportunity to compare their own
monetary system with that of the past and the goods on sale in a general
store with those on sale today. The experience is limited, however. In this
example the children are not in the role of customers and so they have no
opportunity to experience the process of buying, nor do they necessarily
have the opportunity to reflect on their role of customer in a wider economic
context of trade. At Sturbridge I saw the shoemaker attempt to put his work
in such a context that touched on the economies of nineteenth century
America and the Caribbean and the history of shoe sizes. Judging from the
visitors reactions and the lack of questions such an explanation had little
impact. Wider understanding can, after all, only be developed with the
visitors' consent!

The other element that is missing from the example drawn from the
Sturbridge shop is the relationship between employer and employee. As
Leone (1981) pointed out when analysing cookie making at Williamsburg,
such a relationship can only be appreciated if two interpreters are involved
in role-play and visitors can be encouraged to reflect on the economic and
social relationship between them.

## Group political identity

In this section I consider three types of group identity: the citizen of a

Nation as portrayed at Williamsburg, United States, membership of the working class as seen at English sites, and the colonial pioneers and their descendent as encountered in Australia.

## The Citizen of the Nation

Before considering Williamsburg as a major example of a site, where national group identity may be explored and its functioning as a lieux de memoire, I want to mention an incident I witnessed at Berkeley Plantation, Virginia. This is not really a living history site although the guide was wearing period costume. It claims to be Virginia's most historic plantation, the site of the first official thanksgiving in America when on 4 December 1619 early settlers came ashore and gave thanks for finding a safe landing place after a treacherous voyage. In 1621-2 the first Bourbon Whisky was distilled there and in 1862 'Taps', the military bugle tune, was first played for Union forces during the Civil War.

At the end of the guided tour around the beautiful brick plantation house (1726) which included scarcely a mention of a slave, the guide solemnly turned and addressed us:

> We are very proud of our heritage here at Berkeley as I'm sure you are too. So I'd like to say welcome home America - I know you'll enjoy.

The obvious patriotism and the irony that this home of America excluded the Native American population and had prospered on the exploitation of the forefathers of the Black American community, disturbed me. American identity is a complex and contested affair and needs far more exploration than a glib cliche.

Thankfully, other American sites which I visited took the issue of national identity seriously: aware that they could easily promote the propaganda myth of the American dream without a careful examination of the issues involved. To consider some of these issues and to assess the opportunities for national identity exploration and the function of a lieux de memoire, I want to now concentrate on Colonial Williamsburg.

In Part 2 we drew heavily on two major interpretative programmes at Williamsburg: The Family Tour of the Capitol and the three cases tried in the Magistrates Court. These, along with the tour of the Governor's house, which gave an insight into his way of life and the exercise of his power, and Carters Grove Plantation, where the issue of slavery is confronted, offer major opportunities to address modern American identity issues. The tour of the capitol enables visitors to consider the process of democratic legislation in the re-enactment of George Washington's first Bill and the administration of justice in the trial of the indentured servant (see pages 130-131). The Magistrates Court drew our attention to the way in which an official institution dealt with the rights of women and slaves, religious toleration, gender equality and the legal relationship between a man and his wife (see page 126). I am aware that I only saw a snapshot of the considerable interpretative programme at Williamsburg, but I was able to conduct an interview, used in Part 2, which drew attention to some of the issues of identity exploration. The interviewee emphasised the need to examine the histories of all social and ethnic groups who would have lived in Williamsburg and the possibility of showing 'how modern society was born' by comparing the challenge to the class structure in the last quarter of the eighteenth century to similar social fluidity in modern times. (Williamsburg Interview 1) In other words, to explore who has access to the successes of American style democracy and how this political system can be made to work.

This interpretative theme is clearly set out in the draft curriculum statement for teaching history at Colonial Williamsburg entitled 'Becoming Americans : Our struggle to be both free and equal'[3] to which I had access. I want to spend some time considering this document in detail as it demonstrates that identity exploration is an acknowledged part of the 'mission' of this living history site. The title alone 'Becoming Americans' is evidence of that. The plan clearly indicates an intention to explore and inform the identity of American visitors as American citizens. (For those of us visiting from abroad, this is presumably an opportunity to understand the historical roots of the identities of Americans today). It also exposes the values the curriculum planners bring to this process, their view of their visitors as learners, and their understanding of what American identity is.[4]

The plan is in the form of an introduction which sets out the way in which Colonial Williamsburg 'explores the history behind critical challenges that currently divide American Society and the historic forces that simultaneously unite it.' (frontispiece). The plan sets out a common interpretative programme intended to guide the specific 'stories' told at different locations around the historic town to 'show thoughtful men and women how Americans have always been engaged in reinventing the nation and redefining the qualifications for citizenship.' (p.3). It is the intention of the tours and interpretations at Colonial Williamsburg to find ways to present the larger story of American history 'in a miniature version appropriate to the restored streetscapes and furnished buildings of the eighteenth century town that serves as our classroom.' (p.7). To do this six themes or 'fields' are identified in the document's written text: diverse people, clash of interests, shared values, mediating institutions, partial freedoms and revolutionary promise. These themes are first applied to the history of Virginia and then used to outline six story lines covering the issues of:

1. land acquisition by European immigrants and the resistance to this by the local American Indian population (p. 23);
2. slavery as a defining characteristic of eighteenth century Virginian society (p. 27);
3. the changing nature of relationships within gentry families and parallel changes taking place in African American and Native American families and how certain family values, practices and structures became shared by the different groups (p.31);
4. the dramatic rise in consumerism (p.33);
5. independence from Great Britain through revolution (p.38) and finally
6. the religious lives of people from gentry to slaves and the push towards disestablishment precipitated by dissenters (p.42).

These themes are interesting as they typify key ways in which a modern capitalist democracy might be identified through addressing the key concerns of its citizens as identified by Colonial Williamsburg's curriculum planners: the relationship between different ethnic and social groups, the generation and distribution of wealth between these groups, the provision for economic well being and consumer choice, the role of the family in society, political independence and self determination and freedom of thought and the expression of those thoughts. I do not think that it is stretching the point too far to suggest that in these areas citizens identify themselves, positively or negatively, with their State and that this State identifies itself to the citizens of other states through the values expressed in this relationship.[5]

The document sees visitors as actively engaged in the clarification of these issues and the need to present them in a demythologised way:

> So indelibly is 'America's Williamsburg' inked into the mythology of our national heritage that those of us whom the foundation employs as educators are often hard pressed to help visitors see beyond the popular image to the substantive historical issues that we are eager to teach them. (p.1)

Such is the power of a lieux de memoire.

Moreover there is a recognition that the interpretation must make connections with the visitors present day concerns about the state of America, American values and its place in the world. I indulge in the following lengthy quotation because it sets out the mission of Colonial Williamsburg to educate American citizens in the nature of their citizenship in times of international and domestic tension. It is the tone of this document that fascinates me. There is a faint echo of Colonel Pitt Rivers. Life will improve without recourse to revolution if the evolutionary process is allowed to take its course. (Chapter two). In the Williamsburg document there is a clear commitment to the American constitution with all its faults and a belief that 'history' can help to appease 'informed' citizens concerns. Note the way in which the language is used to persuade the reader that this interpretation must be reasonable. It is also interesting that the planners are looking for a coherent narrative whilst acknowledging conflict and tension. It might be suggested that they will search in vain as different contesting groups construct different versions of the past.

The planners:

> start with the visitors own personal interests and concerns about contemporary life, which shape - or sometimes misshape - their understanding of the past. (p.2)

There follows a credo:

> We stand committed to teaching a history of early Virginia that describes and celebrates the diverse backgrounds of Indians, slaves and settlers. (p.2)

Americans...are mindful as never before of their diverse origins, resilient ethnic and cultural traditions, and long history of unequal and contentious relations. At the same time, growing numbers of men and women are coming to realize that they also believe - or want to believe - that 'We the People' represents a whole that is greater than the sum of the nation's many parts. In the search for a more coherent national narrative, including the part that Colonial Williamsburg can tell, we cannot minimize minority rights, smooth over the reality of social conflict in American history, or de-emphasize the country's extraordinary patchwork of unassimilated ethnic cultures and customs.

Informed citizens openly acknowledge the differences that divide us and the inconsistencies of our governing philosophy. Consequently, now more than ever, history learners anxiously seek historical precedents to bolster their hope that greater social diversity need not end in the disintegration of American institutions. They look to the past for guidance at a time when ethnic and racial hatreds are tearing apart settled societies around the globe and poisoning living communities closer to home. (pp..2-3)

And in a similar way the visitors:

need to know that our institutions have stood the test of time. Little by little, and often slowly and reluctantly, those who control society's institutions have yielded to irresistible pressures to share the country's opportunities more widely and to include an ever broader segment of the population in the civic enterprise. The narrative of this continuing struggle to expand or to limit the universal citizenship promised by the Declaration of Independence is the dynamic plot running through the story that we have taken for our central theme and call ('Becoming Americans'. (p.4)

The document proceeds to consider the 'distinctive values and beliefs that give this nation its identity' (p.8 of the document) and list the shared values and assumptions that were discernable by the middle of the eighteenth century which have become fundamental rights that all American's expect, (p.8):

- This country is a place where a person is free to improve his or her circumstances.
- Every citizen is entitled to pursue a private vision of personal happiness.
- Life and individual liberty are essential to that pursuit.
- These expectations are tempered by one more equality, which Americans understand to be every person's equal worth with rights to equal justice, equal opportunities, and equal access to the civic enterprise
- Every citizen has a right and a duty to participate in the governing of society. (p.8)

This sets a clear agenda for the content of the interpretations and the notion of citizenship to be developed at Williamsburg. Although this document acknowledges diversity, there does not seem to be much space for the visitor to develop and discuss alternative views of American democracy, to propose political alternatives or to be radical in their interpretations of the past and its illumination of the present. In practice, however, visitors may well disagree with the version of their identity presented here and dispute the liberal good intentions of the architects of 'America's multicultural experience and its experiment in secular democratic capitalism.' (p.5).

The examples taken from Williamsburg in Part 2 show attempts at explaining the ways in which the government and legislature operated in the colony and the administration of justice. But in neither of these controlled programmes was there much opportunity to question the interpretation. The visitor receives the interpreter's view. Identity exploration in this context is clearly intended and possible through the comparison of one's own views and those of the interpretation but it depends on the disposition of the visitor to pursue the inquiry.

The sites on the east coast of America visited for this study all dealt in some degree or another with national identity and were themselves, or at least contained, lieux de memoire. At Plimoth the myth of the pilgrim settlers, a lieux de memoire in itself, is confronted and attempts made, through rigorous historical research to display to the visitor the reality of the pilgrims' lives and their relationships with the Native Americans. This approach has brought the plantation into conflict with the almost sacred view held by some Americans that their founding fathers were genial, benign and reasonable men rather than those espousing less attractive bigotries current in the seventeenth century.

Old Sturbridge Village is making attempts to portray the stories of those who are not easily visible from the historical record. I was told of shifts in the interpretation to make the poor labourer, Native Americans and African Americans more visible. There were also attempts to interpret the more controversial and perhaps less marketable aspects of New England life as in the funeral. This is important, otherwise Sturbridge, in portraying the ideal of New England life, is in danger of reinforcing visitors stereotypes of rural wholesomeness, ignoring the hardships of country life, and the disputes and conflicts in small town society.

*English working class identity.*

The main sites visited in England were all concerned with industrial heritage and in particular the lives of the working classes. These sites have been subjected to considerable criticism for the view of working life portrayed and the irony that the identity most celebrated, that of the industrial labourer, are now cruelly dislocated by the global economics of the latter half of the twentieth century. The industries interpreted, particularly coal mining, have all but disappeared and the daily life and routine relating to these industries, vanished.

There is a good case here then for representing for future generations a way of life that was pursued by a large percentage of the working population and to which the identities of many people are related. There are, however, problems at these sites for identity exploration. When I visited Beamish the year chosen for interpretation was 1913, the most prosperous year for mining in the north East. This feeling of prosperity was reinforced by the way that the shops were stocked with a wide range of products and the positive tone of the interpretation. There is a grave danger that class relations are romanticised and portrayed only in the shopping street and at the funfair: the working classes in their Sunday best. The apparent prosperity may be falsely read as the general level of comfort experienced by working families in England on the eve of World War 1. There was a general lack of political discussion and little if any representation of trades unionism, industrial action, poverty, drunkenness and outbreaks of violence. It is to other sources that the unemployed of the present must turn to gain some historical insight into their own circumstances.

*Australian Identity: the early colonial settler.*

The main problems for the visitor to Old Sydney town in search of their early colonial roots are the quality of the reconstruction and the tone of the interpretation. This example of Australian living history is not distinguished by the care of reconstruction noticeable in America and England or the seriousness of the interpretative stance. Many of the buildings did not have interpreters on my visit but were peopled by rather ridiculous mannequins. A number of the buildings were in a poor state of repair and had to be viewed through chicken wire. The observatory floor had a drinks can crushed into it and there was a mineral water bottle on the table. In an article in the *Sydney Morning Herald* about the future of the 'attraction', Mr Paul Kiley, the manager of the company (Warwick Amusements) that owns an eighty year lease on the property, is reported to have said that 'the town could be described as somewhat rundown because it was trying to represent a town 200 years ago. The buildings and site were not suited to the Australian climate.' http://www.smh.com.au/news 9 September, 1999.

In short, on my visit it was very difficult to make any but an ironic relationship with the past. It was hard to recognise the description on the introductory display board that announced Old Sydney Town as the world's first faithful re-enactment of the Birth of a Nation. (The word faithful had been painted over the word authentic!).

The second problem was the tone of the interpretation that seemed to aim to amuse and titillate as much as to inform. The gaoler's story was full of presumably accurate information but told in a way that relished the gruesome detail. The interpreter made frequent asides to the women. 'You alright there missus.' In some ways this attitude to women and the roughness of his humour had a certain ring of authenticity. The day I visited, a re-enactment was staged of an Irish rebellion and the battle for Old Sydney Town. This was an opportunity to explore the relationship between the British Colonial troops and the Irish settlers, and in a general sense this was played out through the story, with some dialogue that had the tone of a broadsheet. But again the interpretation was often played for laughs. The mustering of the militia was re-enacted at the expense of the volunteering public, the flogging was accompanied by cheers and laughter, and the final battle complete with blood stained exploding dummies.

As an example of burlesque in the tradition of a British 'Carry On...' film it was highly successful and very enjoyable. It certainly raised many questions about the lives of early colonial settlers but serious identity exploration would need considerable support from other sources.

### Identity exploration in terms of gender and ethnicity

As we have seen when considering the relationship between traditional museums and identity exploration, such an activity is only possible when there is an issue or representation with which to identify.

#### *Gender identity*

Unlike many other forms of historical presentation gender issues are highly visible in 'living history' simply because of the number of women employed or volunteering as interpreters. I will firstly consider opportunities for understanding the historical roots of gender formation and then some contemporary issues of gender politics which arise. At all of the sites visited the traditional roles of male and female were observed with a few notable exceptions which will be discussed later. At the English sites working women were portrayed in domestic roles, preparing food, working in dairies, (Beamish and Kentwell), serving in shops (Blist Hills). Aristocratic female characters have also been observed at the Bank of England and as a guide to the state apartments at Hampton Court. At the American sites as in England there were plenty of opportunities to see men undertaking work associated with their gender and class and women doing likewise. In other words, in terms of modern gender politics a reinforcement of traditional gender and class roles. Rarely in these examples were the relationships between the men and women portrayed or reference made to them.

At Plimoth, because of the small site and nature of the interpretation, it might be expected that men and women would have been seen relating to each other. At other times this might have happened but on my visit the men were farming, house building and chopping timber and the women cooking, cleaning and lighting the oven. This reinforces the fact that unless an interpretation is designed to portray a relationship between groups and more than one interpreter is employed at a 'station' a significant element of understanding the dynamics of a social situation, in this instance of gender formation, is left to chance.

At Williamsburg the legal relationship between a man and his wife, for the lower classes at least, was portrayed in the Magistrates Court. A woman was brought before the court for singing bawdy songs, referring to King George III as the spawn of Satan and professing to be a supporter of Bonnie Prince Charlie. In the judgement there was clearly an expectation that the man should control his wife and be expected to pay a fine as punishment for her behaviour. As the man was poor his wife was subjected to the ducking stool.

Gender relations are also interpreted positively at Williamsburg. In the curriculum statement at Williamsburg, referred to above, there is an interpretative theme on the rise of the 'affectionate' family. As the traditionally authoritarian attitude of parents declined in eighteenth century Virginia, both parents began to take more interest in the upbringing of their children (p.30). This programme would provide opportunities to explore the changing gender roles of the sexes, their relationship to the public sphere (p.31) and the cross-cultural influences with African Americans. There is clearly an acknowledgement here that gender identity exploration is an important function for developing an understanding of modern American society.

The accuracy of gender roles is difficult to determine as much historical evidence arises from a man's point of view. How much information would a woman of the time have had of the political situation or contemporary religious views? I witnessed an interesting exchange at Plimoth where the female interpreter referred to her husband's opinions and religious views rather than her own.

Gender politics of the present can effect the historical interpretation in ways that could be seen to compromise its accuracy. At Jamestown I was shown around one of the ships by a female seafarer. I knew that there were female pirates in the seventeenth century, as this is well documented, but I did not have the opportunity to question her on her role and to explore the role of women in early settler voyages. No reference was made to women serving on board ship and so I was left with an uncertainty: was this an 'accurate' representation of the past or an example of a woman choosing to interpret a man's role.

In re-enactment societies, it is much more common to see women fighting alongside the men in order to make up the numbers and enable women who are tired of being confined to domestic duties to play what they see as a more exciting role. ('Women at Play' Channel 4 Television: 5 December, 1996)

This is contentious territory. Given the artificial nature of living history and the ambivalent relationship of modern interpreters to the characters they are interpreting does the gender of the interpreter have to match the role that they are playing? The portrayal of gender specific roles by interpreters of the opposite gender certainly provides a valuable opportunity for exploring identity. In any case, it may be argued that it is more important to observe contemporary ideas of equality of opportunity than submit to oppressive social practices of the period portrayed. From the point of view of identity exploration and the understanding of gender roles in the past, however, it is important that the historical and interpretative position is clear to visitors.

Living history sites are, of course, subject to current equal opportunities legislation. The *Living History Register Newsletter* No2 1995 has an article 'On Canadian Gender Problems.' Citing the BBC Radio 4 programme Woman's Hour, Pat Poppy reported on two Canadian examples where re-enactments had been influenced by equal opportunities legislation. Fort Henry, a re-enactment of 1867 had employed only men and Bellevue House, the home of Canada's first Prime Minister had employed only women. Bellevue house was forced by law to employ men and so had the prime minister's ailing wife visited by her brother and the doctor. Fort Henry changed of its own accord and employed women to depict soldiers. They had to change the drill as apparently some women could not cope. An archaeologist, who had uncovered evidence that women and children had lived on the site, said that the women portraying soldiers had absorbed 'skewed values' that men's work at the time was more fun that women's. The curator said that the site existed in the 1990s, not 1867.

*Ethnic identity*

Examples of the ways in which museums are attempting to democratise access through the representations of different ethnic identities and the increasing control of these presentations by the ethnic group portrayed have been cited above. In this section, I want to turn specifically to the possibilities for exploring ethnic identity at living history sites. There has clearly been a shift in interpretative stance at the sites on the East coast of America which was acknowledged by all interviewees. This has already been discussed in Part 2. At Williamsburg and Old Sturbridge Village there has been a growing recognition of the need to represent African Americans and Native Americans accurately. As a reminder, I think it is worth quoting these interview notes again:

> It's not that all these great white men are bad people but the perspectives of women, Blacks and the British are represented as well. So that people walk away not just hearing how great this wonderful Revolution was, but they have to come to grips with it themselves just like people two hundred and twenty years ago.
>
> (Williamsburg Interview 1)

At Sturbridge the shift has been to include the perspectives of Native American people:

> In 1830, Sturbridge was mostly a homogeneous WASP society. This period is post slavery in New England, in the South it was still strong. Seven percent of the population were Black Americans, Native Americans or Irish living in more urban areas like Boston and Newport. In the past few years, we have worked with local Native American people who have very definite ideas on how the past should be presented. The biggest shift is that ten years ago there was much more denial that native Americans were here.
>
> By 1830's southern New England was pretty much established. The typical average farmer would not meet many blacks or Native Americans. Ten years ago we would have denied and put down their existence. Now we are asking who were they? What do we know? How can we present their story?
>
> (Sturbridge Interview 1)

Part of the motivation for this is, it has to be said, commercial in the need to reach a wider audience:

> Income is an issue. It is a matter of survival. 90% of our income is
> earned on the gate and in the gift shop. How can we present a story
> which will interest and excite people if they don't see anyone black.
> They say 'What has this to do with me?' (Sturbridge Interview 1)

At Williamsburg the representation of African Americans as slaves has been difficult.    At the heart of the problem is the attempt to portray a morally repugnant institution as a part of everyday life with interpreters expressing historically appropriate attitudes. The problem for black interpreters in representing the degrading position of their predecessors was mentioned in interview. This is made harder when racist whites attempt to play the role of the 'massa' (Is this in turn a type of identity exploration?). The interpretation is, however, crucial to any understanding of how Williamsburg operated in the eighteenth century: 40% of the population of Virginia in 1770 were African American slaves. (Williamsburg 1994).

Interpreting controversy is a difficult area for living history exponents. Stacy Roth in her book *Past Into Present* provides an interesting account of the efforts at this site in October 1994 to sensitively present a slave market recreation. It was planned to be presented with a third person introduction and orientation, three different personal stories based on well documented cases, and followed up with a question-and-answer session for the visitors that had viewed it. Stacy Roth provides a full account of the event, the protests made, and the involvement of the press. (pp.169 -172).

The opposition to this theme of slaves and how they were sold at slave markets, raises the question of the right of a museum to present aspects of the past which are morally unacceptable today, and the notion mentioned by Lowenthal, and cited above, that museums can be seen to condone something merely by choosing to interpret it. One justification for the auction is that it is essential in this instance in order to develop an understanding of modern American society today:

> They [Interpreters] can also explore the constant tensions created by
> race-based slavery and the violence that erupted between whites and
> blacks, thus helping visitors to understand the root causes of problems
> that still plague American society. (Williamsburg 1994 p..30)

I would add that it is also important in terms of identity exploration that the historical relationship between blacks and whites be presented as accurately as possible so that ethnic identities and the changes in the dynamics between them can be more fully understood.

The overall impression that I gained from my visits was that the interpretation of African Americans by themselves was more advanced and developed than that of Native Americans. At Jamestown I was told that local communities had been consulted on the interpretation of their way of life but that those interpreters portraying the native Americans could well be from different tribes. At Plimoth Plantation a problem arose in the change of interpretative style in moving from the intense 'first person' atmosphere of the Pilgrim's Village to the roleless, national park ranger style, of the Native American interpretation. This was partly justified by the introductory film which explained that they spoke from a modern perspective and explained the history of the Native American people before and after English colonisation - myths about these people abound but the staff give an accurate look at the people who profoundly influenced the European settlement. (Plimoth field notes). The interpreters were indeed informative but the change of style was so dramatic that it seemed second rate and less interesting. From my perspective, it seemed as though the institution was implying that the identity of the Native Americans was less important than that of the European settlers. The separation of the visitor's experience of both groups also fails to explain the relationship between the different cultures which, as seen at Williamsburg, could help to explain aspects of various group identities in America today.

In Australia, only one interpretation of aboriginal life was apparent. At Old Sydney Town three Aborigines gave a dance demonstration but there was no explanation of their relationship to the European settlers and when BG visited a notice informed the visitor that 'they had gone shopping'. Aboriginal Australians need to look elsewhere to explore the historic influences on their identity. Chinese workers fare better at Sovereign Hill where their role in gold mining is interpreted by Chinese guides who speak different Chinese languages. (Australian Broadcasting Corporation, 11 July 1997)

Throughout this section and indeed throughout this chapter, I have been operating from a White European perspective which values museum presentations and sees them as vital representations of the past having the potential to help us understand ourselves and others. The people discussed here may have no need for such representations. The conceptualisation of the past and history in this way is essentially a 'western' construction. To the Aborigine and the Native American there is no institutionalising of the past in terms of a museum in their traditional culture. I cannot speak for them but would suggest that the search for identity clarification in a museum is a western practice and the need to recognise other identities in museums a western need. Where non-western cultures become involved in their own representation in museums it may not be so that their own people can improve their understandings of themselves but rather that the dominant western culture can. Seen in this way the whole argument for ethnic identity representation in museums and the consequent 'democratisation' might be no more than another strategy by the dominant culture to collect trophies and explain identities in ways in which it can understand and therefore control.

**Moral identity exploration**

So far in this section I have been examining living history as a possible way of exploring the identity of individuals and groups. Here I want to briefly consider another aspect of identity discussed above which has been described as moral identity or identity through judgement.

There are many opportunities in the examples presented here for individuals to identify with or reject the beliefs of individuals and groups in the past. The three cases portrayed in the Williamsburg magistrates court are expressions of eighteenth century values in terms of race, gender and freedom (slavery and religious toleration), demonstrated in a setting which symbolises justice. The puritanical views of the Plimoth pilgrims and the torture and punishment meted out to reprobate 'nasties' at Old Sydney Town all invite a comparison of values held in different historical periods with those a visitor holds today. Through this process the visitor is often involved in making moral judgments thereby identifying themselves with certain behaviours, attitudes and values which can be described as good and rejecting those described as bad.

At this simple level I decide that slavery is morally indefensible and I identify the enslavers as bad, consequently my opposition to slavery and those who share my views are identified as good, thus asserting my moral identity. At a more subtle level, I can begin to reflect on why I make that judgment and why the characters I am observing from the past do not. I begin to understand that moral values have changed and that perfectly decent human beings (by the values generally held at the time) were able to enslave other human beings because they did not see them as equal to themselves.

I will now cite one example which indicates that some visitors are making moral judgments but not necessarily understanding the historical context in which they are made. At Williamsburg, I saw Dr Baker the physician. In a conversation with a number of visitors he referred to 'damned popery' and referred to Native Americans as 'savages' because they were not Christian. These are perfectly accurate views for an eighteenth century Protestant to have but they upset some visitors who challenged him and became offended and somewhat irate. His communication with them had obviously been effective but they did not seem to understand that their modern values were inappropriate for the immediate interaction they were involved in. They had not bought into the game. They were identifying themselves as morally good and the doctor as bad but their apparent offence seems to suggest that they were not taking account of the changes and developments in moral values that had taken place in the intervening years.

## LIVING HISTORY AS IDENTITY EXPLORATION FOR THE INTERPRETER

So far we have considered identity exploration mostly from the point of view of the visitor, but living history also offers interpreters the opportunity to explore their understanding of themselves through developing characters in tune with their own personalities or taking on a persona of someone completely different.

Characters based on the interpreters' personalities are clearly developments and extensions of the interpreters modern identity. In building up a role it was suggested above that immersion in the character might enable individuals to gain another identity from which to view the present. I was told at Plimoth that this could happen and that the interviewee now viewed events in his own life differently as a result of interpreting a seventeenth century pilgrim.

At least one living history society - 'The Tabard Inn' - concentrates on what it calls first person plural recreation and develops its activities purely for the amusement and edification of its members. Interpreting late Elizabethan London:

> A typical TIS event re-creates some sort of social occasion of the
> period, such as an evening at a London Inn, a dinner hosted for
> neighbours, or a village fete; all participants are in costume, and
> represent characters who might have been present in such a setting,
> engaging in conversation and activities appropriate to the milieu.
> (Hadfield and Singman 1996 p.2)

The motivations of members are clearly related to the exploration of alternative identities:

> The first person experience offers an opportunity for a holiday from
> the world we live in: when we are immersed in a successful first
> person event, the worries and stresses of our modern lives are truly set
> aside for a time. It also offers a certain potential for individual growth
> and exploration: we free ourselves temporarily from the constraints of
> our own personal history and environment, and explore what sort of
> person we might be if we were not ourselves. At the level of first
> person plural, there are comparable personal rewards: the shared
> imaginative experience brings about a kind of bonding and mutual
> extroversion and a sense of community in a world where the old
> communities of family, church, and neighbourhood are crumbling
> before the forces of the economic and cultural market place. (Hadfield
> and Singman 1996 p.7).

It is also possible for interpreters to escape from the realities of the present to a time in their own past which they enjoyed. On a recent visit to Skansen in Stockholm, I was told by an interpreter sitting in the main room of a farm house that she had lived in a similar way in the north of Sweden in her childhood. She had followed the cattle up the mountains in the summer and made butter and cheese. She confessed that she was unhappy with modern life and could escape back to her childhood through working at the museum.

## CONCLUSION

Through this chapter I have shown many ways in which identity can be clarified through participating in living history events both for the visitor and the interpreter. I have also shown how such activities can foster and develop 'memories' which can contribute to the identity of individuals and groups, most commonly the nation, through the existence of lieux de memoire. In at least one example - Colonial Williamsburg - the contribution which the site can make to visitors understandings of their identities as American citizens is acknowledged and planned for.

If this argument is accepted, and I think that it is at least plausible, living history activities have the potential to powerfully affect the way in which we identify ourselves and others. This power can, however, only be exerted if the visitor pays attention. As with all such situations they can only have influence if the visitor watches and listens. Given the techniques described in Chapter seven for attracting and maintaining the visitor's interest and the general popularity of living history events, there is probably more chance of the visitor being absorbed by this form of historic interpretation than the traditional museum display. This is, however, only a presumption. The audience is seldom captive and visitors often manage their own pace and are free to walk away as and when they choose. Even if they are stuck in the school room or cannot leave a conducted tour they can switch off and immerse themselves in their own thoughts as a means of escape.

The potential power to influence the visitor is also apparent in the strength of live interpretation to communicate with the visitor: to establish a relationship with the past. We have encountered many techniques for saturating the visitor in more or less consistent representations of different aspects of the period interpreted that are perceived through and in turn stimulate all of the senses. The relationship between the visitor and interpreter can be sensuously contextualised and thereby strengthened. The illusion of travelling back in time or meeting someone from a bygone age is conjured up by the juxtaposition of these images. As we have noticed, however, there are limitations to this magic both in the susceptibility of visitors and in its power to communicate. Some visitors may be overwhelmed or bewildered rather than informed.

The other limitation to the power of this relationship rests in the interpreter's ability to communicate in ways which the visitor understands. This is particularly the case with first person interpretation where language and concepts may be alien to visitors. We have noticed the difficulty in simply understanding the language used at Plimoth, let alone the confusion brought about by changes in the ways concepts are used and attitudes expressed at different periods. The distress caused to some visitors at Williamsburg by aspects of the interpretation is evidence of this.

Not only are there problems in understanding what is presented but, if the relationship is to be two-way, the visitor must have the opportunity, confidence and knowledge to ask appropriate questions. This again can be more problematic in first person where the interpreter can only respond to questions couched in ways that they would have understood at the time being interpreted. There are also occasions when the control techniques used by the interpreters move visitors on before there are opportunities for conversation and the information first presented by the interpreter is difficult to interrogate. Although this relationship has the potential to be two-way it is almost always controlled by the interpreter.

These limitations considered, there is still a reasonable chance that living history establishes a strong and convincing relationship with the past for many visitors. If this is so it has considerable potential for influencing the identities of visitors through the opportunities which it offers for identity clarification by comparison and through exploring a lieux de memoire.

I do not think that it is over-stating the case to say that such activities can affect the way in which we identify ourselves and others. This is the espoused intention of at least one institution and to a certain extent lies behind most educational processes apparent in this study. Herein lies the chief responsibility of the interpreter. If identity exploration is to educate rather than transmit it must be critical. It must allow the visitor to understand what lies behind the ideas presented to them, what principles underpin their presentation, and then allow the visitor the freedom to reflect and reach their own conclusions. This for me would, in essence, be a critical relationship with the past. Is it apparent in 'living history'?

In many living history presentations the critical aspect is missing or relegated to the introductory film that is only seen by some visitors. It is not normally possible, given the desire to create an illusion of complete immersion, to expose gaps in the historical evidence on which the interpretation is based, or to show how the evidence might be interpreted in a variety of ways. It is also difficult to demonstrate longitudinal change except through a direct comparison between the past and the present. These criticisms are particularly appropriate for first person interpretations. Although Williamsburg and Plimoth are well researched and they have a reputation for approaching first person interpretation with care, it is difficult to demonstrate this in an interpretation. It must be taken on trust. In third person it is possible to discuss the sources and to indicate the stages in the development of a particular trade or lifestyle. An examination of alternative views is perfectly possible but was not witnessed at any of the sites we visited.

The responsibility for developing a critical attitude to the interpretations offered by living history exponents must therefore be addressed outside the interpretation itself. This can be undertaken in the introductory films and traditional displays which introduce many sites but I think the issue lies deeper. The ability to read all media critically is a prerequisite for modern life. It is recognised in some school curricula and marginalised in others. The example of living history is a good case for raising the critical agenda with regard to History education and the importance within it of helping children to see how interpretations of the past are constructed and to realise the formative powers that such interpretations may have on them.

People of all ages need to develop an inquiring attitude to all displays of history: in books, in museums, on TV, in advertising, and in the historical re-enactment. They all rest on certain assumptions which need to be shared if the interpretation is to be critically appraised. The alternative is to establish a situation where ideas about the past can be uncritically absorbed: ideas which might well influence our understanding about ourselves and others.

Living history is powerful, it is fascinating, it can be absorbing and entertaining but it can also be dangerous. I think I have shown here that it has the potential to raise questions in our minds about why we and others are the way we are and offers many opportunities for critically appraising our identities. But by its very nature this must be undertaken outside the interpretation by the reflective visitor, who has been helpfully prepared by the site visited and by their general education, to undertake such an activity.

I began this chapter with a quotation from Daniel Mato to which I now return. Identities are not 'legacies' passively received but representations socially produced, and - in a sense - matters of social dispute.' ( Mato, 1998 p. 598) This social disputation must be informed disputation by individuals aware of the ways in which identities may be constructed and explored. I think that if living history is approached with a suitably critical mind it has a great deal to offer such disputation.

---

Footnotes

1   In an analysis of the relationship between narrative forms, historical consciousness and moral identity, Kenneth Gergen has seen this as:
    One's definition as a worthy and acceptable individual by the standards inherent in one's relationships. In western culture, for example, to intelligibly narrate oneself as a stable and coherent individual (stability narrative), who is attempting to achieve a standard of excellence (progressive narrative), and is fighting against earlier setbacks and injuries (regressive narrative), is to approach a state of moral identity, of communal decency in the broadest sense. (Kenneth Gergen: Narrative, Moral Identity and Historical Consciousness: a social constructionist account.
    http://www. swathmore.edu/SocSci /kgergen1/text3.html 30/11/96)

2   In writing about identity this use of the word 'man' is interesting, insensitive, alienating, or irritating to say the least!

3   It is interesting in terms of identity that the term American should be used to relate to only one country - the United States of America - when it can apply to the whole continent: the appropriation of a whole continent by one nation's identity!

4   This links with 'critical literacy' and the notion of the writer's ideal reader. Readers can contest the writer's image of themselves. As Queitzsch (1998, p.288) wrote, 'I am constituted by discourses that have motivated me to work with students to see how language is political and situated, in order that we find ways to reverse discursive practices and open up multiple ways 'to be.'

5   I use the term 'state' loosely to refer to the country; i.e. United States or constituent 'states; i.e. Virginia or New South Wales. There is, however, a sense in which the citizens of a constituent state might be concerned to identify with these issues within their region.

*Chapter ten*

⚜

# CONCLUSION

In this book, we have attempted to explore the rich and complex phenomenon loosely termed 'living history'. We have considered the implications of this approach for history education in a world in which living history is becoming increasingly popular. The chapters of Part 2 have raised many issues for the presentation of history and these have been extended through BG's analysis and discussion of the language used and GB's examination of identity issues. Any conclusions from such a journey must be tentative and temporary but we hope that those of you reading our work will feel that your experiences of living history, either as a visitor or an interpreter, have been illuminated and that future experiences will be more intriguing. You may like to look back at the vignettes which concluded Chapter One to see if you now read them in a different light.

## METHODOLOGY

One of the major problems in undertaking this study has been methodological. Living history is an extremely fluid and ephemeral phenomenon. It is never the same twice, even if scripted, and will be perceived in many different ways depending on the disposition, former knowledge and experience of the visitor. We have attempted to mirror this fluidity in our approach. We visited incognito and only then conducted our interviews so that we had a visitor's context for what we were told. We also attempted to record living history encounters without interpreters being aware of what we were doing. Many visitors record their experiences using cameras and videos but these are obtrusive. The problem for us was in trying to be less noticeable so that we reduced the effect of the presence of the researcher.

On some occasions, we have attempted to illustrate the fact that no two visitors share the same perception of a living history encounter, by observing sites separately and on different occasions. The variables are, however, too numerous to control and the weather is beyond the reach of even the most skilled researcher! The study was essentially qualitative in approach.

Our concluding remarks are therefore based on our shared and various experiences of the process of writing this book. They are predicated on our own disciplinary backgrounds and our individual analyses of language and identity. They are partial, in both senses of the word, and tentative.

## LIVING HISTORY AS AN INTERACTION

The study of the text of the interaction between interpreters and visitors in the context of a museum or historical site suggests that it is usually dominated by a practised and confident interpreter. However visitors' understanding cannot be totally controlled by the interpreter as we saw in Part 2. We are concerned with a living relationship between human beings - confronting all of the problems of everyday communication. The interaction between interpreter and visitor does, however, seem to be dominated by the participant who changes the 'field' or content of the discussion. Furthermore, the visitor will always make their own interpretation of the 'message' of the interaction based on their experience.

One of the major appeals of the living history approach appears to be the way in which it humanises the exploration of the past, since it involves the visitor in some form of 'human' interaction. Here 'feedback' is feasible, whereas in the other methods of peopling historical space, such as models accompanied by audio characters' speech or commentary, it is not possible. This can only be achieved if the interaction allows the visitor to ask about what they want to know. Of course, knowing what you want to know can be problematic.

As we have seen in Part 2, the possibility of feedback is also influenced by the context of situation as identified in the setting. The completeness of setting helps visitors to contextualise historical knowledge making the learning experience more powerful. This brings with it, however, an additional problem. Because the setting is presented as a 'complete' version of the past it is difficult for the visitor to deconstruct the history being presented and to understand the interpretative stance of the reconstruction.

## LANGUAGE AND MEANING IN THE LIVING HISTORY APPROACH

As we have shown, the past can only be a construction through the medium of language that has currency and meaning in the present. By analysing the function of speech in the living history approach, meaning is seen as a form of negotiation in which the utterance or move is a fundamental element. All genres, including speech, use moves to negotiate meanings. The limited analysis of transcripts carried out so far, would suggest that this genre shows that it is as constrained by the rules of functionality as it is spontaneous. Whether the different contexts of situation, such as the museum, historic site, public place or school building, produce different text types using living history is something yet to be discovered.

## LIVING HISTORY AS EDUCATION

Living history is a potentially effective way of interesting people in, and communicating about, the past - but is it History? There are problems in relation to authenticity, the impossibility or even desirability of recreating the past exactly, and how to demonstrate the sources on which the practice and activities are based. The unrealistic conception of living history by some exponents, who see it as a way of *recovering* the past, is hard for traditional Historians to accept. Indeed, we suspect that individual's attitudes to history are an area of great complexity because they result from the interaction of personal, individual experiences within the social mores of the prevailing culture.

Our belief is that the conceptualising of the past is a continuing process of change and flux, to which a variety of approaches can contribute. *Critical evaluation* of this process will help to prevent the conception of the past becoming a mere 'product' of our cultural understanding rather than our experience, learning and awareness of the complexity of the construction of history in actual practice. This critical understanding of the past is particularly important for all involved in living history, whether they are interpreters, visitors, adults or children - in a formal learning situation, as on a school trip, or pursuing a leisure activity or on a family outing. This need to be critical is a basic tenet of our view of education especially in History and literacy.

Given the cultural and linguistic diversity of school students, teachers have the responsibility to continue to critically reflect on their practice in order to achieve equitable outcomes for all students. This necessitates reflection on school visits to elicit students' understanding of their 'historical experience' and its relationship to History-in-school. A school visit to a historic site or museum is not just an 'outing' to be evaluated on the basis of 'value for money' but an experience of learning history to be criticised. This can be done in terms of the method by which the past is interpreted and communicated and the consequent view of the past that it gives us.

For other visitors there are few formal structures for criticising the living history experience in this way. Unless, that is, the museum or site arranges its interpretations to draw visitors attention to these issues. It may well be that the critically reflective habit has to be caught at school - the beginning of a process of lifelong learning.

In England and Wales, it might be argued, there has been a significant switch away from critical education to the delivery of skills particularly focusing on numeracy and literacy. In English primary schools in the past two years, this has meant that the humanities subjects, along with the creative arts and, to a lesser degree, science and technology, have been marginalised. As we saw in Chapter Two, in Australia and the United States, it has been suggested that most of a child's understanding of the past is likely to be developed by museums and heritage sites. This may soon be the case in England and Wales.

History teachers must now be prepared to prioritise a critical understanding of their marginalised subject over an approach which merely rehearses the subject content and teaches research skills.

## LIVING HISTORY AS A METHOD FOR IDENTITY EXPLORATION

We have claimed that the living history approach may be able to help us understand more about ourselves and others. What are we 'buying into' when we view, talk and read about the past? What do we understand about the constructed nature of presentations of 'others' and those with whom we wish to experience feelings of affiliation and shared 'humanity'? Because of problems of falseness, either partiality, mistaken interpretation or just absences of knowledge, it is necessary to be aware of the limitations of the living history approach. Without this awareness, we are basing our identity exploration unthinkingly on a vision of the past, seemingly complete, but which in fact did not exist.

Given this situation, it is even more vital that living history sites explain their methodology to visitors and encourage a critical response to their interpretations. This may enable people to develop a critical attitude to media presentation of which living history is a particularly complex and powerful form and consider more carefully the impact of their experiences of History on their conception of themselves and those around them .

# Appendix I

## The Main Sites Visited

Living History sites and re-enactments in England, the east coast of the USA, and Australia were visited in the period 1994 - 96. This list is provided as very often illustrations and examples cited come from the experience of these visits and the reader may want to check the place or event to which reference is made. The description or argument could be difficult to follow if each time we had to repeat details of the main distinguishing features of the phenomena.

## Sites in England

### Bank of England Museum, Threadneedle Street, London.

Summer 1994 event organised called 'People, Prices and Profits', to celebrate 300 years of history at the Bank of England. *Costumed characters* from the time of William and Mary were used to present the intrigues and power struggles that led to the creation of the Bank in 1694. Characters were people from all walks of life and included the founder of the Bank, William Peterson. Characters usually approached visitors, using the first person.

### Beamish: The North of England Open Air Museum, Beamish, County Durham

This collection of buildings, transport and artifacts, rescued and rebuilt as they once were, tells the story of the North of England just before the outbreak of World War I. Started by Frank Atkinson and his small band of colleagues in 1970, the Museum is a serious museum with large and important collections of historical objects and documents. The displays are based on detailed research and scholarship. Through use of *costumed demonstrators* (Museum staff in costume) the Museum aims to explain the region's history and educate the visitor. The guide book states that the staff are proud of their North-East heritage and are keen to pass on information and answer questions. A town, farm and coal pit village are reconstructed with buses and trams, trains and a railway station ; a park and bandstand; shops, a dentist and solicitor; a drift mine and colliery.

### The Black Country Living Museum, Dudley, West Midlands

A turn-of-the-century community recreated on a twenty-six acre site. Reconstructions including a chemists, hardware store, chapel, boat dock, canal, electric trams, fairground, cinema, pub, and some cast iron houses. *Guides and shopkeepers* in traditional dress answer questions and talk about how their shop was recreated and compare past practice with the present, usually using third person. In the buildings on the site, *craftsmen and demonstrators* recreate the activities of a time when the 'Black Country' was the heart of Industrial Britain, originally based on the mining of coal and the working of iron. It is the name given to a region which is to the west of the city of Birmingham.

### The Ironbridge Gorge Museum, Shropshire.

A World Heritage site occupying the banks of the river Severn which flows under the world's first bridge built of iron. The Museum is a collection of sites dedicated to the industrial past, one of which is Blists Hill Open Air Museum - a reconstruction of a Victorian town with canal tugboat, pub, printing shop, squatter's cottage, chemists, tin church and what is claimed to be the world's only operational wrought-iron foundry. Also has a Victorian fairground with the 'rides' and stalls of the period, a schoolhouse, and a bank which has Blast Hill's own currency which can be spent in the site's shops. Aims to create the atmosphere and way of life of a working Victorian community, which is presented by *costumed demonstrators*.

### Kentwell  Long Melford, Suffolk

Perfectly preserved sixteenth century house where historical recreation takes place at particular times of the year. Recreation aims to be as authentic as possible of everyday life in the year chosen, which is different each year. Those taking part dress, talk (first person) and follow activities of the year chosen so that visitors feel they are meeting *figures from the past*. For what is called the Great Annual Re-creation, a Gatehouse and Time Tunnel are erected across the avenue leading up to the house with everything beyond being 'Tudor'. Our data included experience of one of the writers as a costumed character with a visiting school and other writer as a tourist; both visited the participating school and talked to children and their teachers. Also interview with a 'seasoned' re-enactor.

### Mountfitchet  Stanstead, Essex

Called 'the Castle Time Forgot', a carefully researched reconstruction to show life in eleventh century Britain, provides replication of castle and surrounding village with buildings populated by life-size models of people. Visitors' approach triggers short tape-recorded monologues for the models. However in May 1996, the site had been used by 500 primary school children and their teachers wearing period clothing or armour, to recreate the attack by King John's army on the castle in 1215.

### Royal Armouries  The Waterfront, Leeds

Opened in 1996, being built for £42.5 millions, is Britains' largest post-war leisure development and national museum. 'In every area of the Royal Armouries you'll see stunning demonstrations of combat using real and replica weapons.' 'Some of the collection needs an outdoor setting to be seen in its true glory.' Authentic jousting tournaments are performed in the attached tilting yard. Programme provided of timed, staged, first person lecture/monologues by *costumed interpreters or actor-interpreters*. Museum project is a private and public sector cooperative exercise providing the Royal Armouries, previously housed at the Tower of London, with a new headquarters and more opportunities for displaying extensive collection of arms and armouries from various periods.

### The Sealed Knot, the Battle of Marston Moor, held in the grounds of Rigby castle (2 July 1994), near Harrogate, Yorkshire.

Three hundredth anniversary of two key events in the English Civil War - the siege of York and the Battle of Marston Moor. Included authentic campsite with opportunities to talk to the soldiers; a living history display depicting the Royalist command post in York; miniature war-game of the event; historical exhibitions; period theatre performances; music and other entertainment; a trade show; a themed craft tent; beer tent.

Weekend event organised by John Libourne Productions on behalf of Gillespie's

Scottish Malt Stout who were particularly interested in highlighting the vital part played in the battle of Marston Moor by the Scots army. Estimated that 8,000 took part in the re-enactment event. The Sealed Knot is a re-enactment society established in 1968 by soldier and military historian Brigadier Peter Young with the aim of promoting research and interest in the English Civil War. Claims to be Europe's longest existing and most experienced re-enactment society, with more than 3,000 members.

## Warwick Castle, Warwickshire

Re-enactments are performed in the castle grounds by the Golden Lions of England, a medieval society interested in the order of the Knights of the Garter in the specific year of 1361. Within the castle there is an audio-visual presentation using model people called 'Kingmaker - a preparation for battle'. In 1450, King Henry VI conferred on Richard Neville the title of Earl of Warwick and he became the power behind the English throne for some twenty years. 'Kingmaker' presents the lead up to the events of 1471 when the Earl called his men to arms for what was to prove his final battle, the battle of Barnet. *Costumed interpreters* from the Golden Lions answer questions in this presentation, and also demonstrate at set times, period armour and fighting techniques to visitors and school parties.

## Sites in the United States (East Coast)

### Boston Tea Party Ship and Museum, Massachusetts

On board the brig Beaver I, a full-sized working replica of one of the three original Tea Party ships, visitors are whipped into a frenzy of protest by *costumed interpreters* who lead them around the ship, harangue them with political speeches, and involve them in hurling a bale of tea into the harbour.

### Colonial Williamsburg, Virginia

Virginia's Historic Triangle publicity leaflet claims that Colonial Williamsburg is America's largest living history museum where you can stop and talk with *costumed actor historians* - many demonstrating historic trades and crafts. The buildings of the former colonial capital of 18th century Virginia have been restored on their original foundations and are interpreted through a mixture of first and third person explanation. Original historic buildings, 88 in all, survive including the Governor's Palace, Capitol, Courthouses, Magazine and Guardhouse, shops, workshops, taverns and gardens. The emphasis of the interpretation, involving visitors in semi-scripted re-enactments is on the contribution of the 18th century people to the ideals, ideas and culture of present day America.

Carter's Grove Plantation (eight miles SE of Colonial Williamsburg) presenting the way life was lived along the James River for four centuries, has a stately mansion and slave quarters representing the material conditions of life for the Chesapeake inhabitants - both black and white. The interpretation stresses the richness and complexity of slave culture and the few material goods the slaves possessed.

### Jamestown Settlement, (6 miles from Williamsburg), Virginia

A living history museum using a mixture of first and third person interpretation to recreate life in America's first permanent English settlement of 1607. In a full-scale, reconstructed Powhatan Indian Village *historical interpreters* discuss and demonstrate the Powhatan way of life. They grow and prepare food, tan animal hides, make tools, weapons and pottery. There are reconstructions of several longhouses, a garden and ceremonial dance circle. Visitors may then move on to the pier where there are full-size replicas of the ships which brought the first English settlers. They are able to board a ship and talk with an interpreter about the four and a half month voyage. The visitor then arrives at the Triangular James Fort, a recreation of the original built by settlers in 1607, where interpreters are engaged in military activities and various tasks of daily life such as gardening, using a bow and arrow, playing games and tying nautical knots. Interpreters encourage visitors to handle many of the 17th century reproduction items.

## Mystic Seaport Museum , Mystic, Connecticut

This Maritime museum grew from the Marine Historical Association founded by three Mystic residents in 1929. It actively pursues the collection, presentation and exhibition of artifacts and skills related to the seas and connects people with their heritage by offering a place to explore, study, experience and appreciate the sea's influence on American life. Ships including a whaler, a fishing schooner, and a training ship are preserved alongside workshops, a school, bank, printers, chandlery, shops, and rigging and sail lofts. The exhibits are interpreted by a mixture of *costumed and uncostumed interpreters*, using explanations, re-enactments and role plays which are scripted and improvised. The museum includes a unique preservation workshop where visitors come in contact with the staff, tools and timber needed for this work.

## Old Sturbridge Village, Sturbridge, Massachusetts

An outdoor history museum, non-profit making and educational, presenting the story of everyday life in a rural New England town during the 1830s. The landscape is recreated with original buildings brought to the museum site from all parts of the region. Historical costumed staff members, called *interpreters* , demonstrate and discuss with visitors the life, work and celebrations of early 19th century America. They use a mixture of first and third person conversation as they enact fictional characters constructed from historical sources to be true to the period. The architectural collection, started by the Wells brothers in 1938 , now includes a meeting house, stores and shops, a printing office, bank, parsonage and a fine town house. The rural buildings on the site include a district school, saw and grist mills, a pottery, a blacksmiths, a carding mill, and farm houses. There are special demonstrations of spinning and weaving, basket and broom making, and an extensive education programme and days of special events.

## Plimoth Plantation, Plymouth, Massachusetts

This living history museum brings to life the experiences and concerns of the Pilgrims and the Wampanoag Indians. 'Talk with Pilgrims as they go about their daily tasks, meet members of the crew who helped bring the ship, Mayflower , to its destiny in Plymouth, and come face to face with Native People who will tell how the arrival of these colonists impacted the lives of their ancestors, the Wampanoag, 'People of the Dawn'.' Dressed in reproduction period clothes and speaking in the dialect of their character's home region, museum staff as *interpreters* take on 'the roles of actual inhabitants of the colony; they become living artifacts.' These interpreters inhabit a reconstructed site on land similar to the original settlement at Plimoth. Complete with stockade, fort, fort/meeting house, animal pens and gardens, the diverse housing styles reflect the vernacular buildings of rural England and the colonists' varied backgrounds. They contain painstakingly accurate reproductions of the furniture, tools and cooking equipment known to have belonged to the pilgrims. Food is grown and livestock raised using traditional methods. In Hobbamock's Homesite interpreters discuss the Indians who lived in south eastern New England. The settlement represents the encampment of a Wampanoag family group. Original dwellings of bark are reproduced and ways of growing and cooking are demonstrated.

### Yorktown Victory Center, Yorktown, Virginia

This Museum of the American Revolution invites you to relive the spirit, sacrifices, and the ultimate glory of the men and women who were the Revolution. The struggle for independence is told through thematic exhibits of original artifact, period graphics, documents and objects as well as in film and living history. In the recreated Continental Army camp visitors are invited into the tents of a surgeon, an officer, and soldiers to participate in their daily routines. On a typical post-revolutionary farm site carpentry, cooking and cloth dyeing are demonstrated by *costumed interpreters*. The Centre claims to enrich visitors' understanding 'of the forces that compelled people to offer their lives, fortunes and honor in the cause of independence.'

## Australian Sites

### Hyde Park Barracks, Sydney, NSW

'A modern museum with a rich and dark history' first used as a convict barracks (1819-1848). Linked with Historical Houses of NSW recreation 'Tried and Transported' in which tourists are tried at a court in the Police and Justice Museum, transported on a tall ship around the harbour, and then spend the night in the prisoners' canvass hammocks at the Hyde Park Barracks, where creaks and moans of sleeping prisoners are recreated by the Museum's 'soundscape'. Prisoners are 'freed' next morning after breakfast. Characters such as the Sergeant, Judge, Bosun, Crewman No 1, and the Gaolers use first or third person speech.

### Old Sydney Town, near Gosford, NSW

Recreation of the Birth of a Nation 1788-1810, one hour's drive north of Sydney is 'a living adventure where you will feel the charm of the past mixed with the harsh realities of colonial life.' Land bought by architect Frank Fox in 1969 used to create a replica of the first settlement, the area of the shallow valley of the Tank Stream, Sydney's first water supply. The land chosen is very similar to the original site and buildings including a windmill, church, inn, and various shops continue to be built. *Distinctive characters* in costume make use of first or third person. There is a time tunnel entrance and visitors are supplied with a timed programme of 'street theatre' events such as a convict trial, capture of an escaped convict, and the punishment of flogging are performed in the relevant parts of the site. Horse or bullock drawn wagon rides provide transport to the animal park where native and farm animals can be fed. Craft demonstrations in the shops and buildings throughout the day and there's a programme of Aboriginal education and entertainment at Bungaree's camp as well as educational activities in the model classroom for visiting school parties.

**Sovereign Hill, Goldmining Township,** Ballarat, Victoria

One and a half hour's drive from Melbourne, this is a non-profit community based organisation run by the Ballarat Historical Park Association which opened in 1970. Employs '150 people including professional museum staff and, most importantly, tradesmen, craftsmen, builders and others with special skills necessary to its historical presentation.' Period represented is 1851-1861, the first ten years of the township. 'Underground Mining Museum tells a more recent story when company mines developed and engineering techniques overtook muscle power.' 'Thrust is towards an activated museum with heavy emphasis on working machinery and exhibits, and a reliance upon costumed *interpreters*, to tell the story.' Time tunnel entrance and use made of first and third person speech. Visitors can try their hand at panning for gold, ride in a 'Concord coach hauled by a team of five-in-hand', see re-enactments, shop in the various main street shops, and have their photographs taken in period costume. Volunteers known as Friends of Sovereign Hill also appear in costume.

**Swan Hill, Pioneer Settlement,** Victoria, Australia.

'Australia's original Heritage park' is 'an inland river township where townsfolk carry on their everyday business and tradesmen toil at bygone activities. ' 'Wander through the homes of our pioneer grandparents, the Log Cabin, the Station Homestead, Keats Cottage and Australia's first Kit-Home shipped out from England in a wooden crate - the Iron House.' Recreates late 19th century era of the paddle steamer on the River Murray. At night there is Sound and Light Show in which visitors are driven around the settlement in a special transporter. Uses *costumed guides* to explain the various activities, usually using third person.

# *Appendix II*

## Two examples of different interpreters using first person with a group of visitors

*Example 1*

*Sovereign Hill, gold rush town, Ballarat, Victoria, Australia*

Costumed interpreter dressed as a salesman of the period (mid nineteenth century) was using first person to address a large group of men, women and children in the open air whereas the interpreter described at the Black Country Living Museum used third person with a small group of three visitors in the overcrowded confines of the recreated pawnbroker's shop.

| | |
|---|---|
| <u>Interpreter</u> | I had hoped to attract the attention of a large group of working diggers up from the diggings of Ballarat to witness my device in operation, but I dare say that those gentlemen who are here are just that, hard working miners up from the diggings of Ballarat ....(indistinct) .. I'll call upon your vast local experience ..... you as a working miner here on the diggings of Ballarat, as you go deeper and deeper in your quest for gold are you, or are you not, required to undertake one particular task which literally requires great care.... perhaps you explain to the ladies what that most dangerous of tasks is, Sir ? |
| <u>Man in crowd</u> | Something to do with the timbers.... |
| <u>Interpreter</u> | I think we're getting there, Sir. Now you're talking about the placing of the explosive charge. How about once you set a charge and light your fuse, what do you do? |
| <u>Man</u> | Run for hell. |
| <u>Interpreter</u> | Exactly!.... Now we are getting some where. Perhaps I should explain. This good gentleman here and the other hard working miners of Ballarat when setting a charge are required to use a length of so called safety fuse. |

The interpreter continued with his talk and a subsequent unsuccessful demonstration that ended with a bang!

**Field:** The interpreter is trying in this section of transcript to get the men in the group, who he addresses as 'miners', interested in what he intends to sell - a new form of 'safety fuse', a 'device' for use with 'explosive charges'. He makes use of technical terms as he describes the process. However this is a demonstration and his choice of words enables him to define and explain both terms and process. The text has something of the characteristics of an instruction register.

He invites a man in the crowd, possibly selected by eye contact, to explain to the 'ladies' what was that 'most dangerous of tasks (in gold mining)'. By means of rising intonation he prompts the man to complete the utterance with the expected noun (nominal) group 'the placing of the explosive charge'. The man guesses 'something to do with the timbers', an aspect of the setting in which miners worked, whereas the interpreter was concerned with the dangerous task that the miner had to complete - set and light the charge! His choice of 'placing' (of the explosive charge) is an interesting example of **nominalisation**, a term used to describe what we do when we express a process as a 'thing' or Participant and commonly used by writers to pack more meaning into a clause. (e.g. 'create' becomes 'creation' or 'long' becomes 'length). There is only one verb in a clause, but there can be several nouns.

One reason for using nominalisation is that it enables the speaker or writer to move an argument along, to condense what has been described into a 'thing' or 'concept' that can become the subject of a further action or elements to be related. This usually creates a more dense and abstract text and 'in our culture, such use of the language is perceived as more formal and more mature. Often given a high status' (*Exploring literacy in School History* p127). Nominalisation is used extensively in the written texts of science, technology and the humanities. However although this interpreter does use nominalisation it is difficult to know whether he does this consistently to construct and develop arguments or whether this is an aspect of talking 'in period' which of course may be based on familiarity with written primary sources of the period such as instructional materials or advertisments for technical products.

**Tenor:** The interpreter replies to the visitor's tentative answer with the plural 'we're getting there' rather than 'you're' getting there. By using the plural, the suggestion is that he and the visitor are working together to construct for the crowd a consensus as to what was the most dangerous task miners had to complete so that they would therefore be interested in any product that could make the task less dangerous. However the interpreter uses a verbal pattern commonly observed in use by teachers in classrooms, particularly at the secondary stage of schooling. It consists of the teacher asking a question, to which the pupil or learner responds, and then the teacher evaluates the learner's response (Sinclair, J. and Coulthard, R. 1975, *Towards an Analysis of Discourse*, Oxford University Press, Oxford.) The interpreter's second question 'what do you do?' prompts the realistic reply 'run for (like?) hell' from the man in the crowd. The interpreter greets this with an emphatic 'Exactly!' In this context, the reply is seen as an acceptable response to the situation he has outlined and also that the man has at the second attempt, given the answer the interpreter was seeking. A humourous answer is acceptable in this interaction in which entertainment is important to sustain the crowd's interest. Also this three part interaction, (question, response, evaluation) enables the interpreter to maintain control of the situation and to resume his interaction with the larger group - the crowd.

In this example of an interpreter using the first person form of the living history approach, he has assumed the character of a travelling salesman who would need to keep the attention of these 'working diggers' and their women folk. However we don't know and never will, whether such 'hard working miners' would have replied in similar fashion since they might have been more knowledgeable about setting fuses.

The role the interpreter assumes, enables him to structure the interaction and thereby control what is a large audience. He consistently refers to the women in the crowd as 'ladies' and the men as 'gentlemen' (generalised human Participants) and individual women as 'ma'am' and men as 'sir'. In role as a travelling salesman he has perfected a 'turn' in which he carefully controls the crowd by tending to single out individuals by eye contact to whom he asks a question which can be answered briefly and preferably humorously. These interactions with individual visitors could not be described as sustained dialogue - they were if anything, more like interruptions to what at times almost developed into a rambling monologue. The relationship between the crowd and the speaker is unequal. It is the interpreter who asks questions not members of the crowd.

In first person the interpreter used the pronoun 'I' and addressed the crowd as 'you' or more correctly the men, making attributions to them such as 'your vast local experience as a working miner' and ' your quest for gold'. This would seem to be a linguistic technique whereby not only does the interpreter role-play a character but can cast members of his audience, individually or as a group, as a character or type, by means of ascribing human characteristics, personality traits or specific experiences to them.

However, if there is little or no opportunity for visitors to respond 'in character' they will not have had to think or feel in the way in which a 'person from that past' would have done. To formulate a meaningful and quick response in such a jointly constructed conversation the 'man from the crowd' would be more likely to draw from his own (modern) experience. Addressing visitors in the second person may be a means of creating the impression of interaction, but it is probably superficial if the role and identity is only ascribed to the 'other' by the interpreter and the visitor does not have the opportunity to at least experience how they might reply or interact in the role ascribed to them.

*Example 2*

*Old Sydney Town, New South Wales, Australia*

Interpreter in the role of gaoler has been telling a group of visitors (mostly families and young children) about how prisoners in the colony were treated. They are all crowded into a small cell in a stone building. The gaoler spoke in first person as he told the group about the fate of one particular prisoner.

gaoler          ...so we hung him...the rope broke. So we hung him
                again...the rope broke, so we hung him a third time. The
                rope undone. The Rev Marsden said yes. He told us it was
                divine intervention. God did not want this man to die. We
                were forced to let him go....died a week later of internal

|             |                                                                                                                                                                                                                                                                                                                                                                                                                                                                                                   |
| ----------- | ------------------------------------------------------------------------------------------------------------------------------------------------------------------------------------------------------------------------------------------------------------------------------------------------------------------------------------------------------------------------------------------------------------------------------------------------------------------------------------------------ |
|             | injuries from when he'd fell off the platform. But the paperwork was clean for all that (subdued laughter)...any questions before I go?                                                                                                                                                                                                                                                                                                                                                             |
| child       | Mummy I got a ...                                                                                                                                                                                                                                                                                                                                                                                                                                                                                  |
| gaoler      | I don't think I can answer that kidda (laughter) you give it to me in English and I'll give it a go...if I don't know I'll make it up. ..you won't know the difference will yer (laughter)... right anybody got, I'll say that again....anybody like to ask anything, about absolutely anything they have seen today, have not seen, would like to see or would like to know anyway (murmurs from the crowd).. oh you're a boring mob! (some laughter).. you should have gone to the reptile park... they don't swear do they.. they just sit there...what do you want missus? (woman's voice but indistinct) I don't want to know about the programme missus, that's not my problem. |
| woman visitor | ... you asked if we had any questions ...                                                                                                                                                                                                                                                                                                                                                                                                                                                        |
| gaoler      | oh all right....I've got one for you though....where do babies come from? (laughter).... the next thing on your programme (breaks off and addresses the crowd) this 'orrible woman what was coughin before..her health's at fault..she...ah go away I hate yer .. kidda. (laughter)                                                                                                                                                                                                                  |
| child       | I hate you                                                                                                                                                                                                                                                                                                                                                                                                                                                                                         |
| gaoler      | down at the King's Head tavern at half past the hour of twelve, on the earth right out the front or in the beer garden, there'll be a musket demonstration and a bit of a sing song...the story explaining weapons we would use and the way of life for a British soldier..all right?... after that at the lower end of town a bullock yoking ....demonstration ...                                                                                                                                   |

**Field:** This is an extract from a longer transcript and is the section where the interpreter changes from his character role in which he has told an anecdote about the fate of a prisoner, to asking if anyone has any questions. His statement that if he doesn't know the answer to questions he will make it up and his audience will be no wiser, is a criticism often aimed at the living history approach in that information may not be referenced in the same way as written texts, so how can the validity of historical information be evaluated by the interpreter's listeners? A further point about this text is the way in which, although the interpreter has to some extent come out of first person role by inviting questions, he seems impatient about having to address the woman's queries about the events of the programme. Her request is a demand not for historical information but rather information about the events on offer to visitors. The subject matter of her question if answered appropriately would mean the interpreter changing his role to that of the more traditional role of site guide who provides information about facilities and events rather than recreating the past by means of talk.

The strategy he chooses is to answer a question with a question - 'Where do babies come from?' Was this a personal comment because the woman was noticeably pregnant or some form of 'put down' because the woman had taken him literally. She was someone in the crowd who took him 'at his word' thereby accepting his offer to answer questions 'about absolutely anything'. The interpreter eventually brought the episode to a conclusion by changing the theme or field of the discourse to that of directions and details of other events that were shortly due to start. Thus he maintained control of the situation in his own time and way, and by the choices he made from the language resources available to him.

**Tenor:** Indirect ways of negotiating speech purposes, related to cultural conventions concerning power differences and politeness, can be observed in conversations. Identifying the forms of negotiation and the moves that participants make, it may be possible to recognise that what is at stake for the interactants, differs from one participant to another. Those involved in the different roles of interpreter or visitor in an interaction may be involved in a process of negotiation so as to achieve either shared or different aims (Schirato and Yell, 1996, p.83). The maintenance of self esteem for interpreter and visitor, may mean that in an exchange the issue of power is 'at stake' or 'under negotiation' in the speech genre in a way that does not occur in the text types in the written medium. For instance, the interpreter as gaoler may maintain control through a judicious use of anecdote, joking and what Stacy Roth refers to as 'painting a picture in conversation'. (Roth, 1998, p.98) However his invitation to ask any questions can lead to a change in subject matter and he may have seen the woman's question as a challenge. As Roth (p.99) has suggested, unrelated questions may be at the least, an indication of the visitor's interest being else where.

In the living history approach, maintaining dialogue in a conversational form may be particularly difficult where sites have large numbers of tourists, since such visitors may speak a different language, or be only too aware of time constraints and physical exhaustion. A coach may be waiting at a specific time to transport them to another place or event. Their purposes may be at odds to those of the interpreter and both may have more than a single aim in mind. The interpreter as a paid member of staff may be required to entertain, educate and ensure safe crowd movement around the site as well as 'bring the past to life.' Quite a challenging role management task!

# Bibliography

Anderson, David (1997) *A Common Wealth: Museums and Learning in the United Kingdom*, A Report to the Department of National Heritage, United Kingdom: Department of National Heritage

Anderson, Jay (1984) *Time Machines: The World of Living History*, Nashville: American Association for State and Local History

Anderson, Robert *The Daily Telegraph*, UK, 27 Nov 1997

Australian Broadcasting Corporation (1997) *Wish You Were Here - Australian Tourism Studies*: Episode 6: 'Heritage Tourism', 11 July

Baldwin, G. (1996) 'In the Heart or on the Margins: a personal view of National Curriculum History and issues of identity', in Andrews, Richard (ed.) *Interpreting the New National Curriculum*, Middlesex University Press

Benhabib, S. (1987) 'The generalised and concrete other: the Kohlberg-Gilligan controversy and feminist theory', in Kittay, E.F. and Meyers, D.T. (eds.), *Women and Moral Theory*, New Jersey: Rowman and Littlefield, p. 166

Bennett, Oliver (1995) 'Queuing for the dungeons', in *The Sunday Telegraph* Review section, 14 May

Bennett, Oliver (1996) 'Go west and find the child within', in *Weekend Telegraph* Travel section, 9 March

Bennett, Tony (1995) *The Birth of the Museum: history, theory, politics*, London: Routledge

Berry, Kevin (1995) 'Past times revisited', in *Times Educational Supplement* Going Places supplement, 3 February

Berry, Ralph (1986) *How to write a Research Paper*, second edition, Oxford: Pergamon Press

*Black Country Museum* (1994) Pitkin Pictorials

Brennan, Geraldine (1993) 'Getting to grips with history', in *Times Educational Supplement* Going Places supplement, 24 September

Butt, D. et. al. *Using Functional Grammar* National Centre for English Language Teaching and Research, Macquarie University, Sydney, New South Wales

Button, James and Walker, David M (1997) 'Why don't we teach Australian children about their past?', in the Melbourne newspaper *The Age*, electronic version, 7 April

Cassidy, Sarah (1999) 'World view to shrink yet broaden too', in *Times Educational Supplement*, 18 June, p.22

Chadwick, A. and Stannett, A. (eds.) (1993) *Museums and the Education of Adults*, Leicester: National Institute of Adult Continuing Education

Channel 4 Television, UK (1996) *Women at Play* 5 December

Christie, Frances (ed.) (1990) *Literacy for a Changing World* Australian Council for Educational Research (ACER)

Christie, Frances (1997) 'Learning the literacies of primary and secondary schooling', in Christie, Frances and Misson, Roy (eds.) *Literacy and Schooling*, London: Routledge, pp.47-73

Claxton, G. (1993) 'Minitheories: a preliminary model for learning science', in Black, P.J. and Lucas, A.M. (eds.) *Children's Informal Ideas in Science*, London: Routledge.

Coffin, Caroline (1997) 'Constructing and giving value to the past: an investigation into secondary school history', in Christie, Frances and Martin, J. R. (eds.) *Genre and Institutions: Social processes in Workplace and School*, London: Cassell Academic, pp.196-230

Colonial Williamsburg (unpublished) Draft curriculum statement for teaching history at Colonial Williamsburg entitled 'Becoming Americans: Our struggle to be both free and equal'

Cooley, Pam (1997) 'Monsieur's menu', in *Times Educational Supplement* Going Places supplement, 7 February

Cowan, James G. (1992) *The Elements of The Aborigine Tradition*, Shaftesbury, Dorset: ELEMENT

Cummings, Elizabeth (1993) *Assessment of the relative educational value of interpretive techniques used at Hampton Court Palace*, Tyler Jones Designs

Davis, G, (1988) 'The Use and Abuse of Australian History', in *Australian Historical Studies*, **23** (1991) October as quoted in Evans, M. (1991, p.142)

Department of Culture, Media and Sport and the Department for Education and Training, UK (2000) *The Learning Power of Museums - A Vision for Museum Education.*

Department of National Heritage (1996) *People Taking Part*, Historic Royal Palaces Agency (HRPA), United Kingdom

Derewianka, Beverly (1990) *Exploring How Texts Work*, Primary English Teaching Association (PETA), Australia: Newtown, NSW

Derewianka, Beverly (1996) *Exploring the Writing Genres*, Minibook 8, United Kingdom Reading Association

Dingman, Bambi (1996) 'A Guide for Accurate Educational Interpretations'. reprinted from *Recreating History* **5** (May issue), http://www.recreating-history.com/character.html

Dray, W.H. (1995) *History as Re-enactment*, Oxford: Oxford University Press.

Duncan, C. (1991) 'Art Museums and the ritual of Citizenship', in *Exhibiting Cultures: The Poetics and Politics of Display*, Karp, Ivan and Levine, Stephen, (eds) Am Assoc Mus/ Smithsonian Institute Press, Washington, pp.88-103

Duncan, C. and Wallach, A. (1978) 'The museum of modern art as late capitalist ritual: an iconographic analysis', in *Marxist Perspectives*, Winter, pp.28-31

Eggins, Suzanne and Slade, Diana (1997) *Analyzing Casual Conversation*, London and Washington: Cassell

Evans, Michael (1991) 'Historical interpretation at Sovereign Hill', in Rickard, John and Spearritt, Peter (eds.) *Packaging the Past? Public Histories*, Melbourne University Press, Australian Historical Studies, pp.142-152

*Explaining History in School History,* (1996) Sydney: Metropolitan East Disadvantaged Schools Program

Fairclough, Norman *Language and Power,* London: Longman quoted in Schirato and Fell p.85

Falk, John H. and Dierking, Lynn, D. (1992) *The Museum Experience,* Washington, DC: Whaleback Books

Fautley, Chris (1997) 'Of cabbages and kings', in *Times Educational Supplement* Going Places supplement, 26 September

Gilbert, Elizabeth (1996) 'Latter-day knight fever', in *The Sunday Telegraph,* 1 December

Gergen, Kenneth (1996) *Narrative, Moral Identity and Historical Consciousness: a social constructionist account*  http://www. swathmore.edu/SocSci /kgergen1/text3.html

Grosset, S. (1997) 'The ship that's homeward bound', in *Weekend Telegraph* Travel section, 15 March

Guest, C.D. (1994) 'Living History Villages as Popular Entertainers', *New England Journal of History,* 51 (Fall issue), pp. 57-66

Hadfield, V.J. and Singman, J.L. (1996) 'First person Living History: Insights from Amateur Practice', as delivered at the Association of Living History Farms and Museums Union of Spirits Conference, Plimoth Plantation, March

Halliday, M.A.K (1978) *Language as a Social Semiotic: The Social Interpretation of Language and Meaning,* London: Edward Arnold

Halliday, M.A.K. (1985) Spoken and Written Language, Geelong: Deakin University Press quoted in Eggins & Slade, p.37

Halliday, M.A.K. (1994) An *Introduction to Functional Grammar,* 2nd edn., London: Edward Arnold

Halliday, M.A.K. and Hassan, R. (1985) *Language, context and text: Aspects of Language in a Social-semiotic Perspective,* Geelong: Deakin University Press

Halliday, M.A.K. and Martin, J. R. (1993) *Writing Science: Literacy and Discursive Power,* London: The Falmer Press

Hammond, Jenny, Burns, Anne, Joyce, Helen, Brosnan, Daphne and Gerot, Linda (1992) *English for Social Purposes: A Handbook for Teachers of Adult Literacy,* Sydney, Australia: National Centre for English Language Teaching and Research, Macquarie University

Heller, A. (1982) *The Theory of History,* London: Routledge

Hooper-Greenhill, Eilean (1994) *Museums and their Visitors,* London: Routledge

Hewison, Robert (1987) *The Heritage Industry: Britain in a climate of decline,* London: Methuen

Hewison, Robert (1989) 'Heritage: an interpretation', in Uzzell, D.L. (ed.) *Heritage Interpretation Vol 1 'The natural and built environment'* pp.15-23, London: Belhaven

Horne, D. (1992) 'Reading Museums', in *Papers in Museology* 1: Acta Universitatis Umensis: Department of Museology, Umea University, pp.168-175

Horne-Jaruk, Honour (1996) Issue 7, September, *Reading History*

Hudson, Kenneth (1987) *Museums of Influence*, Cambridge: Cambridge University Press

Hunter, Kathleen (1988) *Heritage education in the Social Studies*, ERIC Digest EDO-Sc-88-10

Hunter, Kathleen (1992) *Heritage Education: What's Going On Out There?* ERIC NO ED358002

Husbands, Chris (1996) *What is History Teaching?: Language, ideas and meaning in learning about the past*, Buckingham: Open University Press

Jerman, Betty (1998) 'Take the little urchins to task', in *Times Educational Supplement* Going Places supplement, 6 February

Jeudy, Henri Pierre (1986) Memoires du social. Paris PUF (Collection: Sociologie d'aujourdhui), cited in Andre Desvallees: 'Museology and Cultural Identity' pp.50-77 of *Papers in Museology* 1: Acta Universitatis Umensis: Department of Museology, Umea University 1992

Kaplan, F. (1994) 'Museums and the Making of Ourselves', London: Leicester University Press

Kenworthy, Christopher (1995) 'Dressed to kill', in *Weekend Telegraph*, 1 April pp. 8-9

Kirsch, Fritz (1996) 'Living History Theater', in *Camp Chase Gazette*, http://nememis.cybergate.net/-civilwar/articles.html

Klein, Reva (1997) 'Model of correction', in *Times Educational Supplement* Going Place supplements, 7 February

Leone, Mark P. (1973) 'Archaeology as the science of technology' in Redman, C. L. (ed.) *Research in Current Archaeology*, John Wiley and Sons: NY and London, pp.125-150

Leone, Mark P. (1981) in Gould,R.A. and Sciffer,M.B. (eds.) *Modern Material Culture: The Archaeology of us*, London, Academic Press

*Living History Register Newsletter*, No2, 1995

Lorentz, S. (1966) 'Reconstruction of the old town centres of Poland'. pp.46-7, in *Historic preservation today*, Charlottesville VA: National Trust for Historic Preservation at Colonial Williamsburg, cited in Lowenthal, D. (1985), p.46.

Lowenthal, David (1985) *The Past is a Foreign Country*, Cambridge, England: Cambridge University Press

Lowenthal, D. (1993) 'Memory and oblivion', *Journal of Museum Management and Curatorship*, 12 no 7, pp.171-182

Lumley, Robert (1988) (ed.) *The Museum Time-Machine: Putting cultures on display*, London: Routledge

MacDonald, S. (ed.) (1993) *Inside European Identities*, Providence/Oxford: Berg

Malcolm-Davies, Jane (1995) 'Idle Conversation?', in *Museum Visitor*, pp.23-29

Marshall, Catherine and Rossman, Gretchen, B. (1989) *Designing Qualitative Research*, Newbury Park, London: Sage Publications

Martin, J. R. (1989) *Factual Writing: Explaining and challenging social reality*, 2nd edit. Oxford: Oxford University Press

Marbin, J.R. and Rothery, J. (1986) *Writing Project Report No 4* (Working papers in linguistics), Linguistics Department, University of Sydney quoted in Eggins and Slade p. 57

Martin J.R. et. al. *Working with Functional Grammar* London: Arnold

Marx, K. (1852) *Eighteenth Brumaire of Louis Napolean*

Mato, D. (1998) 'On the making of Transnational Identities in the Age of globalisation: The US Latina/o - Latin American case', *Cultural Studies* 12 (4), pp.598-620

May, Peter (1996) 'Ages Alive', http://www.fijimagic.com/features/agelive.htm

Merriman, Nicholas (1991) *Beyond the Glass Case: The Past, the Heritage and the Public in Britain*, England: Leicester University Press

Middleton, Christopher (1997) 'Once more unto the breeches', in *The Sunday Telegraph* Sunday Review, 5 January

Neumark, Victoria (1997) 'Pinch of salt', in *Times Educational Supplement* Going Places supplement, 26 September

Nora, Pierre (1996) *Les Lieux de Memoire* Editions Gallimard (1992). English Language edition *Realms of Memory* (1996), forward by Krtizman, Lawrence D. , trans Goldhammer, Arthur, Columbia University Press

Norrie, Jane (1996) 'So what did the Romans do for us?', in *Times Educational Supplement* 2 Resources, 1 March

Patrick, John J. (1992) *Heritage Education in the School Curriculum: Defining and Avoiding the Pitfalls*, Heritage Education Monograph Series produced by National Trust for Historic Preservation, Washington, D.C., ERIC NO-ED365600

Pedley, Brian (1996) 'Burning the House of God', in *Weekend Telegraph* Outdoors, 24 August

Peterson, David (1988) 'There is no Living History, there are no Time Machines', *History New* 43 (September/October), pp. 28-30.

Pond, M. and Childs, A. (1995) 'Do Children Learn History from "Living History Projects"?', *The Curriculum Journal*, 6 No. 1 Spring, p.47-62

Paynton, C. *Language and Gender: Making the Difference*, Geelong: Deakin University Press, quoted in Schivato and Fell p.85

Pynsent, R.B. (1994) Czech and Slovak ideas of Nationality and Personality, London: Central European University Press

Queitzsch (1998) *Boys and Literacy*, Australian Curriculum Corporation teaching material, (pp.274-289)

Reeve, John (1996) Review of Graeham Talboy's book *Using Museums as an Educational Resource: An Introductory Handbook for Students and Teachers*, in *Times Educational Supplement*, 10 May

Richmond, Simon (1994) 'A night in the life of a felon' in *Sunday Telegraph* Travel section, 20 November

Robertshaw, Andrew (1997) 'A dry shell of the past: Living history and the interpretation of historic houses', in *Journal of Association for Heritage Associations*, 2 (3: July, Historic Houses)

Roth, Stacy F. (1998) *Past into Present: Effective Techniques for First-Person Historical Interpretation*, Chapel Hill & London: The University of North Carolina Press

Sacks et al. (1974) 'A simplest systematics for the organization of turn-taking for conversation', *Language* **50** (4) pp. 606-735 quoted in Eggins and Slade, p.323

Schatzman, L and Strauss, A (1973) Field research: *Strategies for a natural sociology*, Englewood Cliffs, NJ: Prentice-Hall as quoted in Marshall and Rossman 1989, p.113

Shafernich, Sandra, M. (1993) 'On-Site Museums, Open Air Museums, Museum Villages, and Living History Museums', *Museum Management and Curatorship* **12**, pp.43-61

Schrirabo, Yony and Yell. Susan (1996) *Communication and Cultural Literacy*, Allen and Unwin, New South Wales, Australia

Singman, Jeffrey (1996) 'The Future for the Past: A blueprint for early modern living history', reproduced from the journal *Aristo* at http://users.aol.com/maist/future.htm

Stone, Peter (1988) 'What Value Living History?', in **JEM** 9 Summer, pp.21-23

Slater, Jon (2000) 'Where facts get real', *Times Educational Supplement*, 26 May, p.23

Spencer, Diane (1995) 'Museum staff failing adults', in *Times Educational Supplement*, 10 November, p.15

Stanton, Nicki (1986) What Do You Mean *'Communication'? How people and organizations communicate*, London and Sydney: Pan Books

Sutcliffe, Jeremy (1998) 'Age weakens thirst for knowledge', in *Times Educational Supplement*, 22 May

Sword, Ford F. (1994) 'Points of contact', in *Journal of Education in Museums*, **15**, pp.7-9

Tallboys, Graeham (1996) *Using Museums as an Educational Resource: An Introductory Handbook for Students and Teachers*, London: Arena

The Living History newsletter, Spring 1994

*Timecars*, Designed and produced by The Design Advertising Group, Hanover Square, Leeds. (no date)

Wallace (1981) 'Visiting the past: History Museums in the USA', in *Radical History Review*, **25** (3), pp. 63-69 cited in Merriman, Nicholas (1991) *Beyond the Glass Case: The Past, the Heritage and the Public in Britain*, Leicester, England, p. 15

Wallace, Mike (1996) *Mickey Mouse History and Other Essays on American Memory*, Philadelphia: Temple University Press

Walsh, Kevin T. (1992) *The Representation of the Past: Museums and Heritage in the Post-Modern World*, London: Routledge

West, Bob (1988) 'The making of the English working past: a critical view of the Ironbridge Gorge Museum', in Robert Lumley (ed.)*The Museum Time-Machine: Putting cultures on display*, London: Routledge, pp. 37-62.

Worsley, Giles (1998) 'A Challenge to Berlin', *Daily Telegraph*: UK, arts and books section, 27 June

# Index

*A Common Wealth: Museums and Learning in the United Kingdom* 37
Aborigines 35, 126, 194
ALHFAM; Association for Living Historical Farms and Agricultural Museums 17, 68
Anderson, Jay, *Time Machines* 13-16, 92
Angelcynn 18
armour 9, 13, 83, 87, 114,
armour, accuracy 114
Ashmolean Museum , Oxford, England 48

Battle Abbey, East Sussex, England 72
Battle of Hastings 11, 72
Battle of Marston Moor 11, 23, 108, 113, 126
Beamish, The North of England Open Air Museum (England) 48, 69-70, 73, 183, 189, 190
Bennet, Tony, *The Birth of the Museum* 46
Berkely Plantation, Virginia,USA 184
Black Country Museum (England) 48, 69, 71, 74, 106, 148, 159, 183
Black Country Museum, Tilted Cottage 69, 74-75, 148
Black Country Museum, Pawnbroker's shop 159-161, 166
Blist Hills, England 47, 58, 190
Boston Tea Party, Boston, Massachusets, USA 129
Brigantia 18, 83
British Museum 20, 50
buildings, authenticity 73-77

Cashel Abbey, Eire 53
Chauncey School 85
Christie, Frances 139, 145, 148, 163-164, 166
Circumstance of Place (linguistic) 149
Circumstance of Time (linguistic) 149
Claxton, Guy 30, 168
Coffin, Caroline 140
Collingwood, R.G. 32
communication, one way 51, 53
communication, two way 51, 58
Context of Culture 28, 141-147
Context of Situation 28, 141, 145, 147-162
control, mechanisms of 118
control, use of communication 127
conversation, as exchange 161

conversation, power differences 163
costume, accuracy and authenticity 113
costume, adult discomfort 98
costume, children's embarrassment 96
costumed guides/interpreters 118, 121, 149, 152
culture, Aboriginal 194
culture, definition 141
culture, differences 145

Dark Tourism 81, 90
Department for Education and Training 38
Department of Culture, Media and Sport 38
Department of National Heritage 37, 91
Derewianka, Beverly 139
Disneyfication 20
Dow, George Francis (Salem 1907) 47
Dunham Massey, Cheshire, England 96

edutainment 20
Eggins, Suzanne and Slade, Diana: *Analysing Casual Conversation* 141
electronic field trips 86
Ellis Island Immigration Museum, New York, USA 54
English Civil War Society 19, 92
Ephesus, Turkey 52
Ermine Street Guard 83
Evans, Michael 27, 75-77, 89, 101
explanation, factorial 151
*Exploring Literacy in School History* 140ff

fairs, Living History Trade 88
fairs, Renaissance and Medieval 87
fictionality 8-9
Field (linguistics) 149
Fiji Museum 36
funeral 24, 102, 116, 188

Galleries of Justice, Nottingham, England 80
genres or text types 142
Gergen, Kenneth 170, 199
German Historical Museum, Berlin 178
Ghost Riders 19
groups 12-20
Gunnersbury Park Museum 82

Halliday, M.A.K. 139, 141, 146-147, 152
Havel, Vaclav 171

Hazelius, Artur 47
heritage education 39-40, 43, 168
heritage sites 10-11, 40-41, 44, 64, 69, 91-93
heritage sites, penal 78, 80
Hewison, Robert 10, 44, 173
Historians 153
History and Memory 20, 53, 171-172, 177
History and the media 8-10, 35, 81, 94, 198, 203
History and the past 31
History as a school subject 28-30, 40, 42
History education 32-33, 38-40, 42-43, 50
History education in America 40, 43
History education in Australia 39
History education in Museums 33
History education in schools 32
History education, 'critical relationship with the past' 28-29, 34, 42, 168, 180, 198
History education, discovery methods 28, 40
History education, the role of literacy 40, 42
House of Detention, Clerkenwell, London England 53, 80
Hudson, Kenneth 46, 48, 50
Husbands, Chris: *What is History Teaching?* 29-30, 33, 168
Hyde Park Barracks, Sydney, Australia 54, 79

identity 167-199
identity as narrative 170
identity, Australian, colonial, settler 189
identity, citizen and nation 179-180, 183-190
identity, definition 169
identity, English working class 188
identity, ethnic 192-194
identity, exploration 29, 167, 194-196, 198
identity, gender 190-192
identity, group 17-20
identity, interpreters' 195-196
identity, moral 170, 194-195, 199
identities, multiple 169
identity, museums 177-180
identity, myth 173-4
imagination, historical 32
imagination, romantic 52-53
Information Technology 13, 17
interaction, analysis 149, 158
internet 17-18
interpretation for children 113, 126-132, 135-136
interpreters, alternative names 111-112
interpreters, background of 134
interpreters, expectations of visitors 102

interpreters, first person 9, 12, 59, 101, 105, 108, 114. 118-121, 126-128, 143, 152-153, 155
interpreters, motivation of 135-6
interpreters, speech authenticity 117, 121, 122
interpreters, talk 117-118
interpreters, third person 12, 59, 64, 111, 114, 117, 118-119, 121, 125-128, 134, 152-153, 157-159, 161, 164
interpreters, training of 132-134
interpreters,answering questions 117
Ironbridge Gorge Museum, Shropshire, England 48, 58, 75

Jamestown, USA 70-71, 78, 116-117, 119, 127-128, 132
Jewish Museum, Berlin, Germany 36
John Tradescent 48, 50
Jorvik, York, England 57-58

Kentwell Hall 59, 95, 98, 113, 158, 190

language meanings, Ideational, Interpersonal and Textual 146-147
language, different forms 140
language, functional model 139
language, metafunctions 146
language, Participants - generalised human 151
language, Processes - material, verbal, mental, relational 150
language, resources 152
language, spoken and written relationship 156
Les Lieux de Memoire 170-173, 186, 188
Liebeskind, Daniel (architect) 36
linguistic choice, first or third person 152
living history as an educational technique 11, 28, 40, 42
living history as approach 12, 13
living history as medium 12, 13
living history as method 12, 13
living history as public performance 14
living history, definition 12
living history, groups 12, 14
living history, organisations 17
living history, talk 141
London Dungeon, London, England 56
London Transport Museum England 93
Lowenthal, David: *Memory and Oblivion* 177
Lowenthal, David: *The Past is a Foreign Country* 16
Lumley, Robert: *The Museum Time Machine* 75

Malcolm-Davis, Jane  21, 110
Martin, J.R.  142-143, 154
Marx, Karl  172
Mary Mackillop Place, Sydney, Australia  56, 57
Master John Pore  116
Medieval Combat Society  94
memory  20,31, 53, 168, 170-172, 177
methodology  3, 31, 42, 68, 203
minitheories  30-33, 44
Mode (linguistics)  147-148, 155-156
museum education  36, 38
museum education, the hidden curriculum  43
Museum of London  9, 55, 58, 85,
museums, the democratisation of  35, 37
Mystic Seaport  70-71, 108, 134-135

National Maritime museum, Greenwich, London (UK)  177
National Museum of American History, Washington  55
National Museum of Natural History/ Museum of Man, Washington, USA  55
National Museum of the American Indian, New York, USA  54
Native Americans  54-55, 74, 105, 136, 173, 179, 184-185, 188, 192-95
Nora, Pierre: *Les Lieux de Memoire*  170-171

Old Sturbridge Village, Schoolmistress  47, 49, 181
Old Sturbridge Village, USA  47, 49, 69-70, 73-74, 102-104, 107-108, 116, 119-120
Old Sydney Town, Australia  24-27, 49, 57, 80-81, 126, 189, 194-195
Old Sydney Town, Gaoler  49, 189
orientation films  22, 105-107, 110

personal histories  170,174
Pike and Musket Society, New South Wales, Australia  84
Pitt-Rivers  48-50, 186
Plimoth Plantation  22, 26, 73-74, 92, 105, 107-108,119, 121, 123, 127, 135, 173, 188, 190-191, 194-98
Plimoth Plantation, Mayflower II  53
*Presentation of History* project  35

reconstruction  7-8
recreation  7-8
'Red T-shirts'  119
re-enactment  7-8

Regia Anglorum  84
register (linguistic)  147-149, 155, 157, 158, 162-163, 166
replica church, burning of  115
replica ships  70, 78
reproduction  47, 74
Rievaulx Abbey, England  50, 52
Robertshaw, Andrew  12, 14, 68, 106, 119
Roth, Stacy: *Past into present*  119

safety 74-75, 78
Sancte Albantes Stow  85
school history and written text  139-140
school rooms  82, 181
school subjects, written genres  142, 144-147
setting  68
setting, authenticity  73-78
setting, individual loctions  69-71
setting, of the Fair  87-88
setting, of the school  84-86
setting, re-enactors own  83-84
setting, single theme  78-83
setting, total site  64
setting, virtual  86
shopping  25, 142, 150, 159-160, 180, 182, 189
Sir John Soane Museum, London, England  49
site, locations within  69
site, total  69
Skansen, Stockholm, Sweden  47. 196
Sovereign Hill, Ballarat, Australia  39, 72, 75-77, 93, 101, 111, 136, 183, 194
Stanstead Mountfichet Castle, Essex, England  56-57
studioli  48
Swan Hill Pioneer Settlement, Victoria, Australia  115
Systemic functional linguistics (SFL)  139-140, 162

Tabard Inn  196
Tenor (linguistic)  147-149, 152, 158-159, 161-162
Tetley's Brewery Wharf  109-110
text types, written school subjects  142-143
text types, historical recount  159-160
text types, in school History and social purposes  140-142
text types, Narrative - in school English  143
text types, Narrative - in school History  142
text types, recount  159
text, definition  140

text, dialogic  157
text, written and school history  140
textual choices  18
The 14th Brooklyn New York State Militia International  19
The Clink, Southwark, London, England  80
*The Learning Power of Museums - A Vision for Museum Education*  38
The National Trust  40, 96
The Ragged School Museum  82, 181
The Sealed Knot  23
The Vikings  84
time of day, the effect of  69, 71
time scale  117
Times Educational Supplement  64, 80, 89, 92
Torrington, Devon, England  115
Tower Hill Pageant, London, England  58
transcript, discussion of analysis  158
transcript, example  158

United States Holocaust Museum, Washington  53

Valentine Museum, Richmond, USA  33-34, 54
Viking Middle England  102
visitors, satisfaction  91
visitors, questions  100, 104-105, 107-108
visitors, survey (Hampton Court)  91
visitors, school children  95
visitors, the less able  99
visitors, types of  95
visitors, attention spans 100, 107
visitors, historical knowledge  97, 100, 104-105
visitors, previous museum experience  100, 105-106

Wallace, Mike: Mickey Mouse History  20
Walsh, Kevin: *The Representation of the Past*  37
Warsaw  172
Weald and Downland Museum, United Kingdom  41
weather, the effect of  69, 71-72
Weimar-Buchenwald  172, 174
White, Hayden  31
Williamsburg (Colonial Williamsburg)USA  48, 68, 73, 77, 81, 86, 98, 104-105, 107, 184, 195, 197-198
Williamsburg, American democracy  77
Williamsburg, Family Tour of the Capitol  129-130, 184

Williamsburg, Magistrates Court  126, 184, 190, 195
Williamsburg, slave market  193
Williamsburg: *Becoming American*  185, 187
*Write it Right* project  140, 142

York Town, Victory Center,Virginia,USA  127